Covid-19:
Interdisciplinary Explorations of Impacts on Higher Education

Editors:

Tennyson Mgutshini, Kunle Oparinde and Vaneshree Govender

SUN PRESS

Covid-19: Interdisciplinary Explorations of Impacts on Higher Education

Published by African Sun Media under the SUN PReSS imprint

This publication was subjected to an independent double-blind peer evaluation by the publisher.

The editors and the publisher have made every effort to obtain permission for and acknowledge the use of copyrighted material. Refer all enquiries to the publisher.

Views reflected in this publication are not necessarily those of the publisher.

First edition 2021

ISBN 978-1-991201-18-8
ISBN 978-1-991201-19-5 (e-book)
https://doi.org/10.52779/9781991201195

Set in Calibri Light 10.5/15
Cover design, typesetting and production by African Sun Media

SUN PReSS is an imprint of African Sun Media. Scholarly, professional and reference works are published under this imprint in print and electronic formats.

This publication can be ordered from:

orders@africansunmedia.co.za
Takealot: bit.ly/2monsfl
Google Books: bit.ly/2k1Uilm
africansunmedia.store.it.si (e-books)
Amazon Kindle: amzn.to/2ktL.pkL

Visit africansunmedia.co.za for more information.

Contents

Tennyson Mgutshini, Kunle Oparinde and Vaneshree Govender

Rodwell Makombe

Vasanthrie Naidoo, Nellie Naranjee and Maureen Nokuthula Sibiya

Nduduzo C Ndebele and Victor H Mlambo

Rosaline Govender and Mogiveny Rajkoomar

Lize-Mari Mitchell

Amile Olwethu Mavundla and Tennyson Mgutshini

Prinavin Govender and O.O. Olugbara

Urmilla Bob, Suveshnee Munien, Amanda Gumede and Rivoni Gounden

Cheryl Potgieter and Urmilla Bob

Linda Linganiso and Nobathembu Faleni

LIST OF CONTRIBUTORS

EDITORS

TENNYSON MGUTSHINI
DURBAN UNIVERSITY OF TECHNOLOGY/UNIVERSITY OF SOUTH AFRICA

Tennyson Mgutshini is a multi-disciplinarian with expertise, educational qualifications and publications across a range of areas that include public health, the social sciences, educational management and business. He is a researcher in residence at the Durban University of Technology, and the Director at the School of Transdisciplinary Research and Graduate Studies at the University of South Africa. He has research affiliations with a number of universities in South Africa, through which he continues to support the development of entrepreneurial research and innovation among postgraduate learners. He has extensive experience in research and development and has a history of managing no less than 42 successful research and development projects for a wide range of agencies globally.

KUNLE OPARINDE
DURBAN UNIVERSITY OF TECHNOLOGY

Kunle Oparinde is an interdisciplinary researcher with primary research interests in communication, discourse and sociolinguistics, and secondary interests in decolonisation, and research management. He is the Editor-in-Chief of the African Journal of Inter/Multidiscplinary Studies which is indexed on the Directory of Open Access Journals (DOAJ) database. Oparinde has published his research works in reputable academic journals.

VANESHREE GOVENDER
DURBAN UNIVERSITY OF TECHNOLOGY

Vaneshree Govender is the Manager (acting) - Research and Postgraduate Support Directorate at the Durban University of Technology. She has over 2 decades of experience working in higher education and 18 years' experience in Research Management and Development. Ms Govender serves as the Managing Editor for a local DHET accredited journal and in addition she has served as Chief Editor on numerous in-house publications. Ms Govender's research interests includes research capacity development for knowledge production, decolonisation in higher education and Organisational Communication and Change Management. She is an emerging researcher and has published her work in local and international journals and has supervised and graduated postgraduate students.

AUTHORS

URMILLA BOB
UNIVERSITY OF KWAZULU-NATAL

Urmilla Bob is a full professor of Geography in the School of Agriculture, Earth and Environmental Sciences and University Dean of Research at the University of KwaZulu-Natal, South Africa. She conducts research on a range of developmental and environmental issues, including socio-economic impact assessments of developmental projects in relation to conservation and tourism projects, as well as sustainable livelihoods in both rural and urban contexts. She also undertakes research pertinent to higher education. She has published in these fields in both nationally and internationally recognised academic books and journals, as well as been involved in consultancy-based projects.

NOBATHEMBU FALENI
DURBAN UNIVERSITY OF TECHNOLOGY

Nobathembu Faleni obtained her doctorate degree from the University of Johannesburg. She joined the Department of Applied Sciences at Walter Sisulu University as a lecturer in Chemistry. She has been involved in academic activities such as teaching and learning as an emerging teacher and researcher. Nobathembu is assisting and engaging with local surrounding high schools in teaching and transferring her knowledge and expertise of science. She has collaborated in writing scientific manuscripts and book chapters with regional and national universities such as Durban University of Technology.

RIVONI GOUNDEN
UNIVERSITY OF KWAZULU-NATAL

Rivoni Gounden is a masters graduate in the Geography and Environmental Science discipline at the College of Agriculture, Engineering and Science at the University of KwaZulu-Natal. She is currently undertaking a PhD on the impacts of Covid-19 on tourism-related businesses. She also undertakes research on sustainable natural resource management practices. Additionally, she has been involved in postgraduate capacity development programmes.

PRINAVIN GOVENDER
DURBAN UNIVERSITY OF TECHNOLOGY

Prinavin Govender is an academic in the Department of Information Systems in the Faculty of Accounting and Informatics at the Durban University of Technology. Prinavin's areas of specialisation includes (but not limited to) Information Technology, Software Engineering and the pedagogies of Teaching and Learning. As an emerging researcher, he has published his work in local and international journals and presented his finding at various Teaching and Learning conferences and he is currently supervising postgraduate students in the areas of cloud computing, utilisation of e-resources and teaching and learning. His community engagement activities include teaching computer literacy to high school learners. Prinavin is the faculty e-learning representative and an institutional project base learning trainer.

ROSALINE GOVENDER
DURBAN UNIVERSITY OF TECHNOLOGY

Rosaline Govender has a doctorate in Education from the University of KwaZulu-Natal. She has been working within the field of Academic Development since 2011. Her experience in academic development spans across student, staff and curriculum development. At institutional level she has served as a member of several task teams, including General Education and Siyaphumelela. She is the Convenor of the HELTASA's, Professional Development Collaborative Learning Community (HELTASA PDCLC). She is the Co-convenor of the International Teaching and Learning Collaboration between Durban University of Technology and Dr. SNS Rajalakshmi College of Arts and Science (India). Her research interests include student success, staff development, teaching and learning, academic development and gender issues.

AMANDA NALEDI GUMEDE
UNIVERSITY OF KWAZULU-NATAL

Amanda Gumede is a masters graduate in the Geography and Environmental Science discipline. She is from the College of Agriculture, Engineering and Science at the University of KwaZulu-Natal. She undertakes research on sustainable waste management and renewable energy. Additionally, she has been involved in postgraduate capacity development programmes.

LINDA Z LINGANISO
DURBAN UNIVERSITY OF TECHNOLOGY

Linda Linganiso is a scientist, author and inventor. She has published more than 40 research articles including reviews and 15 book chapters. She has filed a number of patents and continues to work towards generating more for commercialisation in the near future. Linganiso is the author of the "Waste-to-Profit" book series, with two volumes of this series already available online. This academic entrepreneur recently established a waste management consulting firm to help investors invest in profitable businesses and assist companies to establish Sustainable Business Systems. She is currently the director of the Research and Postgraduate Support Directorate at the Durban University of Technology.

RODWELL MAKOMBE
UNIVERSITY OF THE FREE STATE

Rodwell Makombe is an associate professor in the Department of English Literary and Cultural Studies at the University of the Free State, Qwaqwa Campus. He works on postcolonial literary studies, social media, memetics and resistance in and through literature. His publications have appeared in journals such as African Identities, Continuum: Journal of Media and Cultural Studies, Journal of Black Studies and the Nordic Journal of African Studies (NJAS).

AMILE OLWETHU MAVUNDLA
DURBAN UNIVERSITY OF TECHNOLOGY

Amile Olwethu Mavundla is a doctoral researcher in Health Sciences at the Durban University of Technology and is currently involved in the coordination of the extended curriculum program there. As a social worker, she did extensive work with the elderly, but her interest in working with the youth has resulted in her pursuing a career in academia. Amile holds a Master's of Social Work degree (family therapy), as well as a Bachelor of Social Work degree (counselling psychology). Her educational and practical background in social work and counselling psychology has given her a broad basis upon which to approach teaching and learning.

LIZE-MARI MITCHELL
UNIVERSITY OF LIMPOPO

Lize-Mari Mitchell is a lecturer at the University of Limpopo, affiliated with the School of Law. She teaches Jurisprudence, Legal Pluralism and Human Rights. She follows a multi-disciplinary approach to research with a focus on developmental psychology, education, and the rights of the child. She has been a part of the steering committee of the iKudu project, an Erasmus+ funded collaborative online international learning programme, since its inception in 2019 and continues to play an active part in the project as an academic, trainer and researcher. In 2020, she received the top teaching excellence award at her institution due to her ongoing efforts with virtual exchange and the innovative use of technology in her classroom.

VICTOR H MLAMBO
UNIVERSITY OF ZULULAND

Victor Mlambo is a lecturer at the University of Zululand, Department of Politics and International Studies. His research interests revolve around Conflict and Migration Studies, Politics of Geography, International Relations and Public Diplomacy.

SUVESHNEE MUNIEN
UNIVERSITY OF KWAZULU-NATAL

Suveshnee Munien is a lecturer in the Geography and Environmental Science discipline at the College of Agriculture, Engineering and Science at the University of KwaZulu-Natal. She holds a doctorate in Environmental Science. Her research focuses on mixed methodological approaches to examining aspects relating to humanenvironmental systems and vulnerabilities. Her main research focus is renewable energy and society, environmental change and food systems, and community-based conservation.

VASANTHRIE NAIDOO
DURBAN UNIVERSITY OF TECHNOLOGY

Vasanthrie Naidoo is a registered critical care nurse and senior lecturer at the Department of Nursing at the Durban University of Technology, South Africa. Her research interests include Critical Care Nursing Education, Health Sciences Education, Health Services Management and Cross-border Education and Research.

NELLIE NARANJEE
DURBAN UNIVERSITY OF TECHNOLOGY

Nellie Naranjee is an Occupational Health Nursing lecturer at the Department of Nursing at the Durban University of Technology, KwaZulu-Natal. Her research interests include Management Sciences, Public Health, Health Services Management and Education.

NDUDUZO C NDEBELE
UNIVERSITY OF ZULULAND

Nduduzo Ndebele is a lecturer in the Department of Public Administration at the University of Zululand and a doctoral candidate in the School of Social Sciences at the University of KwaZulu Natal. Mr Ndebele's research interests incorporate public policy, local economic development, as well as issues relating to higher education in South Africa. Prior to joining the academia, he worked as a Human Resource Practitioner at Ngwelezana Tertiary Hospital in the KwaZulu Natal Department of Health.

OLUDAYO OLUGBARA
DURBAN UNIVERSITY OF TECHNOLOGY

Oludayo Olugbara is a professor and the Executive Dean of the Faculty of Accounting and Informatics at the Durban University of Technology. He is the founder of the ICT and Society (ICTAS) Niche Research Group and the Vice Chair of Space Science Research Group at the Durban University of Technology. He has successfully supervised over 250 undergraduate degree students, 29 Master's degree students and 13 Doctorates in Computer Science and Information Technology. He has so far published more than 160 research papers in national and international journals, books, book chapters and conference proceeding articles.

MOGIVENY RAJKOOMAR
DURBAN UNIVERSITY OF TECHNOLOGY

Rajkoomar currently serves as a lecturer and postgraduate coordinator in the Information Systems Department at the Durban University of Technology. She is passionate about teaching, learning and research. She is currently involved in the supervision of PhD and Master's students in the fields of Information Science, Information Management, Information Systems and Information Technology. She is a member of the Information and Technology Committee at the Durban University of Technology and a member of the Institutional Research Committee. Her research interest is in information and communication technologies, e-learning, cloud computing and decision support systems.

CHERYL POTGIETER
DURBAN UNIVERSITY OF TECHNOLOGY

Cheryl Potgieter has a doctorate in Psychology. Previous posts include: Dean of Research; Deputy Vice Chancellor and Head of College of Humanities at the University of KwaZulu Natal; Professor in Psychology at the University of Pretoria; Director of Women and Gender Studies at the HSRC; and Head of Woman and Gender Studies at the University of Western Cape. She is also a visiting Professor at University College of London. She heads Gender Justice, Health and Human Development and the Research and Doctoral Academy (RADLA) at the Durban University of Technology. She served as commissioner on the Moerane Commission Investigating Political Killings in KwaZulu-Natal.

MAUREEN NOKUTHULA SIBIYA
DURBAN UNIVERSITY OF TECHNOLOGY

Maureen Nokuthula Sibiya is the Deputy Vice-Chancellor: Teaching and Learning at the Durban University of Technology, South Africa. She is NRF-C3 rated and her research focus areas include Primary Health Care, Nursing Education and Health Systems Research.

ACKNOWLEDGEMENTS

This book project would have been an impossible task without the immense support of the Durban University of Technology, especially, the Research and Postgraduate Support Directorate under the leadership of Dr Linda Zikhona Linganiso.

Entrenched within the university's new strategy – ENVISION 2030 – this book addresses a critical issue that has permeated and disrupted the entire world since early 2020. The global pandemic (i.e Coronavirus Disease 2019 (Covid-19)) has affected virtually all spheres of the world and it is only appropriate that academic enquiries are made on the circumstances surrounding the situation. One such circumstance is the higher education institutions (HEIs) and how they have managed, and are still managing to cope with the affairs and operations of these institutions. Therefore, at this juncture, we must appreciate the academics and researchers who have all contributed to this book through their introspections from within their various academic disciplines. It is no gainsaying that they have worked relentlessly to meet the tedious timelines in which this book was published. Sincere gratitude and thanks must also be extended to DUT colleagues for their professional support in rigourously reviewing and ensuring that the academic quality and integrity of the book meets international standards.

The Research Capacity Development unit within the Research and Postgraduate Support Directorate led by Ms. Vaneshree Govender also needs to be acknowledged. The attentiveness, support and encouragement received from this unit has contributed significantly to the production of this book. Also, the Director of the Institute of Systems Science, where one of the editors is hosted, should be thanked for creating a conducive working environment which also contributes to the realisation of this book.

The Editors

FOREWORD

Sibusiso Moyo
Deputy Vice-Chancellor: Research,
Innovation and Engagement
Durban University of Technology

The year 2020, will go down in history as the year of yet another pandemic. This time, the whole world was brought down to its knees, and the affairs of our societies completely upended due to the Coronavirus Disease 2019 (Covid-19). Despite that, academics, and researchers through worthwhile initiatives around the world have rightly devoted their attention towards addressing and understanding the effects of this unprecedented pandemic. If anything, higher education institutions have been tested on their readiness to respond to change and their agility and capability to continue to provide quality education in the 'changed' world. This peer reviewed book brings to the fore the current status and experiences from the higher education landscape as the sector continues to navigate both the challenges and opportunities that the pandemic has caused.

Having not witnessed such a global pandemic for over a century, given that the last widely known history of such was the 1918 influenza pandemic (Spanish flu), manoeuvring the operations of HEIs is bound to be a challenge, not only for tertiary education managers, but also the entire personnel inclusive of staff and students. In fact, the introduction of concepts such as social/physical distancing is an indication of 'business unusual' in HEIs. Universities have had to, on a daily basis, respond to crisis or rethink alternative measures to ensure teaching, learning, research and innovation continue. HEIs cannot afford to shut down for prolonged periods as they are pinnacles of knowledge production, knowledge transfer, as well as innovation today. Despite the effects of the pandemic, we must remain resilient and find opportunities both for innovating on the teaching and learning front, as well as research. On this note, a special congratulatory note to the editors for putting this book together.

The book, *Covid-19: Interdisciplinary Explorations of Impact on Higher Education,* spotlights the overt and covert observations pertaining to Covid-19 in HEIs. Discordant to the Spanish flu, when technology was still in its infancy, technology has played a tremendous role in advancing the course of HEIs during the current pandemic. Thus rightly, included chapters examine the role of technology as alternative measures in the era of Covid-19. I must note that the contributions to this book are rich, diverse, and cogent. The book also prominently addresses critical issues among which are related to effective leadership in HEIs; the adaptation of multimodal method of teaching and learning; challenges faced by students; and the role of innovation as situated within HEIs. Especially important for the book is the Afrocentric approach adopted by viewing Covid-19 and HEIs from an African lense.

As the Deputy Vice-Chancellor: Research Innovation and Engagement at the Durban University of Technology (DUT), the book came at a time when we are fostering the new university strategy – ENVISION2030. The strategy dwells on the need to improve lives and livelihoods with the 'society' being a robust aspect of this strategy. Therefore, perceiving that Covid-19 is a danger to the society, this book in many ways align with the DUT Strategy especially since HEIs are integral to the adventures of our immediate society.

I conclude the foreword by encouraging students, academics, researchers, and education stakeholders to engage with this book and possibly locate the reasoning and arguments in the journey through the Covid-19 pandemic, as well as any other future challenges that may threaten the affairs of knowledge production, knowledge transfer and innovation.

Managing Higher Education in and after the Era of a Worldwide Pandemic

Tennyson Mgutshini, Kunle Oparinde and Vaneshree Govender

The Coronavirus Disease 2019 (Covid-19) has become a significant global threat which has continued to have wide-reaching impacts on the world, and on South Africa. Society in general, and the academic project in particular, have been similarly affected by this public health threat. Also, given the risks of human-to-human transmission, a range of social distancing measures became necessary, such as South Africa's national lockdown and the blanket closure of all institutions of higher learning. The global pandemic represents an unprecedented risk to everyday life and most notably, it has the potential to destabilise educational, research and innovation endeavours for South Africa as a whole. In spite of the possible damaging effects, Oparinde and Govender (2020) emphasise that it is feasible to have coping strategies in place to cushion the effect of the pandemic, and that researchers, as well as academics cannot be excused from such important responsibilities.

Like many other world leaders, President Cyril Ramaphosa of South Africa also declared that the country is in a national state of emergency, considering that the virus brought the entire country to its knees. With the nationwide lockdown that started as a 3-week event and eventually got prolonged, it soon became clear that the Covid-19 pandemic has come to stay far beyond earlier imaginations. What further became obvious was that the more prolonged the pandemic, the more negative effects materialised. The impending situation ushered in a new phrase referred to as the 'new normal', which ingeniously points towards the creation of fresh ways, methods and strategies of proceeding with our daily lives as Covid-19 has forced an instant departure from what used to be the routine. In response to the disruption brought by the pandemic, it became integral for Higher Education Institutions (HEIs) to seek a redress and prepare for the 'new normal' with respect to the operations and affairs of institutions of higher learning.

The necessity of HEIs is hydra-headed. As crippling as the Covid-19 pandemic is, institutions of higher learning are one of the entities that must continue to function at the highest standard, considering the role they play in the community. Not only do these institutions produce university graduates, but they are also key to the development of the society and economy. While some earlier views of HEIs implied the former, modern views have mostly insinuated the latter or combined the two. For instance, Becker's (1964, 1993) earlier positions suggested that higher levels of education are meant to prepare people for the labour market. Although Becker's view is in some way correct, it does not completely represent the enormous benefits of HEIs which Mokyr (2002) argues should serve the purpose of individual intellectual development, as well as social progression. Just as an individual has a lot to gain from HEIs, so does the society.

HEIs should be perceived from both the epistemological and ontological points of view. While these establishments are meant to produce knowledge, they should also recycle and repurpose produced knowledge within our everyday reality and being. In fact, HEIs should play relevant roles in societal development. Luvalo's (2014) position makes this clear when he pontificates that universities have frequently been regarded as key institutions in the process of social change and development. The implication of this assertion, in the period of Covid-19, is that if HEIs unconsciously concede defeat to the disruption brought about by the pandemic, the resultant situation does not only affect the operations of HEIs, but it equally has dire consequences on the development of the immediate society. It is in acknowledgement of this context that it is momentous to respond quickly to the war the virus has brought upon humanity, by researching mitigating factors to the pandemic with respect to institutions of higher learning. In so doing, the epistemological posture of HEIs as places of knowledge production is safe, while this also assists the ontological stance as a venue where reality and worldview is shaped in the modern community.

The sudden closure of universities coupled with educators and students' unanticipated reliance on technology, as well as many other unexpected challenges, mean that HEIs will indeed face unpremeditated and unprecedented attacks that universities need to pay serious attention to. Rashid and Yadav (2020) state unequivocally that HEIs must be prepared for a tough road ahead and make tough decisions that will continue to shape and steer the future of students and society. Hence, Rashid and Yadav (2020) expect that the university communities will need to reflect on their educational vision and mission to ensure that student learning outcomes and standards of educational quality are not compromised in their intertwined missions of education, knowledge creation, and service to society. In a supporting view, Al-Baadani and Abbas (2020) affirm that education is one of the determinants of economic development and that it plays a crucial role in shaping human capital in the world.

The traditional way of education has completely changed during the Covid-19 era. This book presents interdisciplinary perspectives that focus on what the impact of Covid-19 implies for their discipline-specific scholarship. Contributors have critically and constructively reflected from within their specific academic disciplines in their attempt to proffer solutions to the disruptions brought to the South African higher education space by the pandemic. Academics and education leaders have particularly responded to the objective of this book by focusing on how the academia could tackle the Covid-19 motivated disruption and resuscitate teaching, research and innovation activities in South African higher education.

Contributions to this book have diversely addressed salient subjects, including how the pandemic may serve as a platform to decolonise higher education in South Africa; leadership concerns at institutions of higher learning during the pandemic; challenges associated with specific universities, especially as influenced by demographics; the hybrid model of teaching and learning as a strategy; the nitty-gritties of virtual classrooms; equitable access to education; the application of the constructivist theory to synchronous learning; challenges associated with postgraduate training; perspectives from social sciences regarding Covid-19; and how we can adopt innovation technologies to drive Africa's response to the pandemic.

References

Al-Baadani, A.A. & Abbas, M. 2020. The impact of coronavirus (Covid-19) pandemic on higher education institutions (HEIs) in Yemen: Challenges and recommendations for the future. *European Journal of Education Studies*, 7(7):68-81.

Becker, G.S. 1964. *Human capital: A theoretical and empirical analysis with special reference to education*. New York: National Bureau of Economic Research.

Becker, G.S. 1993. *Human capital: A theoretical and empirical analysis with special reference to education*. Chicago: National Bureau of Economic Research. https://doi.org/10.7208/ chicago/9780226041223.001.0001

Luvalo, L.M. 2014. The role of higher education in social transformation and rural development. *Mediterranean Journal of Social Sciences*, 5(23):1206-1212. https://doi.org/10.5901/mjss.2014.v5n23p1206

Mokyr, J. 2002. *The gifts of Athena: Historical origins of the knowledge economy*. Princeton: Princeton University Press.

Oparinde, K.M. & Govender, V. 2020. Disruptions from Covid-19: Challenges and opportunities for research outputs in South African Higher Education. *Alternation (Special Issue)*, 332-347. https://doi.org/10.29086/2519-5476/2020/sp32a13

Rashid, S. & Yadav, S.S. 2020. Impact of Covid-19 pandemic on higher education and research. *Indian Journal of Human Development*, 14(2):340-343. https://doi.org/10.1177%2F0973703020946700

1

THE COVID-19 PANDEMIC AS A PLATFORM TO RETHINK THE DECOLONISATION OF HIGHER EDUCATION IN SOUTH AFRICA

Rodwell Makombe

The Covid-19 pandemic has brought to the fore numerous challenges that South Africa has been grappling with since the end of apartheid. Higher education in particular has been facing many challenges that have opportunistically become salient in the context of the Covid-19 crisis. This chapter explores a wide range of challenges within the higher education sector that participants (mainly students) on the official Facebook Page of the Department of Higher Education and Technology (DHET) raised in the context of the Covid-19 National Lockdown.[1] I draw on concepts from decolonial theory, particularly the notion of "coloniality", to examine how Covid-19 can be appropriated to rethink the decolonisation of higher education in South Africa. Coloniality refers to the perpetuation of quasi-colonial systems and structures long after the end of official colonialism. Decolonial theory seeks to identify and dismantle logics of coloniality in existing structures, systems and patterns of thought in former colonised territories. Covid-19 has not only highlighted the inequalities that continue to stalk South African society post-apartheid, but also the shortcomings of interventions that the government has put in place to address these challenges. The chapter argues that the Covid-19 crisis has presented an opportunity to rethink the unfinished business of decolonisation in higher education.

---

1 South Africa declared a National Lockdown on 26 March 2020 following the outbreak of the novel coronavirus.

In South Africa, the call for the decolonisation of higher education became a buzzword in the context of the student protests of 2015-2016 which focused on, among other things, removing offensive colonial symbols from public spaces, eradicating racism in universities, and abolishing exorbitant and unaffordable tuition fees. Griffiths (2019:145) argues that although the #RhodesMustFall and #FeesMustFall movements formulated their agenda around "free, decolonized education for black people", what the movement achieved through the promulgation of free higher education in 2017 was a small fraction of what the broader decolonisation agenda entailed. In fact, Covid-19 has demonstrated that decolonisation in the 21st century goes far beyond the provision of tuition-free higher education. Before the Covid-19 pandemic, government-funded students in South Africa enjoyed a reasonable degree of comfort in paid accommodation on and off-campus with access to university facilities such as computer labs and libraries. However, when Covid-19 struck, poor students were once again faced with the reality of academic exclusion based on their socio-economic circumstances. The drastic transition from face-to-face to virtual learning methods affected many disadvantaged students from poor communities such as townships, rural areas and informal settlements.

Drawing on decolonial theory, I argue that Covid-19 has exacerbated the violence of modernity for those who live on its "darker side" (Mignolo, 2007:450). The fact that students from particular geographical and socio-economic spaces suffered the most from the effects of Covid-19 should open a debate about what needs to be done to end the violence of modernity in former colonised territories. Despite the advent of the Fourth Industrial Revolution (4IR), students from poor communities continue to live in the shadow of modernity (without electricity, relevant gadgets or internet connectivity). In Fanon's formulation, decolonisation is a process of reasserting the humanity of the colonised. It "infuses a new rhythm, a new language and a new humanity … [it is] the creation of new men" (Fanon, 1961:2). Fanon's writings affirm the perpetuation of relations of coloniality between the Global West and the Global South even after political decolonisation. For Fanon, national consciousness ought to be accompanied by a complete overhaul of socio-economic structures that continue to exclude the formerly colonised while entrenching coloniality. The building of a post-Covid-19 society (and higher education sector) requires a new theoretical language that can radically dismantle structural inequalities and ensure equitable distribution of the benefits of modernity. To create a new rhythm, a new language and a new humanity in the context of this analysis is metaphorically to reclaim the dignity of the formerly colonised by eradicating social injustice and ensuring that all students have access to opportunities and technologies necessary for learning in the 21st century.

Maldonado-Torres' (2007) three dimensions of coloniality, namely coloniality of power, coloniality of knowledge and coloniality of being, show that coloniality is relentless in its attempt to keep the colonised in the shadow of modernity. In fact, former colonised countries in the Global South continue to be on the receiving end of the negative consequences of modernity ranging from climate change to Covid-19. Covid-19 is in many ways a child of modernity, born through the environmental catastrophes of relentless resource extraction and transported to the world through globalisation. The association between Covid-19 and the environmental ravages of modernity means that countries in the Global South will continue to bear the consequences of a modern project from which they are largely excluded. While the Global North has resources and the latest technologies to alleviate crises of modernity such as Covid-19, the Global South is left to deal with crises of apocalyptic proportions.

In light of the above, it becomes evident that the "soft reform" (Andreotti, Stein, Ahenakew & Hunt, 2015:26) approach to decolonisation that South Africa has arguably embraced (see Vorster & Quinn, 2017) cannot address the inherent violence of modernity and its logic of coloniality. Modernity is prone to crisis because it is sustained by violence inflicted on those on "the other side of the line" (Santos, 2007:1). Scientists have argued that crises such as Covid-19 are likely to recur in the future because of global warming (Brower, 2001). If this is the case, the future of poor, racialised and low-income students (and indeed other populations in the Global South) is subject to the endless ravages of Western modernity. If the logic of coloniality is so pervasive that it permeates every sphere of former colonised spaces, then it goes without saying that decolonisation "cannot be accomplished by the wave of a magic wand" as Fanon (1961:2) argues.

Decoloniality and South African higher education

Previous studies on decolonising higher education (Naidoo, Traher, Lucas, Muhuro & Wisker, 2020; Zembylas, 2018) have generally focused on transforming university curricula to reflect the diversity of current student populations. However, few studies have investigated the socio-economic conditions of coloniality that continue to affect previously disadvantaged students. Le Grange (2016:3) posits that "the transformation of the university curriculum is both a microcosm of and impetus for broader societal transformation". To illustrate this, Le Grange (2016) argues that the curriculum consists of three facets namely, the explicit curriculum (prescribed readings, module guides, theories etc.), the hidden curriculum (the culture and values of the university) and the null curriculum (that which is excluded in the curriculum). When talking about renewing the curriculum, the temptation is always to focus on the explicit curriculum, yet the modern university often perpetuates conditions of coloniality through institutional cultures and values that exclude and "peripheralise" other forms of knowledge. What Grange (2016:7) calls the null curriculum is "what universities leave out – what is not taught and learned in a university". To leave out some knowledge from the curriculum is tantamount to leaving out some people. Given that the violence of modernity is embedded in structures and systems of the modern neo-liberal university, it is people of the Global South who are often left out from the curriculum.

Considering this, decolonising the university becomes a painstaking process of identifying experiences, ways of being and contextual realities of the "other" that have been, and continue to be, excluded from the curriculum. Maldonado-Torres (2007) describes coloniality as a system that defines the organisation and dissemination of epistemic, material and aesthetic resources in ways that reproduce modernity's colonial project. Santos (2014) in Zembylas (2018:2) also highlight that the struggle for global social justice is inseparable from the struggle for cognitive justice. Covid-19 has shown that universities remain entangled in structures of global coloniality. Thus, attempts to decolonise the university without decolonising society are superficial and bound to fail.

In a study of rural students' experiences of the curriculum in South Africa, Naidoo et al. (2020) found that students from rural communities continue to experience epistemic exclusion, because universities disregard the realities of their socio-economic contexts. The neoliberal university is insensitive to the socio-economic realities of poor students, because it is entangled in a neoliberal framework that sustains coloniality. If the triad of education consists of the teacher, the learner and the curriculum, as Vandeyar (2019) argues, changing the curriculum without changing the socio-economic conditions of the learner is likely to reproduce existing inequalities. How do we ensure that students from poor backgrounds (and those whose socio-economic status have been eroded by the pandemic) are included in the new framework of the post-Covid-19 university? Paulo Freire (1992:85) avers that "the liberation of individuals acquires profound meaning only when the transformation of society is achieved". Covid-19 clearly demonstrates that the decolonisation agenda must be aligned to the lived realities of poor, low-income and racialised students.

In an assessment of possible approaches to the violence of modernity, Andreotti et al. (2015) developed a social cartography which consists of three approaches namely, soft-reform, radical-reform and beyond-reform. Andreotti et al.'s cartography is relevant to the way South African universities have implemented the decolonisation/

transformation agenda. The soft-reform approach seeks to decolonise the university by inserting an African voice into its systems and structures. This approach works on the assumption that it is possible for those who were formerly excluded to find space within the structures and strictures of a Western-oriented university. On the other hand, radical-reform seeks to achieve systemic and structural transformation by rejecting values, norms and worldviews that perpetuate coloniality. What distinguishes beyond-reform from radical-reform is that beyond-reform rejects the idea that incorporating other epistemes into existing structures will ultimately change the system. In fact, the beyond-reform approach recognises that modernity itself is flawed and needs to be disbanded.

In the context of this analysis, South Africa's approach to decolonising higher education is located within the soft-reform/radical-reform paradigm which focuses on providing "additional resources to indigenous, racialized, low-income and first-generation students" without "questioning the integrity of the system itself" (Andreotti et al., 2015:32). The question that arises is whether this approach is sustainable especially in the "new age" of pandemics. If pandemics turn out to be the "new normal" of 21st century society, as some scientists have predicted, how will students from low-income, poorly serviced communities cope? Is it not more sustainable to address the structures that reproduce inequalities than to continue to provide support to students in a structurally flawed system?

Grosfoguel (2007) argues that people located in the Global South are characterised by a catalogue of deficits and lacks. Although Grosfoguel's position was meant to theorise the perpetual state of overdraft that colonialism bequeathed to former colonised countries, it echoes the "overdraft" situation of poor students in South Africa which has been aggravated by the Covid-19 pandemic. The township, where the majority of students reside, is reminiscent of Frantz Fanon's (1961:4) Medina, a "hungry town, starved of bread, of meat, of shoes, of coal, of light". The postcolonial township (at least in South Africa) suffers from constant power cuts, poor housing and limited internet connectivity – conditions that make it difficult for students to keep up with the neoliberal call to "save the academic year".[2] Clearly, the new world of pandemics requires a new decolonised education model that recognises the contextual needs of students living on the darker side of modernity. Students from South Africa's townships, informal settlements and rural areas do not only need laptops and data to engage in online learning but also a conducive learning environment. Decolonising the university without decolonising the socio-economic

---

2   The Department of Higher Education and Training articulated its objective in the context of Covid-19 as saving lives and saving the academic year.

conditions of blackness is a superficial exercise that will only postpone the problem. While the South African government has done a great deal to help poor students through the National Student Financial Aid Scheme (NSFAS), more challenges have emerged in the context of the Covid-19 pandemic.

Method

This is a qualitative study that uses textual analysis as its analytical tool and purposive sampling as its method to identify and select relevant data from the DHET's Facebook Page. I purposively selected messages posted by students on the DHET Facebook Page between 1 and 11 June 2020, a period that marked the beginning of the Level 3 National Lockdown which lifted a number of restrictions on businesses and public gatherings. DHET used Facebook to communicate new regulations and government initiatives to students. Comments that students posted in direct response to official posts were included while those that they post in response to other students were excluded.

Data were purposively sampled and analysed using the process of coding described by Miles and Huberman (1994) to identify themes or emergent concepts. In this process, texts that discussed the same theme or topic were clustered together and given particular labels. Data was organised in line with Miles and Huberman's (1994) three stages of data analysis namely, data reduction, data display, and verification and analysis. Data were categorised into eight themes namely, differential treatment of students from different institutions, the rural-urban divide, lack of appropriate gadgets, accommodation challenges, the neoliberal preoccupation with saving the academic year, power outages, delayed government response and the costs of extending the academic year. Comments that did not reveal any new information on a particular topic were excluded. A maximum of four comments under each theme were selected for analysis.

Data were analysed using decolonial theory as a theoretical prism and thematic analysis as an analytic tool to investigate how the challenges faced by students in the Covid-19 context were entangled with modernity and its logic of coloniality. The study followed Wiles, Heath, Crow and Charles's (2005) principles of ethical research, particularly the view that research must not cause harm to participants and that participants should be treated fairly and equally during the research process. Principles of confidentiality and anonymity were observed by identifying participants through pseudonyms (initials).

Student responses to the Covid-19 pandemic: The darker side of modernity

This section presents and analyses data obtained from the DHET Facebook Page between 1 and 11 June 2020. While official messages posted on the Page sought to create the impression that the Department had the Covid-19-induced crisis under control, most of the comments from students expressed frustration with the way the Department and institutions of higher learning addressed challenges posed by the pandemic. The prevalent perception among students was that previously advantaged institutions and universities in general were treated better than previously disadvantaged institutions, especially in relation to the provision of necessary resources for virtual learning. This perceived discrepancy highlighted the perpetuation of quasi-colonial structures in the distribution of resources across universities in South Africa. A cursory analysis of the data showed that most participants on the Facebook Page were enrolled at former black universities, Technical and Vocational Education and Training (TVET) colleges and private colleges. These institutions have experienced numerous challenges since the dawn of democracy, ranging from lack of student funding to lack of resources such as laptops and infrastructure.

Scholars of decoloniality such as Quijano (2017) and Grosfoguel (2007) have argued that former colonised territories in the Global South subsidise the bright shine of modernity in the Global North, an observation that mirrors the situation in South African higher education where former white universities continue to shine while former black universities remain in a state of crisis. The "shine" of modernity in the Global North means that Western countries are likely to be in a better position to respond to the consequences of pandemics than those in the Global South where the majority of citizens are excluded from the global economy. The same can be said about South African universities' unequal capacity to respond to the Covid-19 crisis. Most of the students in South Africa are funded by government through NSFAS. The question that arises is whether this is going to be sustainable given that South Africa's economy has been on a downward spiral even before the outbreak of the pandemic. What does Covid-19, and other pandemics that may happen in the future, mean for those students (mainly black) who live in the shadow of modernity in South Africa? Most of the contributions on the DHET Facebook Page suggest that the decolonisation of higher education in South Africa must include dismantling structural inequalities not only within universities, but also within communities where students live.

Some are more equal than others: Covid-19 and inequality in higher education

When universities announced the migration of teaching and learning to online platforms, the question of access became topical given that South Africa's rural areas, townships and informal settlements do not have reliable access to basic services such as electricity, decent housing and internet connectivity. Although the government announced that it would provide data and laptops to poor students, most of the students said they never received the laptops and data packages as the government promised. Students from different institutions, such as private colleges, TVET colleges and previously disadvantaged universities, felt that they were not being treated fairly. A comment by a TVET college student (SS) suggested that former white universities such as the University of the Witwatersrand (Wits) were treated better than previously disadvantaged institutions because their students "received laptops and 30gig data" in time to prepare for virtual learning.

My observation during data collection was that most of the students who complained about virtual learning were from former black universities, TVET colleges and private colleges. Wits was one of the first universities to announce data packages for students to facilitate online learning. Previously disadvantaged universities took longer to make announcements and when they did, students raised concerns about the inefficiency of the new learning model. In fact, some students at the University of the Free State (UFS) raised their concerns under the hashtag #UFSMUSTFALL which trended for several weeks on Facebook and Twitter.[3] Another TVET student (ENE) expressed disgruntlement with the way TVET college students were treated by DHET. ENE was unhappy that some students received "50GB plus... while some of us received nothing". The comment expressed frustration not only with online learning but also with perceived and/or real inequalities in the higher education sector. ENE's contribution started as a desperate plea for help from the government, but it ended as an insult ("this is bullshit").

The perceived discrepancy in the way students were treated resonates with Fanon's theorisation of the colonial society as a compartmentalised society. The logic of coloniality which drives the modern project is evident in the way universities are disparately resourced in ways that mimic the colonial economic structure. This is why Covid-19 did not affect former white institutions and geographical spaces in the same way it affected black institutions and geographical spaces. ENE's world

---

3   #UfsMustFall, University Of Free State Must Fall and this why it's called to fall, available at: http://bit.ly/3lFegh4

reminds us of Fanon's zone of non-being which breeds frustration and violence. Students from previously disadvantaged universities have been reduced to beggars pleading with government to give them "a tablet that has got a sim with data". Another participant (ZOM) complained that the government was only concerned about students on NSFAS, neglecting other equally poor students who did not qualify for government funding. The DHET's obsession with the so-called poor students has become problematic because of its political implications. Some students felt that the DHET was no longer representing all students, but only those on NSFAS. What the Department overlooked was that Covid-19 had pauperised many families, thus consequently re-designating some previously advantaged students into the "poor and needy" category.

ZOM's comment suggests that the government neglected students from private colleges and left them at the messy profit-seeking institutions who he calls "money chasers". The comment shows that South Africa's private education sector faces challenges such as lack of qualified personnel and profiteering. The fact that students in private colleges are taught "ten subjects by one lecturer" implies that there is limited government oversight in these institutions. As a result, students continue to pay for poor quality education. Another participant (TTFS) highlighted discrepancies in the way different institutions responded to Covid-19, raising questions about persistent racial inequalities in post-apartheid South Africa. TTFS felt that the DHET treated students from under-resourced institutions as "the step child(ren) of the family" fed on false promises of free data and laptops. Thus, TTFS considered e-learning an "anti-Black" initiative that expected poor black students to "watch countless videos" without taking cognizance of data costs. The idea that black students were treated as stepchildren of the Department suggests the persistence of quasi-colonial structures in higher education. Black students felt as if they were second-class citizens, always grovelling for handouts from government. TTFS posed a series of questions that highlighted the challenges faced by black students, namely high data costs, government neglect of non-NSFAS students and lack of appropriate gadgets such as laptops and tablets.

The rural-urban divide: Covid-19 and connectivity inequalities

Covid-19 put many previously disadvantaged students in a conundrum where, on the one hand, they were expected to heed the neoliberal call to save the academic year, while on the other, they had to deal with limited resources and unsupportive social contexts. When universities relocated to online platforms, they only addressed issues of curriculum delivery and ignored and/or superficially addressed a wide range of socio-economic realities that affected student access to the curriculum. One participant (BTM) pointed out that virtual learning favoured students from urban environments, such as Johannesburg, "where there are WIFI hotspots everywhere". The implication is that the online learning approach adopted by universities reinforced existing inequalities by ignoring the lived realities of students from the rural areas. BTM complained that students from villages in provinces such as the Eastern Cape (EC) did not have reliable "power supply and it cost a fortune to get to town". The EC is the poorest province in South Africa, hence issues such as power cuts and poor internet access are a reality that students experience on a daily basis. In an article that reflected on connectivity challenges in rural spaces, Ndepa (2020:2) argued that online learning "only benefits the children of the rich and middle class, who are mostly located in urban areas and big cities".

Other participants such as BT opposed the phased reopening of colleges and universities, arguing that institutions in the rural areas were not ready to reopen. BT questioned the DHET's criteria for assessing institutional readiness saying the Department only visited institutions in the cities. What is evident in BT's comment is that the DHET's phased reopening agenda was influenced more by the need to save the academic year than the readiness of colleges and universities. The plight of students from previously disadvantaged rural universities was aptly captured by TTL, who argued that "our institution doesn't have a plan for online learning". TTL also pointed out that even if the institution had a plan, rural areas "face[d] challenges such as connection and time to study". The living conditions of students in rural areas and townships are generally not conducive for learning from home. This explains TTL's plea for the government to "allow us to go back to our residence[s] and study". TTL's plight underscored the coloniality of life for poor black students in post-apartheid South Africa who can only study outside the discomfort of their homes. For most poor students, the home space is not associated with comfort and tranquillity, but with lack of basic amenities and violence. The crude reality of studying from home amid Covid-19 is aptly captured by NZN who submitted that some students lived in small home spaces where they were "overcrowded by siblings" and drunken parents (*abazali bayasela*) who often communicated through violence.

NZN's desperate plea for government to allow students to go "quarantine themselves in their respective residences" suggested that the Covid-19 university posed serious challenges for students who could not study from home. Perhaps the question is: what is the meaning of free education in the context of Covid-19? Free education comes with paid tuition fees, accommodation, transport and meal allowances. However, students lost some of these privileges when they were forced to finish the academic year at home. In this context, students from poor communities are likely to struggle academically. Other participants, such as VDF, raised the issue of residence allowances, which they claimed universities did not pay given that students were not staying on campus. In most cases, universities eventually paid the allowances, however, the delays negatively impacted the academic welfare of students who relied on government funding. Other students, such as NN, complained that bursary funds took a long time to be paid, putting students in situations where they had to "study on empty stomachs". An important point to make is that not all students used NSFAS funds for prescribed purposes such as accommodation and meal allowance. Some students used NSFAS and bursary funds to support families at home. One student (WS) mentioned that "NSFAS money" was for taking care of "the struggles we have at our home". The fact that students used NSFAS funds to support families at home vindicates the view that transformation of the university must be complimented by transformation of society.

The Eskom problem: Power cuts in townships

Load-shedding is one of the major challenges faced by students from townships, rural areas and informal settlements. Lack of electricity usually results in poor or no internet connectivity, making it difficult for students to engage in online learning. One participant (SM) asked what the department was doing about load-shedding that lasted "for over 5 hours almost every day, disrupting internet connectivity and online lessons". Another participant (SM) also indicated that power outages were serious "in the townships where our black students are". These comments highlighted the coloniality of service delivery in post-apartheid South Africa where black communities continued to receive substandard services.

Poor students and the N+2 rule

Covid-19 also amplified shortcomings of government interventions designed to address issues of access to higher education. Students who participated on the DHET Facebook Page used the platform to contest the N+2 rule which the DHET put in place to cap the number of years that beneficiaries of NSFAS benefitted from the funding. According to this rule, NSFAS can only fund a student for the total number of years it takes to complete a degree plus two years. Thus, a four-year degree is funded for a maximum of six years. Although students have contested this rule since its inception, Covid-19 has highlighted its shortcomings especially with regard to students from poor communities. Given the litany of challenges highlighted above, students from poor communities are likely to fail because of socio-economic circumstances beyond their control. Participants, such as SM, wanted the N+2 rule to be revised so that NSFAS can count only those years that a student was on NSFAS funding.

Currently, the N+2 rule considers the number of years that a student appears in the system regardless of whether those years were funded by NSFAS or not. The N+2 rule is problematic because it cannot distinguish between students who fail out of negligence and those who fail out of genuine financial problems.

The fact that the majority of the students who raised concerns on the DHET Facebook Page were black does not only reveal the slow pace of transformation in South African institutions since 1994, but also the continuation of quasi-colonial structures and systems within the higher education sector. When the DHET posted a message saying that the Deputy Minister was going to visit colleges and universities to evaluate their state of readiness to reopen, students from previously disadvantaged institutions pleaded with the department to visit their institutions. Participants from institutions such as the University of Zululand (UNIZULU), the Mangosuthu University of Technology (MUT) and the University of Venda (UNIVEN), pleaded with the department to visit their institutions, which they believed had many issues that needed "serious attention". Although the participants did not mention specific challenges faced by their institutions, the comments suggested that students were aware of numerous problems at their institutions.

Summary of findings and recommendations

The study has revealed, through an analysis of messages posted by students on the DHET Facebook Page, that Covid-19 poses a threat to the welfare of poor, low-income students in South African universities. The results show that students were unhappy with the way the government treated different institutions, especially with regard to the provision of data and laptops for e-learning purposes. Previously disadvantaged institutions were most affected, because they were already experiencing problems before the outbreak of Covid-19. Students from rural areas and informal settlements also raised concerns about poor internet connectivity and power outages, which adversely affected their ability to engage in elearning. The prevailing perception among participants was that online learning favoured students from urban communities where power cuts were less frequent and internet connectivity was more reliable. The study also found that students were unhappy with the DHET's focus on NSFAS students at the expense of other students (especially the missing middle) who were equally affected by the pandemic. Government response to the pandemic was seen as slow, because some students received their allowances late while others never received the laptops and data packages that the government promised. Concerns were also raised about NSFAS's N+2 rule which stipulates that students can only be funded for the maximum number of years it takes to complete a degree plus two years. In the context of Covid-19, the N+2 rule is likely to affect students from poor communities who may fail modules because of reasons beyond their control.

In view of these findings, it is evident that universities in the Global South in general, and South Africa in particular, need to adopt a beyond-reform approach that addresses the inherent violence of modernity. In the past, the violence of modernity manifested through Western projects such as slavery, colonisation, globalisation and neoliberalism. In the 21st century, pandemics have become the new vehicle through which modernity unleashes violence on the peoples and economies of the Global South. While the form and scope of the beyond-reform approach may differ from university to university and country to country, there is no doubt that the current approaches to the decolonisation of higher education are inadequate and unsustainable. Therefore, I recommend that universities should not only focus on delivering epistemic justice, but also work with the government to find ways of addressing systemic inequalities that continue to deny poor students access to the benefits of the 4IR. While I recognise the immense difficulty associated with dismantling the current modern project, the beyond-reform approach requires the dismantling of existing structural inequalities that keep poor students in the shadow of modernity. However, in the short term, the government should dismantle historical inequalities among universities and ensure that all universities are adequately resourced and equipped to respond to crises. The current situation where some universities (previously advantaged) are better resourced than others (previously disadvantaged) perpetuates the violence of modernity on vulnerable social groups. It is also important for both universities and the DHET to take the socio-economic realities of students seriously.

The post-Covid-19 university (and world) needs to be vigilant so that vulnerable students (and groups) are better prepared to survive pandemics. A starting point would be to deliver social justice to all students through the provision of relevant gadgets, internet connectivity and liveable home spaces that can facilitate learning in the 21st century. An important point to note is that the decolonisation of the university is not possible without the decolonisation of society. The Covid-19 pandemic has starkly reminded us that the university is not an island. Societal challenges such as power outages and poor service delivery have a direct impact on the operations of the university, especially in the context of a pandemic. This study recommends that universities and the DHET should be more flexible in times of crisis and be ready to change rules and policies to alleviate the impact of the crisis, especially on poor students and communities. In the South African context, this may require broadening the scope of NSFAS to include students in the missing middle and those whose incomes have been eroded by the crisis. Rules such as N+2 may need to be revised to cater for students who have been economically downgraded by the Covid-19 pandemic.

Conclusion

If any lesson has been learnt from the Covid-19 crisis, it is that universities need a complete beyond-reform approach to decolonisation rather than the current additive-inclusive approach that seeks to include marginalised students into universities modelled on the logic of coloniality. The beyond-reform approach recognises that social justice cannot be delayed any further because it is intricately intertwined with epistemic justice. The decolonisation of the university should of necessity include the decolonisation of society otherwise students from poor backgrounds will continue to be treated as second-class citizens of the higher education sector. While pandemics such as Covid-19 affect all nations across the globe, nations on the "darker side of Western modernity" suffer the most because they do not have big budgets to cushion their populations. The irony, however, is that the bright shine of modernity in the West is subsided by the darkness it creates in the Global South. Given that the world is becoming more and more prone to pandemics and other natural disasters, the situation of poor students in the Global South (including South Africa) is likely to get worse.

Students who participated on the DHET Facebook Page in the context of the Covid-19 pandemic lamented the perpetuation of conditions of coloniality in the post-apartheid higher education system. Poor black students from low-income communities were left with no choice but to contend with a litany of challenges that, overnight, turned education into a privilege rather than a right. If the advent of pandemics signals the beginning of the end of the four-walled university as we know it, the implication is that South Africa's higher education institutions would need to rethink the decolonisation of the university. In the 21st century, the decolonisation of the university should entail making the benefits of the 4IR accessible to all students. Learning in a world of pandemics and natural disasters is only possible when all students have access to the internet, appropriate gadgets and habitable home spaces. Participants on the DHET Facebook Page highlighted that students from poor households faced numerous challenges such as lack of data, lack of appropriate gadgets, power outages and hostile home-learning environments. Clearly, Covid-19 has not only given South Africa an opportunity to reset the economy, but also to broaden its scope of transformation/decolonisation.

References

Andreotti, V.O., Stein, S., Ahenakew, C. & Hunt, D. 2015. Mapping interpretations of decolonization in the context of higher education. *Decolonization: Indigeneity, Education & Society*, 4(1):21-40.

Brower, V. 2001. Vector-borne diseases and global warming: are both on an upward swing? Scientists are still debating whether global warming will lead to a further spread of mosquitoes and the diseases they transmit. *EMBO reports*, 2(9):755-757. https://doi.org/10.1093/embo-reports/kve193

Fanon, F. 1961. *The wretched of the earth*. New York: Grove Press.

Freire, P. 1992. *Pedagogy of hope: Reliving pedagogy of the oppressed*. London: Continuum.

Griffiths, D. 2019. #FeesMustFall and the decolonised university in South Africa: Tensions and opportunities in a globalising world. *International Journal of Educational Research*, 94:143-149. https://doi.org/10.1016/j.ijer.2019.01.004

Grosfoguel, R. 2007. The epistemic de-colonial turn: Beyond political economy paradigms. *Cultural Studies*, 21(2-3):211-223. https://doi.org/10.1080/09502380601162514

Le Grange, L. 2016. Decolonising the university curriculum. *South African Journal of Higher Education*, 30(2):1-12. https://doi.org/10.20853/30-2-709

Maldonado-Torres, N. 2007. On the coloniality of being: Contributions of the development of a concept. *Cultural Studies*, 21(2-3):240-270.

Mignolo, W. 2007. Delinking: The rhetoric of modernity, the logic of coloniality and the grammar of de-coloniality. *Cultural Studies*, 21(2-3):449-514. https://doi.org/10.1080/09502380601162647

Miles, M.B & Huberman, A.M. 1994. *Qualitative Data Analysis*. London: SAGE Publications.

Naidoo, K., Traher, S., Lucas, L., Muhuro, P. & Wisker, G. 2020. 'You have to change, thecurriculum stays the same': decoloniality and curricular justice in South African higher education. *Compare: A Journal of Comparative and International Education*, 50(7):961-977. https://doi.org/10.1080/03057925.2020.1765740

Ndepa, M. 2020. The use of learning technology or online learning is a pipe-dream for mostrural students and learners. *Daily Maverick*, 11 May.

Quijano, A. 2017. Coloniality and modernity/rationality. *Cultural Studies*, 21(2-3):168-178. https://doi.org/10.1080/09502380601164353

Santos, B.S. 2007. *Beyond abyssal thinking: From global lines to ecologies of knowledges*. Revista Critica de Ciencias Sociais, 80. Available at: https://bit.ly/3rcIbOT [Accessed 20 June 2020].

Santos, B.S. 2014. *Epistemologies of the South: Justice against Epistemicide*. Boulder, CO: Paradigm. https://doi.org/10.4324/9781315634876

Vandeyar, S. 2019. Why decolonising the South African university curriculum will fail. *Teaching in Higher Education*, 25(7):783-796. https://doi.org/10.1080/13562517.2019.1592149

Vorster, J.A. & Quinn, L. 2017. The 'decolonial turn': What does it mean for academic staff development? *Education as Change*, 21(1):31-49. https://doi.org/10.17159/1947-9417/2017/853

Wiles, R., Heath, S., Crow, G. & Charles, V. 2005. *Informed consent in social research: A literature review.* NCRM Methods Review Papers, 1:1-26. Available at: https://bit.ly/3tMX0JD [Accessed 25 November 2020].

Zembylas, M. 2018. Decolonial possibilities in South African higher education: Reconfiguringhumanising pedagogies as/with decolonising pedagogies. *South African Journal of Education*, 38(4):1-10. https://doi.org/10.15700/saje.v38n4a1699

EFFECTIVE LEADERSHIP AT A HIGHER EDUCATION INSTITUTION DURING THE COVID-19 PANDEMIC

Fostering social cohesion in the face of social distancing

Vasanthrie Naidoo, Nellie Naranjee and Maureen Nokuthula Sibiya

Introduction

James Lane Allen, an American 19th century writer, put it very aptly when he stated, "adversity does not build character, it reveals it" (Syracuse University Libraries, 2011). This quote has certainly proven itself true time and time again, and more so recently, in the troubled and uncertain times we are living in. The repercussions of the Coronavirus (Covid-19) pandemic has notably devastated lives and livelihoods and its consequences for businesses, organisations, economies and societies will play out for years to come. Right now, what the world needs is smart, values-driven, and focused leadership. While there is no specific 'rulebook' for leadership when the stakes are high, like we have all witnessed, there is no 'rulebook' for what to do in the face of a 21st century pandemic either. The manner in which organisations intervene in the midst of crisis to bring about safe and sustainable change does matter. Globally, people are facing threats on multiple fronts all at once. Threats to oneself, one's family, employees, customers, financial well-being, social and physiological well-being has the potential to threaten the very fabric of one's existence.

So, whilst leaders may be on differing scales and exist on various levels, such as leading a country, managing an organisation, a lecturer in a classroom or just a person spearheading one of the many "Task-Teams" that have emanated as part of crisis management of the Covid-19 pandemic, leadership dexterity, skill and quality have become more crucial than ever. Leaders are faced with difficult choices and are recognising that terms, schedules and even regulations are changing on a daily or even hourly basis due to crisis management. Although there is no crystal ball that can influence decision-making, it becomes imperative that those in positions of power and tasked with making decisions do so by integrating new and relevant information to make strategic decisions, whilst igniting commitment from every member of the organisation or team. So how does a leader help to ensure that the rest of the team feels engaged, informed and physically and psychologically safe?

In this chapter, we reflect on the implications of the current Covid-19 pandemic for academia and higher education and the need for responsive leadership. We examine leadership in the face of adversity, emphasising the need for university leadership that nurtures a culture of innovation, change, empathy and integrity. It provides evidence that during a crisis, leaders do not need predefined response plans, but behaviours and approaches that will assist them to effectively respond and improvise in navigating crises such as the Covid-19 pandemic. This entails not only adjusting current practices or strategies, but also adopting new ones, which can prove beneficial to maintain even after the crisis has passed.

This chapter will therefore share insights into the leadership skills that academic leaders require in the face of adversity, to deal with the challenges of colleagues and students, as well as the restructuring of the existing curriculum outcomes. It proposes answers to the following questions pertaining to higher education in times of crisis management:

- What factors influence the current practices of academic leaders' leadership roles during crises intervention?
- What support strategies are in place to assist academic leaders to achieve success in leading and managing employees and students during times of crises?

Leadership and higher education

Leadership in higher education needs to move beyond just the recognition of the leader as a change agent. It needs to consider a leader as one who leads, but is willing to be creative, share ideologies and ensure a collaborative approach to the field of education (Marinoni, Van't Land & Jensen, 2020:16-21). Given the complexities and the uncertainties of leadership in times of disrupted change, such as the current pandemic, leaders need to learn to shift their decision-making styles to match the changing environment. This kind of leadership style should also embrace a connected world, borrowing ideas and possible best operating practices. Traits, skills and behaviours of leaders in higher education often determine the way they utilise their power and influence to relate to each other. While there are numerous examples, models and frameworks in existence that attempt to distinguish effective leadership skills from poor ones, it is the contention of the authors that these often have far more commonalities than differences when one examines their essential elements. It is further posited that poor implementation strategies and accountability are far more frequently the root cause of problems. Although there may be acceptable methodologies for establishing priorities, decision-making and strategic planning for any higher education institution, the greatest challenge comes in the face of adversity when leaders have to orchestrate policies and plans in a way that produces desired and accepted results.

Impact of Covid-19 on higher education

The current Covid-19 pandemic has markedly placed unexpected and overwhelming demands on global health, educational and economic systems alike. No one ever assumed or envisioned the magnitude of the Coronavirus pandemic and its impact upon the world and higher education in general (Catton, 2020:1-3). The pandemic developed very rapidly and apart from all its observable undesirable effects, it has brought on many challenges in the field of academic leadership.

The massive scale of the outbreak and its sheer unpredictability, together with a high degree of uncertainty, gave rise to feelings of fear, disorientation, a sense of loss of control to some and a strong emotional disturbance in others. Rashid and Singh Yadav (2020:1-4) agree that these and other uncertainties evoked by this pandemic, have undoubtedly made it challenging for leaders of higher education institutions to respond. The authors also state that whilst the Covid-19 pandemic is considered a global humanitarian tragedy that continues to disrupt the lives of millions of people, it has become a major challenge for most learning institutions across the world. This crisis has undoubtedly presented an opportunity for higher education leaders to create more team cohesion while suggesting numerous innovative ways of curriculum conceptualisation, interpretation and implementation. In times of crisis, leaders within the different rungs of the higher education hierarchy, such as executive management, lecturers and team leaders of various departments, should be actively involved in coordinating and taking collective action (Rashid & Singh Yadav, 2020:1-4). The current pandemic has undoubtedly disrupted the balance of teaching and learning globally. This has forced academic leaders to face the monumental task of reassuring their peers, colleagues and the general university population, as well as persuading them to follow through on government decisions and its knock-on effect on university policy and protocol.

Since South Africa recorded its first confirmed case of Covid-19, universities have experienced entirely unexpected changes in the way they operate and in the way they deliver the academic programme. With the national lockdown in place, universities have had little option but to carry out different methods of teaching and learning to save the 2020 academic year. The Department of Higher Education and Training (DHET) has ordered curriculum coverage of the current programmes and for higher education institutions to manage the educational consequences of this crisis. Proactive and effective leadership was obviously needed to allow these curriculum imperatives to be met. Given the prolonged lockdown, insecurity and uncertainty of the Covid-19 pandemic, universities began progressively encouraging better relationships across the system; sharing existing resources and mutually creating solutions for what might well become a new standard in upcoming curriculum delivery (Universities South Africa, 2020:1).

In addition to upholding their core functions, universities have fully responded to and collaborated with other organisations in finding solutions to this unprecedented pandemic. This has undoubtedly stimulated a call for educational experts and formulation of task-teams to discuss, debate and examine possible solutions for the multitude of complex concerns that face higher education institutions (Universities South Africa, 2020:1). Although the custodians of higher education delivery are entrusted with the safety of students, faculty and staff, they have a mammoth task in leading the institution and getting all stakeholders to respond to policies and protocols. At many universities, teaching and training activities are occurring remotely to ensure the continued functionality of the organisations (Daniel, 2020:1). Although remote working may represent new and uncertain challenges for many organisations, there appears to be conflicting role functionality related to controlling and managing the change-readiness in organisations through such a platform. Those involved in complex social systems, like universities, play increasingly interdependent roles. It is therefore essential to understand how institutions are steering teaching and learning in the present situation. Adoption of best operating practices and sharing of guidelines and resources from other universities add to collective learning and cross-enrichment (UNESCO: International Institute for Higher Education in Latin America and the Caribbean (IESALC), 2020:6).

Need for leadership dexterity in higher education

As a result of the Covid-19 pandemic, higher education institutions throughout the world are on high alert. Those in leadership positions have been obligated to reflect on the institution's educational vision and mission to ensure student learning outcomes and standards of educational quality are not compromised. While the Covid-19 crisis requires a clear understanding of the threat, focusing on the challenges it brings, allow those in positions of leadership and governance to strategise in the face of this unprecedented hardship. Maringe (2020:1) agrees that this pandemic presents a historic opportunity to entrench a joint response in the educational system that includes a focus on social determinants of effective leadership to inform decision-making whilst addressing challenges such as inequities in risk factors and accessibility. Recent turn of events such as the "second wave" of the pandemic has heightened the need for robust decision-making and recognises the importance of social solidarity within the realms of the higher education sector. Strengthening the educational system and its processes from registration of students until graduation requires effective leadership from all vantage points and is more important now than ever. Strielkowski and Wang (2020:1) assert that academic leadership might benefit from the Covid-19 pandemic in a way that no one foresaw and is receiving much attention and importance as people have to face many unusual challenges. The authors also note that it is ironical that all these changes happened without any specific leadership or leaders leading the way.

Bureaucracy and "red-tape" in the higher education sector, that once could have clogged the channels of effective governance, have now been replaced with continuous discussions amongst key stakeholders in higher education in a decentralised approach (Marinoni, Van't Land & Jensen, 2020: 24-38). Many things that would be impossible, or next to impossible, to implement in academia and the higher education sector, due to the administrational rules and codes, are being implemented in a matter of days. This has further allowed for the latest developments regarding the impacts of the Covid-19 pandemic on the education sector to be reviewed and debated, while strengthening and enhancing the leadership skills and qualities of those participating in such robust discussions.

According to Marinoni, Van't Land and Jensen (2020:16-21), leadership in difficult times can be developed, and the abilities of those that have been long-standing leaders are tested. This goes beyond the obvious examples of professors, deans and heads of departments, to lecturers, students and many others. Leaders hold positions of power and how each chooses to wield such power plays out in numerous ways. This ultimately defines the shift from responding to the crisis to recovering from it and require leaders to help move from an internal, functional view to a view focused on all stakeholders and organisational outcomes (Bell, 2013:83).

Leaders depend upon their followers and their definitions and thoughts about leadership. One cannot exist without the other and followers need to see their leaders as trustworthy, charismatic and transformational (Felfe & Schyns, 2010:393).

21

Presently, leaders dealing with this unforeseen pandemic are being analysed by their followers. What makes a person a leader is compound, especially during crises such as the one we all face now. Nair (2020:2) reports that the response of people during a crisis is often to look to leaders to do something. How do leaders respond in ways that still uphold their standing as leaders, but permit them to be adaptable and accommodating during a pandemic? It would be useful here to look at how leaders seem to perform against the expectations of the staff, students and the public.

Types of leadership required in higher education

Leadership is a multifaceted experience and can mean many things. Maringe (2020:1) found that many people define leadership simply as the act of influencing others to think and act in certain ways. However, the same author reports that, while this is true, it does not go far enough to capture what is really needed to lead others in times of crisis. In this context, it can be argued that there is a need for transformational leaders who display confidence, are able to inspire and are seen as collaborative and inclusive. During transformation, there is also an anticipation that leaders should take charge and provide clear directions for crisis management (Hui, Sajjad, Wang, Muhammad, Khaqan & Shafi, 2019:5). What then emerges is an approach to transformational leadership.

Problems that arise every day do not have easy or singular solutions, and leaders who merely give directions and expect them to be followed will not succeed in this environment. What is needed is a style of leadership that involves working with others as full partners in a context of mutual respect and collaboration (Al Khajeh, 2018:1-10). The benefits of collaboration amongst diverse professionals have frequently been documented. Interdisciplinary teamwork is frequently not the norm within the university culture. However, in the face of adversity, such as the catastrophic effects of the Covid-19 pandemic, changing this culture is often not easy, but essential.

What is desperately needed is a new kind of leadership that flows in all directions and at all levels. Everyone from the classroom to the boardroom must engage colleagues, subordinates and executives, so that together they can identify and achieve common goals (Taher, 2018:1). Higher education professionals need to work together to break down the walls of hierarchical silos and hold each other accountable for improving quality whilst employing the principles of crisis management. There should be a display of capacity by all concerned to adapt to the continually evolving dynamics of the educational system under threat.

Literature review

Leadership

Management and leadership are key components for service delivery and although the two are similar in some respects, Al Khajeh (2018:1-10) notes that they may involve different types of outlook, skills, and behaviours by different people managing and leading a particular unit or sector. Recently, the responsibility of managers has become more important than ever due to demands for the development of policies and strategies in order to salvage the academic year (Taher, 2018:1). Leadership has become an important aspect of managing colleagues or fellow employees, especially in a changing and challenging environment. As educational organisations restructure to meet the demands for accessible, efficient, safe and affordable education delivery, people in management roles are under constant pressure to develop new skills and strategies to meet the challenges that accompany system changes (Zhao, 2020:29-33). Leaders need to be mindful of how complex factors such as the environment, diversity of staff members, resources and organisational policies and protocols affect the effectiveness of academic team functions. Duffield, Roche, Diers, Catling Paull and Blay (2010:2242-2251) note that good managers should strive to be good leaders, and good leaders need management skills to be effective in their roles.

Leadership and people management

According to Bell (2013:83-91), leadership is the kind of power where one person has the ability to influence or change the values, beliefs, behaviour and attitudes of other people. Leadership effectiveness is displayed based on staff motivation, productivity and the ability to develop and nurture fellow staff members, using good communication skills. Effective leadership involves having a clear vision and a clear plan of action of how to turn it into reality, whilst dealing with industrial relations in order to minimise friction amongst the staff. A study done by Amanchukwu, Stanley and Ololube (2015:4) found that leadership empowerment could be utilised as a tool to get better outcomes amongst employees and thereby promote job satisfaction. Hughes (2018:3-5) adds that to empower means to delegate the responsibility and therefore people that are delegated tasks should also understand that responsibility goes hand in hand with accountability. Therefore, the strength of every organisation lies with leadership empowerment.

This crisis has called for many leadership skills to come to the fore for many people "captaining their ship." Skills such as interpersonal skills, the ability to think strategically, prioritising and the ability to empathise with fellow employees are vital components of effective leadership. Boamah, Laschinger, Wong and Clarke (2018:180), agree that although key characteristics of leadership include establishing principles for strategic planning and empowering and mentoring the team to lead them to their goals, it also means that leadership is not necessarily getting caught up in all the details, but rather setting the plan and inspiring people to follow it. Al Khajeh (2018:1-10) adds that a leader who empathises with employees can emerge from any crisis stronger and better than before. Armstrong, Rispel and Penn-Kekana (2015:24-26) agree with the above authors and state that people inherit certain qualities that make them better suited to leadership. It is particularly important for organisations to have the right kind of leadership in order to cope with the complexities and competitiveness that prevail in such an environment.

The current unprecedented Covid-19 complexities have redefined the landscapes of not only the teaching and learning sectors of higher education, but also disrupted the research outputs of scholars and students alike. The organisational challenges that appear to affect other structures of the university functionality require strong leaders in all spheres (Rispel, 2015:1-4).

Transformational leadership

Transformational leaders work to enhance the motivation and engagement of followers by directing their behaviour towards a shared vision. Rispel (2015:1-4) agrees that transformational leaders seek to motivate and inspire workers, choosing to influence rather than direct others.

They can also articulate the organisational vision, conform to values and norms, build trust and motivate other staff members to achieve organisational goals (Ramesh & Hegde, 2017:552). This type of leadership is defined as a leadership approach that causes valuable and positive change in individuals and social systems with the end goal of developing such followers into leaders. This kind of leadership also enhances the motivation, morale and performance of followers, allowing them to connect themselves to the mission and identity of the organisation. The application of these theories depends on the situation at hand (Hughes, 2018:4).

While organisations and employees may feel "bruised" by lockdown rules due to the Covid-19 pandemic, recovery states appear to be aligned to a transformational leadership model. This allows for a positive organisational performance and the achievement of strategic goals (Amanchukwu et al., 2015:4). The same authors note that effective leadership is driven by an appropriate leadership style, which is exhibited within environmental contexts and contingencies. The current pandemic has highlighted the need for leadership that requires a new way of thinking and doing.

Theoretical underpinning

From a holistic perspective, an image of a leader during challenging times emerges as someone who can work collaboratively, obtain the best information possible, engage in thoughtful planning, execute well, act decisively and inspire confidence. It is an almost impossible task and no one person ever gets it completely right (Rengen, 2020:1). Leadership comes with its own difficulties and growing pains as being decisive and taking responsibility for others is not easy. The Covid-19 pandemic has made leadership roles even more challenging as leaders are faced with anxious students and staff.

The authors of this paper have posited Burns' Transformational Leadership Framework as its theoretical underpinning. This framework illustrates that those in leadership roles have an ongoing task to consider ways beyond being just a manager, especially when dealing with crisis intervention. Strategic discussions pave the way for sharing and implementation of knowledge, experience and wisdom. Therefore, Burns' Transformational Leadership Framework challenges leaders to take ownership of their work and understand the strengths and weaknesses of followers, so that the leader can align followers with tasks that optimise their performance (Choi, Kim, Ullah & Kang, 2016:459). This framework (see Figure 2.1) also emphasises the importance and support of governance structures in any institution.

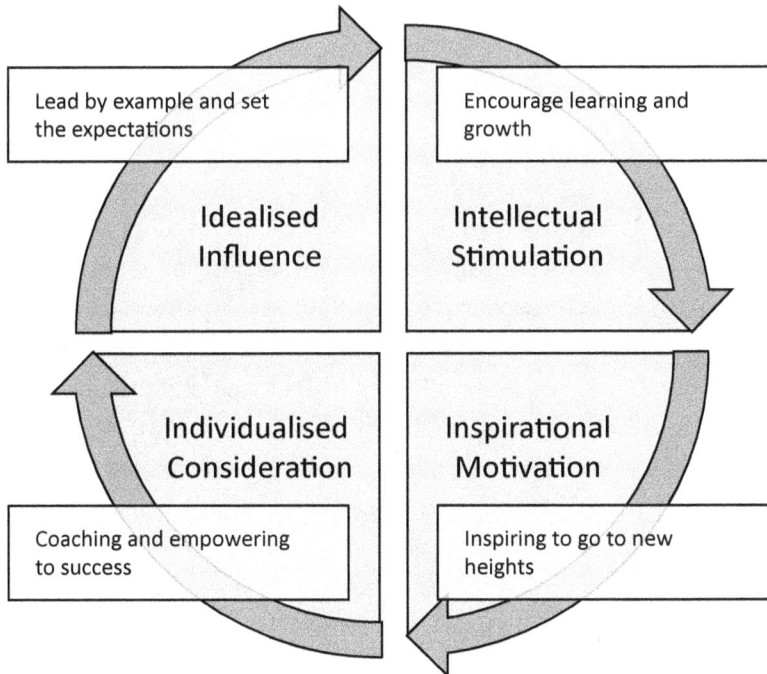

Figure 2.1   Burns' Transformational Leadership Framework (Hughes, 2018:4)

Application of the Burns' transformational framework

Idealised influence

This implies that a leader should serve as a role model for persons that they are responsible or accountable for and should therefore be respectable and trustworthy. Subordinates or followers should be able to emulate this individual and internalise his/her ideals (Hughes, 2018:4). In the context of the current crisis facing the higher education sector, this component will serve to ensure that all academic leaders are role models to their team members and should lead by example.

The role of leadership in planning for and managing crises is considered within the contextual dimensions of responsible leadership, stakeholder management and sustainability. Most of the academic processes and practices that are currently in use are not designed for the high levels of instability of the academic environment and potential crisis. That is why many academic models are altered or even completely changed in times of crisis. A leader's behaviour is rarely, if ever, the issue planned for, debated or even considered a potential risk. Since they are monitors, inspirers or sponsors of the overall crisis readiness process, it is assumed that leaders would not be part of the problem, but of the solution. Yet in practice, it is often just the opposite and the crisis occurs as a result of the inadequate behaviour of leaders and, more frequently, the crisis is not resolved efficiently due to inadequate leadership (Tafra-Vlahović, 2016:57-63).

Inspirational motivation

Transformational leadership is the promotion of a vision, a mission and a set of values to the members of the team. This allows for teamwork, and commitment is therefore guaranteed because of enthusiasm and optimism (Choi et al., 2016:459). Thus, this type of leader can inspire and motivate his/her team through their behaviour and actions and successfully steer them towards their goals. Within the context of uncertainty, due to the restructuring of the academic year, a manager who inspires his/her team will positively influence his/her staff and thereby increase job satisfaction and productivity (Hughes, 2018:4). People normally think of educational leaders as principals, superintendents, and higher education leaders in our schools, communities, and even businesses. However, educational leadership also exists outside of the classroom, for example, whenever someone in a position of influence works to guide teachers, students, parents, or policymakers towards a common education-related goal (Felfe & Schyns, 2010:393-410).

Intellectual stimulation

Transformational leaders do not only challenge the status quo, but also encourage creativity amongst followers as they allow the team to explore new ways of doing things and new opportunities to learn (Hughes, 2018:3-5). This component can be applied to the lack of understanding and fear of the unknown that the restructuring of academic programmes has had on staff and students. Working remotely can have its challenges, but a positive practice environment is achievable if managed by a team leader who regularly engages with and involves staff in decision-making. Higher education leadership is more important now than ever before. Covid-19 has changed universities' reality in general and the concept of teaching in particular. University leaders are looking for a new world of teaching that will cater to the diverse needs of their students. In order to learn how to operate in challenging and unpredictable circumstances, leaders need to create a culture of innovation within their organisations (Tamrat & Teffera, 2020:1).

There is a need for transformative leaders to support a collegial and innovative culture that fosters motivation and commitment, and that can strengthen the collective efficacy beliefs of their academic staff. Covid-19, which is currently putting the global education system to the test, creates stress that can undermine academic staffs' self-confidence. Developing a culture of innovation is directly attributed to leadership behaviour. Accordingly, leaders must act in ways that promote and support organisational innovation (Baqutayan, Jamaluddin, Hazizi Omar & Parvez, 2018:33). As transformational leaders, the focus must be on fostering educational processes and personal commitment, while leading their educational staff to change their teaching practices. Moving people towards new challenges emphasises the transformational approach to leadership that calls for emotional support, interpersonal relations and the creation of a safe environment which allows both right and wrong answers (Litz & Blaik-Hourani, 2020:1).

Individual consideration

Transformational leaders offer support and encouragement to their team and the lines of communication are always kept open to foster supportive relationships (Hui et al., 2019:5). In this context, all academic leaders should be able to employ the principle of transparency, working together as a unit and supporting one another. This will not only encourage effective communication, but will also establish a trust relationship amongst staff members.

Leadership is associated with a position that has authority and is accompanied by clear line management responsibilities and the professional support of others. Covid-19 has dramatically changed conceptions of leadership and leadership practices. Educational leadership in times of the Covid-19 crisis is particularly demanding (Harris, 2020:321). Prior to Covid-19, the type of leadership most typically found in educational institutions could be described as traditional, following the contours of role and position.

Although higher education institutions cannot fully plan for crises, they can, and many do, engage in developing responses and processes to mitigate the short and longer-term impact of university closures (Azorin, 2020:1). In these processes, roles of educational leadership need to be given special emphasis and consideration for various reasons. As indicated by Tafra-Vlahović (2016:57-63), the leader is usually a decision maker who only makes decisions based on the assessment and proposals of the team. Yet, he/she nevertheless remains the most important individual in times of crisis.

As pointed out by Kerissey and Edmondson (2020:1), communicating with transparency means providing honest and accurate descriptions of reality, being as clear as humanly possible about what is known, what is anticipated, and what it means for people. It is crucial to convey the message in a way that people can understand, but communication cannot be utterly devoid of hope or people will simply give in to despair. Somewhere in that communication must be a hopeful vision of the future towards which people can direct their energy, because without hope, resolve is impossible. The authors of this chapter sought to identify the challenges facing academic leaders and therefore propose recommendations that can offer assistance to academic leaders to navigate the Coronavirus pandemic and other future crises.

Recommendations

The roles and responsibilities of leaders and managers have dramatically changed in the past few months. This is probably not an easy transition, as those in charge will be tested in areas where they may not have fully developed their leadership and management muscles. No doubt, the learning curve will be steep and they will need coaching, mentoring and support from relevant people. Before Covid-19, academic leaders focused on fostering innovation, as well as driving teaching and learning initiatives. Today, these leaders must make rapid decisions about how they react should they and the departments that they manage, encounter unforeseen obstacles, team shortages and operational challenges that drastically alter the scope of their roles and priorities. This is done whilst they and their teams are navigating personal and work-related health and safety concerns, working remotely and supporting their families, friends and colleagues through the pandemic. There are lessons to be learnt when thrown in this so-called "deep end". Those in positions of leadership need to decide with speed over precision, adapt boldly, deliver reliably and engage for impact. The following key areas are recommended for enhancement of sound decision-making when leading team members:

Defining priorities

Individualised consideration affords leaders the opportunity to make interactions with followers more meaningful. Leaders who personalise and encourage two-way communication can find it to be an asset for their organisation (Choi et al., 2016:460). Leaders should:

- Identify and communicate factors that might affect employee safety and care, ensuring that the issues identified are fully aligned with corrective actions as events unfold.
- Be aware that conflicts might arise amongst the priorities outlined and must decide between what is urgent and what is important and communicate accordingly.
- Empower other members of the academic team to make decisions where possible, clearly stating what needs to be escalated, by when and to whom. Those leading in the face of crises should drive decisions downward to all.

Adapting to circumstances

Intellectual stimulation involves transformational leaders resolving problems with new and innovative thinking and indirectly encouraging followers to think creatively in solving problems (Zhu, Newman, Miao & Hooke, 2013:94). Leaders should:

- Do a situational analysis early and often. They must identify those that can influence other team members and those that are knowledgeable about the impact of the Covid-19 crisis.
- Look at best operating practices and offer innovative ideas and solutions to the identified problems. Effective leaders should be aware of how to manage employees that are resistant to change and allow them to extend their antennae across all the systems but arrive at a win-win situation for the department.
- Communicate to all what is to be done. Correct and aligned policies and protocols need to be communicated and enforced, especially in view of the pandemic.

Many aspects of the Covid-19 pandemic are unprecedented, and dealing with situations of this magnitude is completely new to educators. On a smaller scale, the Human Immunodeficiency Virus (HIV) crisis and school shootings are examples of past and current issues education administrators have had to grapple with. Despite their differences, two things remain consistent: the importance of communication and the responsibility to protect vulnerable populations (Kozak, 2020:1).

Taking ownership

Through role modelling and idealised influence, transformational leaders help to build follower commitment to organisational goals and challenge followers to take greater ownership for their work (Boamah, Laschinger, Wong & Clarke, 2018:180). Leaders should:

- Align the team's focus and monitor their performance to create a culture of accountability.
- Maintain their composure even when others are uncertain or losing control and utilise coping mechanisms to deal with difficult employees.
- Ensure that their line managers are kept informed of departmental operations.

Engaging with team players

In the context of higher education, transformational leaders must be able to inspire and motivate their followers. For continued commitment, leaders need to continually send signals that encourage follower commitment, respect and loyalty. When leaders share in the sacrifice of an organisation, it can signal that there is a combined effort taking place. It can be positively interpreted and it can increase idealised influence (Shandraconis, 2013:3).

- Effective leaders should understand their team's circumstances and find ways to engage with them.
- All goals and new information should be clearly and thoroughly communicated to all. During remote work, relationships need to be strengthened and trust needs to be built to avoid a communication breakdown.
- Empathy is vital when leading in turbulent times. A leader showing colleagues or staff that he/she understands how they feel will help co-workers face the uncertainty with a lot more resilience.

For many educators, this is their first venture into teaching online. In addition to these new challenges, many of them are balancing more familial responsibilities, including taking care of children or other relatives. Administrators need to be conscious of this and make certain allowances to support their staff. Leadership also means looking out for the physical and mental well-being of students. This may mean turning to networks they have built within the community. Mental health centres, faith-based organisations, nursing and health centres, social services and administrators can utilise these connections to create a network that parents and students can turn to for help (Kozak, 2020:1).

Sharing of knowledge

The transformational style of leadership encourages leaders to empower followers, and allows them to draw on the collective intelligence of their followers and seek to create novel solutions to treat a crisis (Shadraconis, 2013:11). Navigating unchartered territories like the Covid-19 pandemic is frightening and investments in support, mentoring and training can go a long way towards motivating and boosting a team's morale.

- Crisis intervention can reveal a great deal about a person's leadership quality, and it is important to assess how team members function in a time like this. A leader may have to consider the redistribution of tasks and allocate workloads in the best interest of the employee, student and department.
- A leader should constantly engage with those who are willing to share practices that are helping to overcome hurdles and adapt them to suit their department. They should utilise departmental expertise that can offer education and training within and outside the faculty. This will not only allow for the growth and the development of fellow colleagues, but also give them a sense of purpose in trying times.

In times of crisis, leaders have to put in place teams and people who are capable of dealing with the unexpected, people who have a capacity for making and implementing, as well as reviewing and recalibrating decisions. It is a time to set up such crisis teams across all levels of the organisation rather than expect everyone or, least of all, the usual organisational structures to deal with the crisis.

Creating opportunities for constructive engagement

Intellectually stimulating leaders help make their followers more innovative and creative by creating opportunities for constructive engagement with other organisations. The desire to outsmart others and to be the most successful creates self-imposed solitary confinement which rarely breeds success, especially in the context of a global pandemic (Maringe, 2020:2).

- Educational leaders need to convene frequently, not just to share intelligence, but, more importantly, to create the shared wisdom required for joint decisions and action. Similar structures are necessary in higher education, health and other sectors (Maringe, 2020:2).

Planning beyond the Covid-19 pandemic

Unlike other globally disruptive events, such as natural catastrophes or terrorist events, determining the potential scope of such an extraordinary pandemic event is extremely difficult. Notably, the fear it has generated can be as devastating as the pandemic. Therefore, one has to step back and reflect on what lessons are learnt from this and what strategies can assist in coping with future catastrophes of this kind. Even after the pandemic subsides, a growing prevalence of online learning will be seen at all educational levels, further highlighting the importance of technology in teaching and learning (Maringe, 2020:2).

Higher education institutions need reimagining, not just repairing. Educators, policymakers, employers and investors must urgently give thought to what a post-Covid-19 world should look like and what role higher education institutions must play to make that world a reality (Marmolejo, 2020:1). Crises tend to consume leaders in the here and now and sometimes understandably so. Organisations rarely move back to the status quo after a crisis. Failure to plan for the post-crisis era is the worst form of short-sightedness. Efforts must be made to prepare for the new organisation, which always emerges from major crises such as the current pandemic. Leading in times of crisis goes beyond mere adaptation of an organisation, requiring a strong people-first approach, as well as a desire to connect with and not outshine others. It also requires reorganisation of the institution to face the crisis squarely and robustly and, above all, a vision that goes beyond the crisis (Maringe, 2020:2).

Conclusion

For educational and academic leaders, the Covid-19 pandemic is a classical transformative challenge that one must adapt to (Reimers, Schleicher, Saavedra & Tuominen, 2020:1). Educational leaders must swiftly design responses to the emerging education challenges as the pandemic runs its course. The goal is to protect young people's educational opportunities during and following the pandemic. What leaders need during a crisis is not a predefined response plan but altered behaviours and mind-sets that will prevent them from overreacting to yesterday's developments and help them look ahead. As much as the journey of recovery will be a critical one for the entire global community, it will require a leadership style that aligns with and is successfully able to navigate the turbulent terrain that is the repercussion of such a pandemic. Massive challenges still lie ahead as this global crisis is not yet over. Educational leaders have a crucial role to play in steering a safe, ethical, and shared passage through, so that all learners will see better days (Harris, 2020:326).

References

Al Khajeh, E.H. 2018. Impact of leadership styles on organizational performance. *Journal of Human Resources Management Research*, 8(1):1-10. https://doi.org/10.5171/2018.322892.

Amanchukwu, R., Stanley, G. & Ololube, N. 2015. A review of leadership theories, principles, styles, and their relevance to educational management. *Management*, 5(1):6-14. https://doi:10.5923/j.mm.20150501.02

Armstrong, S.J., Rispel, L.C. & Penn-Kekana, L. 2015. The activities of hospital nursing unit managers and quality of patient care in South African hospitals: A paradox? *Global Health Action*, 8(1):24-26. https://doi.org/10.3402/gha.v8.26243.

Azorín, C. 2020. Beyond Covid-19 supernova. Is another education coming? *Journal of Professional Capital and Community*, 5(2):1-5. https://doi.org/10.1108/JPCC-05-2020-0019.

Baqutayan, S.M., Jamaluddin, N., Hazizi Omar, H. & Parvez, D.H. 2018. Leadership framework intensifies innovation culture in an organization. *Journal of Advanced Research in Social and Behavioural Sciences*, 10(1):33-49.

Bell, R.M. 2013. Charismatic leadership case study with Ronald Reagan as exemplar. *Emerging Leadership Journeys*, 65(1):83-91.

Boamah, S.A., Laschinger, H.S., Wong, C. & Clarke, S. 2018. Effect of transformational leadership on job satisfaction and patient safety outcomes. *Nursing Outlook*, 66(2):180-189. https://doi.org/10.1016/j.outlook.2017.10.004.

Catton, H. 2020. Global challenges in health and health care for nurses and midwives everywhere. *Nursing and Health Policy Perspectives*, 67(1):1-3. https://doi.org/10.1111/inr.12578

Choi, S.B., Kim, K., Ullah, S.M.E. & Kang, S.W. 2016. How transformational leadership facilitates innovative behavior of Korean workers: Examining mediating and moderating processes. *Personnel Review*, 45(3):459-479. https://doi.org/10.1108/PR-03-2014-0058

Daniel, S.J. 2020. Education and the Covid-19 pandemic. *Comparative Journal of Curriculum, Learning, and Assessment*, 48(3-4):1-21. https://doi:10.1007/s11125-020-09464-3.

Duffield, C., Roche, M.A., Diers, D., Catling-Paull, C. & Blay, N. 2010. Staffing, skill mix and the model of care. *Journal of Clinical Nursing*, 19(15-16):2242-2251. https://doi.org/10.1111/j.1365-2702.2010.03225.x

Felfe, J. & Schyns, B. 2010. Followers' personality and the perception of transformational leadership: Further evidence for the similarity hypothesis. *British Journal of Management*, 21(2):393-410. https://doi.org/10.1111/j.1467-8551.2009.00649.x

Harris, A. 2020. Covid-19: School leadership in crisis? *Journal of Professional Capital and Community*, 5(3/4):321-326. https://doi.org/10.1108/JPCC-06-2020-0045

Hughes, K. 2018. 4 elements of transformational leaders. *American Journal of Operations Research*, 9(5):3-5.

Hui, L., Sajjad, N., Wang, Q., Muhammad Ali, A., Khaqan, Z. & Shafi, A. 2019. Influence of transformational leadership on employees' innovative work behavior in sustainable organizations: Test of mediation and moderation processes. *Sustainability*, 11(6):1-21. https://doi.org/10.3390/su11061594.

Kerrissey, M.J. & Edmondson, A.C. 2020. *What good leadership looks like during this pandemic*. Harvard Business Review. Available at: http://bit.ly/3shUWcf [Accessed 13 April 2020].

Kozak, M. 2020. *Tips for principals and superintendents on leading during the Covid-19 pandemic*. Drexel University. Available at: http://bit.ly/31bwfSN [Accessed 13 April 2020].

Litz, D. & Blaik-Hourani, R. 2020. *Transformational leadership and change in education*. Oxford Research Encyclopedia of Education. Available at: http://bit.ly/3vTghLq [Accessed 20 April 2020].

Maringe, F. 2020. *Lessons for university leaders from the Covid-19 crisis*. University World News. Available at: https://www.universityworldnews.com [Accessed 20 May 2020].

Marinoni, G., Van't Land, H. & Jensen, T. 2020. *The impact of Covid-19 on higher education around the world*. International Association of Universities, Covid-19 Global Impact Survey, 16-38. Available at: https://bit.ly/2QvQIzQ [Accessed 12 June 2020].

Marmolejo, F. 2020. *We need to reimagine higher education, not just repair it*. University World News. Available at: http://bit.ly/3ccRb27 [Accessed 12 June 2020].

Nair, V. 2020. *Leadership during Covid-19*. Available at: https://www.csagup.org. [Accessed 20 June 2020].

Ramesh, R.S. & Hegde, M. 2017. The impact of transformational and transactional leadership on organizational performance: References in literature. *Paripex-Indian Journal of Research*, 6(3):552-554.

Rashid, S. & Singh Yadav, S. 2020. Impact of Covid-19 pandemic on higher education and research. *Indian Journal of Human Development*, 14(2):1-4. https://doi.org/10.1177/0973703020946700

Reimers, F., Schleicher, A., Saavedra, J. & Tuominen, S. 2020. *Supporting the continuation of teaching and learning during the Covid-19 pandemic*. OECD. Available at: https://bit.ly/3falrN0 [Accessed 13 July 2020].

Rengen, P. 2020. *The heart of resilient leadership: Responding to Covid-19. A guide for senior executives*. Available at: http://bit.ly/3f5Z3o1 [Accessed 11 July 2020].

Rispel, L. 2015. Transforming nursing in South Africa. *Global Health Action*, 8(1):1-10. https://doi.org/10.3402/gha.v8.28005

Shadraconis, S. 2013. Organizational leadership in times of uncertainty: Is transformational leadership the answer? *LUX: A Journal of Transdisciplinary Writing and Research from Claremont Graduate University*, 2(1):1-28. https://doi.org/10.5642/lux.201301.28

Strielkowski, W. & Wang, J. 2020. An Introduction: Covid-19 pandemic and academic leadership. *Advances in Social Science, Education and Humanities Research*, 441(1):1-6. https://doi.org/10.2991/assehr.k.200526.001.

Syracuse University Libraries, Special Collections Research Centre. 2011. Available at: https://bit.ly/39uUBeY [Accessed 1 April 2020].

Tafra-Vlahović, M. 2016. *Leadership in crisis management*. The World Guide to Sustainable Enterprise, 3(1):57-63. Available at: https://bit.ly/2PD7NXS [Accessed 1 April 2020].

Taher, R. 2018. What is the role of the unit manager in creating an environment conducive to innovation with reference to continuous improvement and innovation of the unit? *Innovations*, 8(7):1.

Tamrat, W. & Teferra D. 2020. *Covid-19 poses a serious threat to higher education*. University World News. Available at: http://bit.ly/3fjH3XB [Accessed 13 June 2020].

UNESCO: International Institute for Higher Education in Latin America and the Caribbean (IESALC). 2020. *Covid-19 and higher education: Today and tomorrow*. IESALC. Available at: https://bit.ly/316Ni8N [Accessed 13 April 2020].

Universities South Africa. 2020. *Public universities have either embraced emergency teaching/ learning, or are getting ready for the inevitable, in the Covid-19 era*. Available at: https://bit.ly/2PhatKM [Accessed 14 June 2020].

Zhao, Y. 2020. Covid-19 as a catalyst for educational change. *Prospects*, 49(1):29-33. https://doi.org/10.1007/s11125-020-09477-y

Zhu, W., Newman, A., Miao, Q. & Hooke, A. 2013. Revisiting the mediating role of trust in transformational leadership effects: Do different types of trust make a difference? *Leadership Quarterly*, 24(1):94-105. https://doi.org/10.1016/j.leaqua.2012.08.004

COVID-19 HIGHLIGHTS INEQUALITIES BETWEEN HISTORICALLY BLACK AND HISTORICALLY WHITE SOUTH AFRICAN UNIVERSITIES

A comparative analysis

Nduduzo C Ndebele and Victor H Mlambo

Introduction

Under apartheid, higher education in South Africa was skewed in ways designed to entrench the power and privilege of the ruling white minority. The Bantu Education Act of 1952 for example, ensured that black South Africans received an education that would limit their educational potential and thus, remain in the working class. However, Case, Marshall, McKenna and Mogashana (2018) lament how apartheid had developed a two-tier higher education system in the country. The first tier was for the privileged and the haves; they were afforded to study in universities that were from a developmental perspective prioritised by the apartheid regime. These institutions were characterised by the availability of infrastructure, human capital, and were mostly located in metropolitan areas. The second tier was to cater for the previously disadvantaged, mostly the African population (black South Africans, Indians and coloureds). Their location was away from the metropolis, they were structurally challenged, and were not viewed from the same confines as their white counterparts (Case et al, 2018).

South Africa has 11 historically black universities that played a crucial role in shaping the development of the higher education sector in the country. These are: The University of Bophuthatswana – recently renamed the North-West University

(NWU); the University of Durban-Westville (UDW); the University of Fort Hare; the Medical University of South Africa (MEDUNSA); the University of the North-Turfloop (main branch); the University of the North-Qwaqwa; the University of Transkei; the University of Venda (UNIVEN); Vista University; the University of the Western Cape (UWC); and the University of Zululand (Unizulu) (Badat, Barron, Fisher, Pillay & Wolpe, 1994 in Subotzky, 1997). When apartheid ended in 1994, there were 36 higher education institutions in the country. Of this number, ten were historically disadvantaged universities and seven historically disadvantaged technikons which were solely meant for the use of black South Africans (Bunting, 2006:35), while ten historically advantaged universities and seven historically advantaged technikons were designated for the exclusive development of white South Africans. Two distance learning institutions catered for all races.

However, more than two decades after the end of apartheid and the consolidation of multiparty politics in South Africa, Carolissen and Bozalek (2017:346) explain that the higher education sector, like other levels of education, has been, and continues to be, deeply affected by its apartheid past. The author reveals that despite the existence of national documents such as the Ministerial Committee on Transformation and Social Cohesion, the education landscape has not considerably changed and remains skewed with historically white universities still at the apex in terms of research and development, and teaching and learning. Carolissen and Bozalek (2017:347) further attest that even today, the concept of dualism in higher education still exists, i.e. institutions and academic developments associated with whiteness are normatively considered excellent and desirable; in this case universities. The converse is conceptual blackness where institutions and practices associated with blackness are normatively considered to be mediocre and less desirable. For Bozalek and Boughey (2012) this mismatch between the higher education sector today is largely because apartheid impacted the higher education system in numerous ways. Not only were separate institutions for black and white population groups established, but the programs these different kinds of institutions could offer were also defined by apartheid beliefs about the roles considered appropriate for different social groups.

It is with this contention that this chapter argues that Covid-19 has, to a great extent, laid bare the structural inequalities that exist between historically black universities (HBUs) and historically white universities (HWUs) in South Africa. The chapter, therefore, seeks to examine how HBUs and HWUs have responded to the raging pandemic.

Methodological issues

To gain a deeper understanding of this subject matter, this chapter first seeks to systematise the existing empirical literature on HBUs, HWUs and Covid-19. By addressing existing empirical literature, the chapter provides a sound basis for a more evidence-based discussion of this highly-debated issue. However, the chapter takes into consideration that Covid-19 is a recent issue, hence there are still few empirical studies that have been done to effectively document the phenomenon within the context of South Africa's higher education sector. Nonetheless, the chapter did its best to synthesise the existing literature (incorporating global examples) to answer the objectives of this chapter. Taking into account the historical debates around the 'un-equalness' of South Africa's higher education sector, secondary sources will provide an exhaustive pool of information, hence, aiding the study to reach meaningful conclusions informed by current debates and narratives.

Higher education enrolment in a pre and post-apartheid South Africa

South Africa has 26 public universities with nearly one million students, while 700 000 students are registered at more than 50 higher education training colleges (TVET colleges – Technical Vocational Education Training). An additional 90 000 students can be found at various private institutions (Tjønneland, 2017). The establishment of the South African College in Cape Town in 1829 for people of European descent marked the beginning of tertiary education in South Africa. The apartheid regime, as argued by Raju (2006), was successful in creating a higher education system that was complex and discriminatory. The higher education system of the 1990s consisted of 21 universities, 15 technikons, and a host of colleges including teacher training colleges, agricultural colleges, and colleges of nursing. However, under apartheid, African students were legally prohibited from attending the 19 white higher education institutions and could only enrol in six institutions designated specifically for their use (Bunting, 2006:38-40). In essence, this meant that higher education for blacks was to take place exclusively in the homelands, in colleges that were defined in tribal, as well as racial terms, i.e. Zulus would attend classes with Zulus, Xhosas with Xhosas, and so on for each of the major ethnic groups among South Africa's black majority. Moreover, a HBU was, therefore, more likely to offer nursing rather than medicine and public administration or political philosophy. Under apartheid, research was structured to serve the white population and the need for the security of this group on a continent wracked with wars for independence (Bawa & Mouton, 2001). This segregation created a dual education system that was unequal and unjust. Subscribing to the above, Carolissen and Bozalek (2017:347) argue that the concept of dualism, as reflected by Plumwood (1993), arises when there are two opposites, which are then hierarchised.

For McKeever (2017:117-124), the establishment of English schools in 1902 resulted in the government importing teachers from abroad, and created a structure and curriculum to match the English system of education. This arrangement was rebuffed by many whites in South Africa who did not want a predominantly English curriculum with English as the medium of instruction. Afterwards, disgruntled by the thought of an English curriculum, this group, mostly Afrikaaners but also other whites of non-English descent, set up a parallel system of schooling based on principles known as Christian National Education (CNE) (McKeever, 2017:118). These two parallel systems were developed to serve whites, whereas the third system of education, for black South Africans, coloureds, and Indians, consisted primarily of schools established and run by Christian (usually foreign) missionaries. This segregation ultimately found its way to higher education, where universities were predominately seen as white, whereas those which were meant for blacks were pushed to the confines of rural areas.

The racialisation of higher education ought to achieve one element, restrict quality education for blacks and deepen the divisions among them to preserve the white rule. Rural-based colleges for blacks were not on par with that of their white counterparts, hence the education offered in terms of quality was skewed. The quality of academic programmes and teaching was uneven, as were the qualifications of academics (Rensburg, 2006; cited in Stanfordmagazine, 2007). While some HBUs can enrol students (and thus earn input subsidy), their ability to earn output subsidy based on graduation and throughput rates is negatively affected because of their inability to provide the sort of intense teaching and support these students need (Bozalek & Boughey, 2012). Observing this from the realms of Fraser's normative framework on social justice, Bozalek and Boughey (2012) expounded that social arrangements must be such that they allow individuals to participate as equals in the following spheres: economic, cultural, and political. However, within the context of higher education, even though one may be able to vote and participate in social movements, Fraser introduced a second level of representation, which pertained to the aspect of boundary setting. This happens when higher education establishes boundaries that exclude some groups or institutions and includes others, which Fraser terms as mis-framing them. Educational differences created from the apartheid era onward have great importance for understanding continuing inequalities in contemporary South Africa, especially within the context of the black population.

The 1994 democratic elections in South Africa signalled the need for change in the higher education sector. This sector witnessed significant changes in the 1990s as a result of post-apartheid legislation, as well as global and national changes in the economy. Post-apartheid legislation de-radicalised universities and other institutions in the higher education sector (Raju, 2006). Immediately after this, the higher education sector was a less regulated market atmosphere. However, this de-regulation of higher education came with its consequences, for example, it resulted in a widening of gaps in higher education. Exemplifying this, Raju (2006) argued that HWUs and technikons were able to consolidate their leading positions within higher education in the country, whereas HBUs were plagued by administration and governance issues and were losing students in massive numbers. Bozalek and Boughey (2012) explained that the functioning of the higher education sector in the apartheid era was governed and resourced differently. HWUs were given the administrative and financial power to make decisions concerning the spending of government subsidy, the setting of tuition fees, the number of staff to employ, and how any surplus should be invested. This, however, was not the case for HBUs who were considerably more constrained in the decisions they could make. Moreover, budgeting for these HBUs involved gaining approval for expenditure from the controlling government department. This means they did not possess the operational autonomy as their white counterparts, which further impeded their effective functioning.

To address these injustices, firstly, there was the urgent need to increase the enrolment of those who were previously disadvantaged and secondly, there was the need to ensure that HBUs eventually match HWUs in terms of development and educational output. However, what these urgent needs failed to reflect or perhaps take into consideration was that for HBUs to catch up to HWUs, significant investments would be needed. These would range from infrastructure development, human capital provision, and Information and Communications Technology (ICT).

HBUs during apartheid were poorly funded compared to HWUs. Library facilities were minimal and teaching venues were poorly equipped. One significant feature of black campuses was the architecture that was designed to impede movement in cases of civil unrest. Such poor design continues to impact learning environments to this day (Bozalek & Boughey, 2012). Nevertheless, South Africa has seen a major expansion of student enrolment. University enrolment (including technikons and teacher training colleges) has increased from about 500 000 in 1994 to 938 201 in 2011 in public universities and universities of technology (Tjønneland, 2017). However, the chapter contends that the increase in student enrolment has not corresponded with the development of HBUs. Twenty-seven years after the demise of apartheid, HBUs are still experiencing problems inherited from the legacies of apartheid. It is with the above deliberation that this chapter argues that Covid-19 has laid bare the inequalities that exist between HWUs and HBUs. This chapter, however, acknowledges that while successive governments (post-1994) have been committed to redressing past injustices within the higher education sector, most of the HBUs have continued to remain completely black and have not witnessed significant changes that allow them to be on par with their white counterparts. While Covid-19 is just one of many issues that have plagued South Africa's higher education sector, it has, however, allowed one to observe how unequal the higher education system in South Africa continues to be. Post-1994, policy development with regards to higher education in South Africa had to deal with both the need for equity in the higher education sector and the need to prioritise development necessary for South Africa to engage with a rapidly globalising economy coupled with the influence of the internationalisation of higher education (Bozalek & Boughey, 2012; Mlambo, Ogunnubi & Mlambo, 2020).

Inequality, Covid-19 and higher education in South Africa

Conceptualising the concept of inequality within the context of higher education in South Africa is largely premised on the inability of HBUs to catch up with levels of development attained by HWUs. This was reinforced by Chetty and Knaus (2016), who pointed out that higher education is increasingly racially stratified, and it is particularly apparent in the concentration of black and coloured students at HBUs. Most of the white students attend the HWUs i.e. the University of Cape Town (UCT), the University of Witwatersrand (Wits), Stellenbosch University (SU), and the University of Pretoria (UP). These universities, before 1994, catered predominantly for the white minority, and even today, these institutions occupy top positions in local and international research rankings. Moreover, they charge much higher fees than HBUs. In a post-apartheid South Africa, this sadly maintains the class structure of apartheid society (Chetty & Knaus, 2016). Significantly, the long term lack of resourcing and continuing financial struggle appear to have impacted HBUs in other ways.

Access, success and completion rates continue to be racially skewed, with white completion rates being on average 50% higher than that of Africans (Smith, 2013). However, Bozalek and Boughey (2012) argued that the skewed higher education system in South Africa cannot be observed in isolation, rather, there is a need to look at the fragmented public schooling sysyem. Since 1994, the public schooling system is widely acknowledged to have failed, with the result that the majority of schools open to black learners continue to be marked by the sort of conditions characteristic of apartheid. This means that the impoverished nature of the educational experience offered at the secondary level eventually makes its way to higher education.

The 2015 #FeesMustFall protests marked a turbulent year for higher education in South Africa. Students protested against institutions' language policies, high fees, structural inequalities, and colonial symbols. It was poor and working-class youth who drove the protests – a clear indication that it is a class struggle. This is further emphasised by the fact that most of the students who protested, whether during 2015 or on other occasions, were black (Chetty & Knaus, 2016). Race and class lie at the heart of opposition to South Africa's existing exclusive university system. Needless to say, the debates around the #FeesMustFall movement have raised different narratives. Lekaba (2016) argued that the movement missed the opportunity to address imbalances of the past; rather it focused on the vandalism of properties and the violence emerging from the protests. For HBUs, the #FeesMustFall movement was just one of many examples of South Africa's unequal higher education sector (Mlambo, Hlongwa & Mubecua, 2017). Years of student riots and protests have dilapidated infrastructure which has compounded their ability to respond to Covid-19. Even though it was HWUs (with their high fees) that protested the most, some HBUs used this time to vent out their issues. However, media coverage was not evenly distributed, hence HWUs were seen as being at the forefront of the #FeesMustFall movement.

Covid-19 has therefore reinforced the inequalities that exist in South Africa's institutions of higher learning. Apart from racial observations, inequalities also exist in the form of lack of infrastructure in HBUs, the failure to attract and retain students, and the failure to attract skilled human capital. These challenges have existed for decades, but the academic fallout from Covid-19 has laid bare their colossal impact. Highlighting the negative impact of the pandemic, Mamokgethi Phakeng, the Vice-Chancellor of UCT, contended that the pandemic has 'fast-tracked conversations' about online learning (Kelly, 2020). Conversely, the Vice-Chancellor fails to reflect on the inequality that exists among universities in South Africa. Arguably UCT, considering its global reach and levels of development, may be able to manoeuvre quickly and introduce alternative learning systems, however the same cannot be said about HBUs who serve a student base largely from remote areas. However, Phakeng acknowledged that Covid-19 is exposing many of the country's problems as inequality and poverty have become much more pronounced (Kelly, 2020).

Additionally, Petersen (2020) argued that Covid-19 has unearthed inequalities that were not seen as less important, for example online learning systems and the need to incorporate technology in modern-day teaching. However, since 1994, such challenges have been in the public domain especially within the context of HBUs where issues of infrastructure and remote learning systems have always been seen as key challenges. While Covid-19 has had a ripple effect on HBUs, it becomes cumbersome to make sense of why these universities have not invested in remote eLearning systems. While salvaging the academic year remains a top priority in the higher education sector, salvaging the academic year ought to be underpinned by the need to ensure that no student gets left behind.

The chapter ponders how this will be accomplished as the majority of students in HBUs are contact students.The pandemic, however, has suspended such contact sessions and has forced universities to rethink how they deliver the academic programmes. This has left institutions with little choice, but to embark on wide-scale emergency teaching and learning to salvage the 2020 academic year, which has in most cases been online learning. It is with disputation that this chapter contends that while HBUs do have systems for online learning and support, historically however, they have not sufficiently entrenched them in their curricular of teaching and learning. In essence, the face of higher education in South Africa is a poor, black working-class young person who comes from the townships and villages that do not have the basic infrastructure that students need to function. Also, most households and communities are not conducive spaces for a fulfilling learning experience. Therefore, it becomes evident that the urgent rush to implement online learning in the hope of salvaging the academic year will present significant challenges for HBUs.

Responding to Covid-19 within the context of HWUs and HBUs: The question of teaching and learning

The quest to respond to the crippling effects of Covid-19 on higher education has rested on the following: the need to salvage the 2020 academic year; the need to ensure students, despite being away from campuses, are engaging in teaching and learning processes, and, more importantly, to prepare for the re-phasing of students back to campuses depending on the trajectory of the virus.

Saving the 2020 academic year

Salvaging the academic year is imperative, however, the chapter critiques the formula used to decide how universities ought to go about issuing laptops. The chapter acknowledges that the Department of Higher Education and Training (DHET) has been central in the process, however, the prioritisation of the NSFAS-funded students as key recipients of laptops and data bundles fails to reflect that many students are self-funded and are not under any form of sponsorship. This criterion, sadly, goes against the emphasis of not leaving any student behind. Moreover, the National Planning Commission, in its 2011 National Development Plan: Vision for 2030, proposes that the number of PhD graduates per year, which was 1 421 in 2010, be increased to 5 000 by 2030 (Mohamedbhai, 2012). However, the DHET and by extension many universities, both HWUs and HBUs, have been rather silent about how postgraduates are going to be catered for during this period.

Therefore, the chapter argues that the DHET's focus on the NSFAS-funded students sidelines the purpose of inclusivity, hence concluding that some students will be inevitably left out. Reinforcing this, Tawana Kupe, the Vice-Chancellor of UP as cited by Bothell (2020), argued that the Covid-19 crisis is likely to undermine the progress that South Africa has made post-apartheid in providing equal access to quality higher education. The Vice-Chancellor argued that a significant number of students in the country do not have the devices or stable enough electricity to study online and internet data costs were "very high". In essence, despite the pledge from universities to send laptops and data bundles, the issue of internet connectivity is still a problem; hence sending laptops does not guarantee that students will be able to partake in online learning processes. For HBUs, being able to cater for students who are located in rural areas will be difficult, hence implying the need for alternatives, for example physically delivering learning materials.

Engaging students in teaching and learning processes away from campuses

It becomes imperative for one to understand that the role of Covid-19 in exposing the inequalities in South Africa's higher education sector is not an isolated occurrence. Galvin (2020) noted that the same situation can be observed in the United States of America (USA), where African American, Latin American, and Native American students were educated in wholly segregated universities who are disadvantaged and underfunded. The National Academies and Issues in Science and Technology explained that historically black colleges and universities in the USA have struggled to respond to Covid-19. Such problems are compounded by financial challenges that the pandemic is bringing, a lack of technological set-up for online learning, and a need to help students returning to homes where they may not have had computers or connectivity. Black universities had fewer resources than their white counterparts and the financial structure of many black universities has left them especially vulnerable (Galvin, 2020). However, Bozalek and Boughey (2012) argued that the first issue in comparing educational standards is that we tend to ignore the problem itself, which is the system. In higher education, the first problem is mis-framing in that individual students, lecturers, and institutions, are held accountable for success in higher education endeavours, rather than the entire education system, which is inequitable. The authors argue that systems in HBUs struggle because of poor teaching practices of lecturers, the inadequate mix of programmes and qualifications offered by some institutions, the failure to align curricula, or in mismatches between mission and vision statements and what an institution is doing.

HBUs in South Africa show-case similar characteristics, hence the chapter argues looking at the response patterns between HBUs and HWUs. The latter has been able to take the lead in ensuring a seamless flow of teaching and learning without waiting on government support, nor direction, especially when it comes to online learning preparation; while the former has shown signs of uneasiness and a lack of resolve. One cannot blame HBUs for their lack of resolve, for Subotzky (1997) argued that the government, since 1994, has failed to address the governance problems that have plagued HBUs and these problems have become observable in a time of crisis. In 2009, Professor Jonathan Jansen was appointed as an administrator to head Mangosuthu University of Technology. In November 2011, Walter Sisulu University was placed under administration. In the same year, the University of Zululand was placed under administration for two years. In 2019, maladministration continued unabated as the University of Fort Hare was placed under administration (Hweshe, 2011; Mbanjwa, 2009; News24, 2011).

The above reflects that institutional governance issues have long plagued HBUs. Covid-19 has gone further expose these institutional shortcomings. On the contrary, no HWU was placed under administration in the same period. The chapter, therefore, argues that governance issues, provision of technological systems, sufficient human capital, infrastructure provision, and the location of HWUs have made major differences in how they managed to mitigate the impact of Covid-19. However, contrary to the above view on governance, Bozalek and Boughey (2012) argued that HBUs are struggling today not only because of governance-related issues, but also because of the legacy of apartheid. They were considerably more constrained in the decisions they could make and as such they were not able to build financial reserves. The controlled nature of the budgeting processes meant that the capacity to plan and handle financial resources was not always developed. After apartheid, this legacy had gone on to impact the ability of the HBUs to manage their finances in substantial ways. Hence, several HBUs have been placed under administration in recent years, because of the perceived failure to manage their affairs appropriately. Although corruption cannot be dismissed in such cases, neither can the fact that HBUs were systemically denied the opportunities to develop the capacity to manage their affairs under apartheid.

Nonetheless, it becomes narrow to view the response to Covid-19 within the realms of universities, without considering the location of their student population. That is, HBUs despite their shortcomings have made attempts to reach out to their students, but attempts have been hampered by the location of students. Most HBUs serve rural-based students, hence transporting study materials and laptops to these students may be cumbersome. Moreover, data usage may be hindered by the lack of telecommunication support in such areas. While HWUs also serve students in rural areas, their well-integrated online learning portals tend to mitigate the lack of communications support. Moreover, Bozalek and Boughey (2012) revealed that location, therefore, impacted academic life by contributing to the social segregation already introduced by apartheid legislation. Post-apartheid, this historical legacy continues to be significant. Universities in remote rural areas are, for example, less likely to attract highly-qualified staff than their HWU counterparts.

The DHET acknowledges that higher education is confronted by the very same inequalities it seeks to address. Institutions have taken a variety of actions to respond to the needs of their students. Sadly, the responses to Covid-19 have laid bare the considerable differences between HWUs and HBUs. Universities such as SU, WITS, UP and UCT have all prioritised the allocation of free data bundles (in collaboration with network providers and support from the DHET) and laptops to students for online teaching during Covid-19 (IOL, 2020; Macupe, 2020; & Shoba, 2020). Notably, these are well-established universities that were predominantly white universities in the apartheid era. HBUs such as the University of Fort Hare, Unizulu, UWC, UNIVEN, and the Walter Sisulu University have indicated that they will also support students, but one cannot deny that without substantial government support, they might have little room to manoeuvre.

The re-phasing of students back to campuses

The DHET argued that to save the academic year, there is a need to gradually phase-in the return of students back to universities. This was to be done in phases and in line with the lockdown levels. Under levels 5 and 4, no students were allowed on campus. Under level 3, 33.3% of students were allowed back to campus, and these were students in the natural sciences and those who needed laboratories and practicals to complete their qualifications (Ngqakamba, 2020). Under level 2, another 33.3% of students were allowed back, bringing the total to 66.6%. Under level 1, all students were allowed to return. Nonetheless, the chapter argues that what the rephasing in process failed to reflect was that not all universities could welcome 66.6% of students back while at the same time maintaining strict Covid-19 regulations (Nqakamba, 2020). For HBUs, the shortage of residences, congested spaces, and the overcrowding of lecture halls compounds the planned phasing in of students. In HWUs, with infrastructure in place, the process has become seamless, evident by some HWUs already welcoming students back to campus (for example the University of Johannesburg (UJ) and the University of KwaZulu-Natal (UKZN)). This again shows the disparity in the higher education sector in South Africa.

Looking at HBUs in the USA, the concept of online learning has become an important element to ensure continuity. However, resembling HBUs in South Africa, DePietro (2020) argued that in the USA, the requisite change to online learning has been challenging for HBUs, especially those campuses that emphasise an intimate college experience. Moreover, with online learning not well integrated, the interaction between lecturers and students affects knowledge generation. Reinforcing this, the European Data Portal (2020) contended that in Europe, while countries are adapting to the 'new normal' with education from a distance, nonetheless, three requirements need to be fulfilled: access to the internet, the right technology, and the skills to use the technology.

Taking this into account, the use of digital content in education worldwide was relatively uncommon before the crisis started. Only 20% of countries had digital learning resources in teaching, while no country has a universal digital curriculum for teaching and learning (European Data Portal, 2020). These revelations highlight three elements from a South African perspective. Firstly, concerning internet access, many students in HBUs access internet services on campus through Wi-Fi hot spots or computer labs. However with Covid-19, students in rural areas may battle for the internet services needed for online learning. Even though the government has arranged for educational websites to be freely accessible even without data, the concept of online learning and its operation is still a barrier for HBUs and their student populace (McKane, 2020). Moreover, the rush to implement online learning has reduced the training time needed for staff, especially in HBUs. Finally, for those who do have access to the internet and the necessary technology, there is evidence that learning online can be more effective. However, for those who do not, this will likely prolong the divide in South Africa's higher education systems.

The following section intends to unpack the transition from face-to-face teaching and learning to online teaching and learning in the institutions of higher learning.

Readiness of higher education institutions for blended learning

Covid-19 is a global phenomenon and will leave no sector in any country in the world unaffected, and its consequences will be felt for years to come (Mohamedbhai, 2012). Although education is becoming a ubiquitous service delivered anywhere and anytime over the global network, higher education institutions have embarked on a journey to implement elements of e-learning in traditional course delivery, to prepare their students, as well as the institution, for the future participation in education (Bonk, 2009; McCradie, 2003). However, the reality is that universities offering contact learning, whether HBUs or HWUs, are not ready for a complete transition to online teaching and learning. Furthermore, the provision of laptops, data, and delivery of study materials does not guarantee effective teaching and learning. Amid Covid-19, methods and practices of teaching have come under the spotlight as students and lecturers are expected to transit from face-to-face to online remote learning and teaching in a short space of time.

This chapter maintains that there is a considerable gap among institutions of higher learning. Some universities, predominantly the better-resourced universities (HWUs), have been able to carry on with teaching online whereas, in other universities (HBU), students have had to make do with WhatsApp voice audio, YouTube videos, and accessing slides on data free learning websites, such as Moodle. Evidently, within universities, there is also unevenness in the distribution of devices, as not all lecturers possess smartphones or laptops to be able to teach online (Moeng, 2020). As a result, training is required to better equip lecturers for the changes brought by Covid-19 and online pedagogical expertise that many of our lecturers lack. Despite the clear demonstration of the benefits of using technology in education, there continues to be a marked reluctance by academics to engage with online learning (Anderson, 2008). Even though many lecturers from HWUs and HBUs have made efforts with online skills and expert guidance in creating online classrooms on multiple platforms, Becker and Jokivirta (2007:7) found in their study that academics worldwide reported low enthusiasm for using technology in learning.

Throughout the discussion, it becomes observable that Covid-19 has brought numerous challenges for the higher education sector around the world, especially for disadvantaged universities. In Indonesia, online learning faces similar challenges to those in South Africa, for example, only 56% or 150 million of Indonesia's 268 million population have access to the internet and of those who do, many cannot afford unlimited, stable, and speedy connections (Yamin, 2020). Bandwidth and server capacity have also been issues. In Thailand and Cambodia, less than 60% of the population has access to the internet, while only around 40% have access in Myanmar and Vietnam (Jalli, 2020). In Asia, another key issue is how prepared systems, students, and teachers are to adapt to online learning as having the infrastructure in place makes the transition to remote teaching and learning much easier (Jalli, 2020). In Latin America, the response has been similar to that of South Africa (ensuring no one gets left behind and establishing alternative teaching and learning methods), in Costa Rica, hard copy resources have been handed out to students with no access to the internet (Cobo, Hawkins & Rovner, 2020). In El Salvador, a national call centre (accessible via email and WhatsApp) was set up to provide support to students in the delivery of educational activities. In Peru, the government is adopting a strategy to use different channels to distribute content: internet, TV, radio, and phones. In

Paraguay, an agreement with a large technology company was reached to offer an educational package at "zero cost" to benefit 60 000 teachers and 1.2 million students (Cobo et al., 2020).

In Colombia, the strategy combines online, offline and broadcasting. For those families with internet access to "Aprender digital", a national platform with over 80,000 digital resources organised by grades (in different modalities, such as games, videos, etc.) is available (Cobo et al., 2020). However, Adeotey (2020) argued that the coronavirus pandemic has exposed the unpreparedness of many higher education institutions in Africa to migrate online. While countries such as Egypt, Ghana, South Africa and Rwanda are among those countries who have moved some of their programmes to online platforms and partnered with network providers to zero-rate these platforms, students continue to face several challenges. According to UNESCO, 89% of students in sub-Saharan Africa do not have access to household computers and 82% lack internet access (Adeotey, 2020). This means that online classes cannot cater to all students as this has been the case with South Africa's HBUs.

The effects of Covid-19 on the quality of education provided and the quality of students produced in HBUs/HWUs

The global lockdown of education institutions has caused a major and unequal interruption in students' learning; disruptions in internal assessments; and the cancellation of public assessments for qualifications or their replacement by an inferior alternative (Burgess & Sievertsen, 2020). Educational access has become a noticeable issue during this period of Covid-19. Some students have access to information and technology, particularly those from HWUs, but even then, the process of learning is difficult, including a lack of study space in many homes as rooms are taken up by family members since there is a national lockdown. It is important to understand that access to gadgets (i.e. laptops, smartphones) and information does not always result in learning taking place. Mohamedbhai (2012) cautioned that quality online learning requires that the teaching material is prepared by a professional instructional designer, that the lecturer is pedagogically trained for delivering the programme, and the students are equally exposed to the pedagogy of online learning. The careers of this year's university graduates may be severely affected by Covid-19.

The interruptions in learning and the untested and unprecedented scale shift to online learning will harm the quality of graduates to be produced in the 2020 academic year. Furthermore, the vast majority of HBUs student enrolments comprise of underprepared black students who have for years depended on face-to-face lectures. Additionally, in the lens of this chapter, HBUs under the discriminatory and repressive conditions of apartheid are subjected to severe financial and other disadvantages, with the result being that their institutional infrastructure is poor and does not reflect the internationalisation of higher education. In all, this chapter evaluated the educational and structural challenges that are compounding South Africa's higher education sector. More worryingly, however, is the unequal development of universities in South Africa. Undoubtedly, the period of 1994 was meant to radically alter the way higher education was undertaken. There were greater calls for inclusivity, doing away with the racial element in higher education, and promoting a higher education system that was characterised by accessibility and a system that would respond to the challenges of a democratic South Africa. However, 27 years after the consolidation of multiparty politics in South Africa, the higher education sector has been observed as being one of the most unequal sectors in the country. HBUs have failed to catch up to the levels of development that characterise their HWU counterparts. The South African government has realised that HBUs are characterised by governance issues, corruption, and maladministration, all of which have hindered their ability to catch up with HWUs.

Covid-19 has further reflected on these inequalities by laying bare the effects of the unequalness of higher education in South Africa. Students in HBUs are mainly rural-based, lack internet connectivity and are not well entrenched in the concept of online learning. Moreover, academic staff at HBUs are also greatly challenged in terms of online teaching and there has been a general fear that teaching and learning taking place via online platforms will compromise the quality of education offered to students from HBUs. Finally, there have been arguments and debates at the slow pace at which HBUs have integrated online learning in their curricula development. Arguments have contended that while no one expected a sudden halt to higher education owing to the pandemic, HWUs should have long integrated online learning into their curricula development. Unfortunately, this chapter argues that the sudden rush to integrate online learning will impede a staff and the student population that is neither well-trained nor well equipped to make the best use of such, hence, this questions the rationale behind the inability of HBUs to integrate online learning in their curricula.

Recommendations and conclusion

The takeaway point from this discussion rests on the premise that the responses towards Covid-19 will greatly differ between HWUs and HBUs. These differences will be buoyed by the differences in resources and levels of development that differentiate HWUs and HBUs, thus implying that HWUs might have more room to manoeuvre apart from government intervention. For HBU's there seems to be significant reliance on government support rather than taking the lead in developing mechanisms that ought to ensure the seamless integration to online. However, one ought to take into cognisance that many HBUs are still struggling in terms of ICT support, hence setting up the necessary and student-friendly online portals might take some time, which might inconvenience students and further disrupt the teaching and learning process. However, what gives rise to the different responses to Covid-19 between HBUs and HWUs, and why are HWUs perceived to have manoeuvrability with regards to Covid-19? Covid-19 has exposed the inequalities that currently exist in the South African higher education sector. The consequences have been felt by all sectors in the country and the education sector is no exception. The sector as a whole needs to reflect, recalibrate, and reimagine the best way forward during and beyond Covid-19. The approach must be holistic and multi-dimensional and should involve all relevant stakeholders, including the private sector, students, policymakers, researchers, and civil society.

A specific task force on higher education under the leadership of the Departments of Basic Education, Higher Education and Training, and Science and Technology must survey the situation, suggest immediate and short-term measures, and be ready to effect redress when the crisis is over. Additionally, the global community will offer lessons through which South Africa should learn from, especially within the higher education sector. However, going forward the focus must be directed towards gradually developing HBUs. The reality is there is an increasing demand for higher education in South Africa, and coupled with this demand is the need for expansion of higher education institutions. However, the chapter contends that the inequality of higher education needs to be addressed first before such expansion can be consolidated. Moreover, HBUs ought to integrate online learning in their curricula. Sadly implementing it in such a rush will cause more problems rather than solutions. Also, issues of corruption and maladministration ought to be addressed in HBUs, thus enabling conducive teaching and learning environments. This chapter, however, concludes that it will be difficult for HBUs to catch up to their HWU counterparts as they are compounded by a plethora of issues that have multiplied in their appearance, and sadly, these issues have hindered their ability to respond to the pandemic.

Covid-19 demands a swift shift to online learning in higher learning institutions, both HBUs and HWUs. The development and adaptation of new technologies; as well as a sufficient level of absorptive capacity from HBUs (i.e, the ability to adopt new technologies) are required as a core condition for successful leapfrogging. This capacity includes technological capabilities, knowledge, and skills, as well as supportive institutions. There is a range of policies that can be implemented to develop this capacity. Evidence suggests that a mix of generic functional policies (for example, to strengthen the levels of education) and more specific policies (for example, to stimulate innovation in the education sector) are required. To this end, forming partnerships between institutions of higher learning, both HBUs and HWUs, and the basic education sector, both private and public, is essential and will enable them to share scarce resources, learn innovative educational practices, and apply them from a collaborative perspective. Furthermore, deploying and improving digital infrastructure in HBUs is important. The application of ICT in education necessitates digital equipment and internet access, which has proved to be a cross-cutting enabler for education during the current Covid-19 pandemic. Lastly, more effort is needed to train and retrain teachers and ensure that they are appropriately allocated and adapting to technological changes.

References

Adeotey, S. 2020. *What will higher education in Africa look like after Covid-19?* Available at: https://bit.ly/3f6hGbz [Accessed 22 August 2020].

Anderson, T. (ed.) 2008. *The theory and practice of online learning.* Edmonton: Athabasca University Press.

Badat, S., Barron, F., Fisher, G., Pillay, P. & Wolpe, H. 1994. *Differentiation and disadvantage: The historically black universities in South Africa: Report to the Desmond Tutu Educational Trust.* Bellville: University of the Western Cape, Education Policy Unit.

Bawa, A. & Mouton, J. 2001. Research. In: N. Cloete, R. Fehnel, P. Maassen, T. Moja, H. Perold & T. Gibbon (eds.), *Transformation in Higher Education: Global pressures and local realities in South Africa.* Cape Town: Centre for Higher Education Transformation, 296-333.

Becker, R. & Jokivirta, L. 2007. *Online learning in universities: Selected data from the 2006 Observatory report.* London: Observatory on Borderless Higher Education (OBHE).

Bonk, C.J. 2009. *The world is open: How web technology is revolutionizing education.* San Francisco: Jossey-Bass.

Bothell, E. 2020. *Pretoria v-c: Covid-19 will 'undermine' post-apartheid progress.* Available at: https://bit.ly/3u2AvAL [Accessed 31 May 2020].

Bozalek, V. & Boughey, C. 2012. (Mis)framing higher education in South Africa. *Social Policy & Administration,* 46(6):688-703. https://doi.org/10.1111/j.1467-9515.2012.00863.x

Bunting, I. 2006. The Higher Education Landscape Under Apartheid. In: N. Cloete, P. Maassen, R. Fehnel, T. Moja, T. Gibbon & H. Perold (eds.), Transformation in Higher Education. *Higher Education Dynamics,* Vol 10. Dordrecht: Springer, 35-52. https://doi.org/10.1007/1-4020-4006-7_3

Burgess, S. & Sievertsen, H.H. 2020. *Schools, skills, and learning: The impact of Covid-19 on education.* Available at: https://bit.ly/2PrcBj1 [Accessed 4 May 2020].

Carolissen, R. & Bozalek, V. 2017. Addressing dualisms in student perceptions of a historically white and black university in South Africa. *Race Ethnicity and Education,* 20(3):344-357. https://doi.org/10.1080/13613324.2016.1260229

Case, J.M., Marshall, D., McKenna, S. & Mogashana, D. 2018. *Going to university: The influence of higher education on the lives of young South Africans.* Cape Town: African Minds. https://doi.org/10.47622/9781928331698

Chetty, C. & Knaus, C. 2016. *Why South Africa's universities are in the grip of a class struggle. The Conversation.* Available at: https://bit.ly/3sgTCGt [Accessed 7 June 2020].

Cobo, C., Hawkins, R. & Rovner, H. 2020. *How countries across Latin America use technology during Covid-19-driven school closures.* Available at: https://bit.ly/3tSF1RU [Accessed 21 August 2020].

DePietro, A. 2020. *Here's a look at the impact of coronavirus (Covid-19) on colleges and universities in the U.S.* Forbes. Available at: https://bit.ly/3sgWB1N [Accessed 21 August 2020].

European Data Portal. 2020. *Education during Covid-19; moving towards e-learning.* Available at: https://bit.ly/2QqrB18 [Accessed 19 August 2020].

Galvin, M. 2020. *Historically black colleges and universities take center stage as the nation responds to Covid-19 and systemic racism*. Available at: https://bit.ly/3sc9sSR [Accessed 19 August 2020].

Hweshe, F. 2011. *WSU placed under administration*. Available at: https://bit.ly/2QDgmTr [Accessed 19 August 2020].

IOL. 2020. *UKZN rolls out free data bundles and laptops to students for online teaching during Covid-19*. Available at: https://bit.ly/3cW8MdW [Accessed 13 June 2020].

Jalli, N. 2020. *Lack of internet access in Southeast Asia poses challenges for students to study online amid Covid-19 pandemic*. Available at: https://bit.ly/3chtCWc [Accessed 21 August 2020].

Kelly, E. 2020. *Covid-19 is ushering in a new way to do research and teaching*. Available at: https://bit.ly/3rhGEqX[Accessed 14 June 2020].

Lekaba, F. 2016. *#FeesMustFall presents us with a golden opportunity*. IOL. Available at: https://bit.ly/2QBFmu7 [Accessed 19 August 2020].

Macupe, B. 2020. *UCT to loan (some) students laptops during Covid-19 lockdown*. Available at: https://bit.ly/3lKz6eY [Accessed 15 June 2020].

Mbanjwa, B. 2009. *Criminal case for ex MUT head?* Available at: https://bit.ly/395LPE3 [Accessed 19 August 2020].

McCradie, J. 2003. Does IT matter to higher education? *Educause Review*, 38(6):15-22.

McKane, J. 2020. *Here is the full list of zero-rated websites in South Africa*. Available at: https://bit.ly/3tQeQvc [Accessed 23 August 2020].

McKeever, M. 2017. Educational inequality in apartheid South Africa. *American Behavioral Scientist*, 61(1):114-131. https://doi.org/10.1177/0002764216682988

Mlambo, V.H., Hlongwa, M. & Mubecua, M. 2017. The provision of free higher education in South Africa: A proper concept or a parable? *Journal of Education and Vocational Research*, 8(4):51-61. https://doi.org/10.22610/jevr.v8i4.2160

Mlambo, V.H., Ogunnubi, O. & Mlambo, D.N. 2020. Student mobility, brain drain and the internationalisation of higher education in Southern Africa. *African Journal of Development Studies*, 10(2):59-82. https://doi.org/10.31920/2634-3649/2020/10n2a3

Moeng, M. 2020. Education is a political and ethical matter. *Mail & Guardian*. Available at: https://bit.ly/2NLuHMi [Accessed 15 June 2020].

Mohamedbhai, G. 2012. *Are national goals for doctoral education realistic?* Available at: https://bit.ly/3f8VCNn [Accessed 6 June 2012].

News24. 2011. *Zululand: University put under administration*. Available at: https://bit.ly/3cW9ms8 [Accessed 19 August 2020].

Ngqakamba, S. 2020. Under Level 3.33% of student population meant to return - but TUT's final-year students amount to 36%. *News24*. Available at: https://bit.ly/3cgsQIV [Accessed 19 August 2020].

Petersen, F. 2020. Covid-19: An opportunity for universities to regain public trust. *Mail and Guardian*. Available at: https://bit.ly/3cgrzBJ [Accessed 10 June 2020].

Plumwood, V. 1993. *Feminism and the Mastery of Nature*. London: Routledge.

Raju, J. 2006. *The historical evolution of university and technikon education and training in South Africa and its implications for articulation between the two types of higher educational institutions with particular reference to LIS education and training.* Durban: Institute of Technology. https://doi.org/10.4314/innovation.v29i1.26489

Shoba, S. 2020. *Universities gear up to save the academic year.* Available at: https://bit.ly/3celu8z [Accessed 12 June 2020].

Smith, D. 2013. South Africa's universities 'racially skewed', claims watchdog. *The Guardian.* Available at: https://bit.ly/3rg5pUl [Accessed 7 June 2020].

Stanford Magazine. 2007. *Education After Apartheid.* Available at: https://bit.ly/3vPLO0R [Accessed 7 June 2020].

Subotzky, G. 1997. Redefining equity: Challenges and opportunities facing South Africa's historically black universities relative to global and national changes. *Journal of Negro Education,* Autumn:496-521. https://doi.org/10.2307/2668176

Tjønneland, E.N. 2017. *Crisis at South Africa's universities–what are the implications for future cooperation with Norway?* CMI Brief. Available at: https://bit.ly/2NPioyE [Accessed 12 June 2020].

Yamin, K. 2020. *Mixed response but online classes to stay post Covid-19.* Available at: https://bit.ly/3vPNCXH [Accessed 21 August 2020].

4

A multimodal model for learning, teaching and assessment in higher education

Rosaline Govender and Mogiveny Rajkoomar

Introduction

The Covid-19 pandemic has had a cataclysmic impact on all aspects of human existence, including the higher education sector. This pandemic has forced contact Higher Education (HE) institutions to move to emergency remote teaching with a shift to blended or online teaching or adopt a hybrid approach of combining print materials with online learning. Whilst some educators were prepared for online teaching, others who were not so tech-savvy had to quickly adapt to teaching online.

Due to the Covid-19 pandemic, many institutions of higher learning were forced to suspend the planned curriculum as the academic calendar was restructured and universities had to adapt for remote emergency teaching. Planned assessments and exams were suspended and educators had to find innovative and alternative assessment strategies. More flexible ways of incorporating online content and assessments had to be considered. Many institutions turned to continuous assessments conducted on online platforms. This radical shift from a face-to-face and/or blended approach to online and/or hybrid platforms have raised serious questions about the readiness of higher education (staff and resources) for the 21st century student, referred to as Generation Y (millennial) and Generation Z.

Higher education and generational diversity

A generation is a social construction in which individuals born during a similar time period and is influenced by, historic and social contexts in such a way that their experiences differentiate from one generation cohort to another (Lester, Standifer, Schultz & Windsor, 2012:341). Karl Mannheim (1928) postulates that people belonging to the same age group who witness common crucial, socio-political and historical events during developmental stages of their life, form a generational group. Lyons and Kuron (2014:141) argue that Mannheim's theory is not specifically concerned with the impact of generation on individual attitudes and behaviours, but rather the dynamic interaction of generations as a mechanism for social change. The Generation Theory was made popular by William Strauss and Neil Howe's book *Generations: The History of America's Future, 1584 to 2069* (1991). Currently, there are five living generations namely the Greatest Generation, the Silent Generation, Baby Boomers, Gen X, Millennials, and Gen Z (Hodges, 2019).

It is important to also note that although Generation Z students are described in literature as a homogenous group, there exist anomalies in the characteristics between first world countries and developing countries. These anomalies are entrenched by socio-economic factors which include the disparity in educational provision, unemployment, urban versus rural and the digital divide (Duffet, 2017:4). Brown and Czerniewicz (2010) argue that what is clearly evident from research in higher education is the varied set of digital skills of South African millennials.

There seems to be a paradoxical situation in higher education as millennials, Generation Z students (with varying digital competencies) and the Baby Boomer and Generation X educators all occupy the same space (Robson, 2015:1). The Covid-19 pandemic has had widespread impact on HE and educators must be knowledgeable about the factors that affect Generation Z students which Trevino (2018:88) outlines as:

- Student well-being
- Technology
- Parent involvement
- Flexible classroom modalities
- Campus safety

In addition to the above, educators must be cognisant of the types of devices that students have access to, data and other contextual constraints, and structure their teaching accordingly.

The Covid-19 pandemic has brought about tremendous distress to both students and educators who are experiencing high levels of burnout and depression (Marshall & Wolanskyj-Spinner, 2020). Both students and staff are undergoing a change in the learning environment and plans for the future are changing in a relatively short period of time. It is imperative that educational institutions play an active role in addressing distress management. Educational institutions should provide access to trained personnel in stress management. As students and staff move primarily to online learning platforms it is imperative that online support communities are provided. We must be cognisant that the HE sector in South Africa services primarily Generation Z students with educators who hail primarily from a different generation. Generation Z students are true digital natives: they are able to access information online, they have a very short attention span and connect to and switch between a variety of devices (Hart, 2018). In order for HE to be germane, it is imperative that they "adapt their courses, programs, processes, environments, and initiatives" (Trevino, 2018: 44).

HE institutions in South Africa are faced with further challenges with the high intake of first year students who come from diverse socio-economic backgrounds. Many of these students come from under-resourced schools with very little or no exposure to Information and Communications Technologies (ICTs) in teaching and learning (Strydom, Mentz & Kuh, 2010). HE is still grappling with issues of equitable access and social justice. Covid-19 compelled HE institutions to revise the curriculum and change the mode of delivery in order to salvage the 2020 academic year. Both educators and students had to quickly assimilate 21st century digital skills. These transitions were done under emergency conditions so there was very little time to plan for students who come from diverse backgrounds and have different learning styles and abilities.

The lockdown during Covid-19 has placed the spotlight on the South African HE landscape and its under-preparedness for 21st century teaching to Generation Z students. It has forced HE to re-examine its current teaching, learning and assessment strategies. University education should be flexible, inclusive and adaptable and Generation Z students should be offered multiple ways of acquiring knowledge, applying this knowledge and engaging in learning (Alexander, Ashford-Rowe, Barajas-Murphy, Dobbin, Knott, McCormack, Pomerantz, Seilhamer & Weber, 2019). It is crucial that HE takes full advantage of this 'pause' that Covid-19 has provided to address the expectations and needs of Generation Z students in order to attract and retain these students. This will definitely impact on the retention, success and graduation rates of students. Teaching and learning practices also need to be re-evaluated in line with Generation Z student needs. HE staff must be cognisant of the students' contextual realities and have a responsibility to help students achieve both epistemic access and success. This includes providing disadvantaged students with data and devices and adopting a more flexible approach in the delivery of the curriculum.

Covid-19 has foregrounded that HE must cater for the diverse student body with different learning preferences and expectations of personalised learning. HE institutions are compelled to leverage innovative teaching and learning approaches. The increasing use of the internet and digital technologies by HE students also calls for a transformation of the teaching and learning environments in HE institutions that should be facilitated by an effective combination of various modes of delivery, models of teaching and styles of learning. One such approach discussed in this chapter is multimodal teaching, learning and assessment, which should be implemented by HE contact institutions as it has the propensity to provide more engaged learning experiences while recognising the potential of ICTs.

Learning theories for multimodal teaching and learning

The Covid-19 pandemic has certainly changed the face of teaching and learning in HE which has helped usher in a new dispensation for teaching and learning. For the first time students from predominantly contact HE institutions had to grapple with teaching and learning happening outside a traditional classroom. In HE educators draw from a variety of learning theories and teaching strategies as they traverse the teaching terrain (Ershler & Stabile, 2015). Before the onslaught of the Covid-19 pandemic, there were significant shifts in HE as many educators moved from Behaviourism to Constructivism to underpin their work (Ershler & Stabile, 2015).

Constructivism is a philosophy of learning that articulates mechanisms by which knowledge is co-constructed by students. Constructivism expects students to "engage in interpretation, organisation and inference creation about knowledge, with the cognitive structures they have previously constructed" (Ershler & Stabile, 2015:14). As students interact with the material and each other, meaningful learning takes place. Constructivism tends to emphasise knowledge construction, rather than knowledge transmission (Beyers, 2009:220). Constructivism emphasises the building or construction that takes place when people engage in learning activities by active engagement and understanding the environment according to their experiences, perceptions and mental models. In constructivism, learning is seen as a personal interpretation of the world where the learners construct or interpret their own reality based on their perceptions and experiences (Alonso, López, Manrique & Viñes, 2008:390). "The learning environment based on constructivist and socio-constructive setting" is a key component of active learning (Gazibara, 2018:184) and it empowers students through the integration of ICTs into all aspects of the teaching and learning process (Beyers, 2009:224). Constructivism is strongly aligned with an outcomes-based curriculum and the teacher has the responsibility of guiding students to achieve the module outcomes (Starkey, 2015). Scardamalia and Bereiter (2006) critiqued constructivism by saying "if learners construct their own knowledge, how is it possible for them to create a cognitive structure more complex than the one they already possess?" (Scardamalia & Bereiter, 2006:103).

It is clear that students in the digital era can network and collaborate in online spaces and constructivism does not account for the learning that takes place in digital spaces (Siemens, 2004).

Theory of connectivism

The Covid-19 pandemic has forced the 21st century students to process and apply information in a very different way and at a different pace than was the case in previous centuries. The span of time between learning something new, being able to apply it and finding that it is outdated and no longer useful, continually decreases. Gonzalez (2004) refers to this as the "half-life of knowledge", which is the time span from when knowledge is gained until it becomes obsolete. The cycle of knowledge development, from personal to network to organisation, enables students to remain current in their field through the connections they have formed. Students create knowledge as they attempt to understand their experiences (Siemens, 2004).

The learning landscapes in the digital age are networked, social and technological (Dunaway, 2011:678). Generation Z students have available a wide range of online information resources, collaborative knowledge systems, open access publications of scholarly communication, online databases and other library resources. This is made possible by networked information using the internet. Students use technology to form their own information networks which include learning communities where students participate in the knowledge creation process (Dunaway, 2011:675). The inclusion of technology and making the connection using technologies as learning activities begins to move learning theories into a digital age.

According to Siemens (2004):

> Connectivism is driven by the understanding that decisions are based on rapidly altering foundations. New information is continually being acquired. The ability to draw distinctions between important and unimportant information is vital. The ability to recognize when new information alters the landscape based on decisions made yesterday is also critical.

Connectivism can therefore be seen has having evolved with the growing interest in the teaching and learning potential of Web 2.0 technologies and practices. Connectivism is "the integration of principles explored by chaos, network and complexity and self-organization theories" (Siemens, 2004). Central to connectivism is the idea that learning takes place across networked communities and information technologies (Dunaway, 2011:675). Connectivism sees learning as residing outside oneself, which can be within an organisation or a database, where learning is focused on connecting specialised information sets, where the connections that enable learning is more important than the current state of knowing. Connectivism is the ability to learn from both animate and non-animate sources. The nurturing and maintaining of connections are required to facilitate continual learning. Current and accurate knowledge is the intent of connectivist learning activities. Connectivism also sees decision-making as a learning process. The starting point of connectivism is the individual where personal knowledge comprises of a network, which feeds into organisations and institutions, back into the network, then continues to provide learning to the individual. Connectivism emphasises the importance of the ability to be able to recognise connections, patterns and similarities and the ability to synthesise ideas and information (Dunaway, 2011:676). Siemen's (2004) theory also acknowledges that real-life learning is messy and complex and that acquisition of knowledge takes place in a nonlinear manner.

Multimodal learning environments

Multimodal learning environments can be defined as learning environments that use verbal and non-verbal modes to present subject matter. In multimodal learning environments, academics present the learning material by using both verbal and visual means. Modules that are multimodal provide a dynamic learning space for students, as it combines the use of multimedia and ICT, and can be presented in various modes and cater for different learning styles as discussed below (Gilakjani, Ismail & Ahmadi, 2011).

During the unprecedented situation of Covid-19, HE intuitions in South Africa and around the world have implemented e-Learning platforms for teaching and learning. Many HE institutions have not considered the perceptions of students, particularly Generation Z students, with regards to the use of e-Learning platforms. An interesting study conducted by Pikhart and Klimova (2020) reported that some of the current e-Learning platforms are not attractive to Generation Z students. They want to participate in the creation of its content and collaborate and interact with each other in ways that they are used to in other social media platforms, such as Facebook. Academics and e-Learning course designers should heed to this. The implications of the research findings by Pikhart and Klimova (2020) are important as they also suggest a new approach to the exploitation of e-Learning platforms connected to Web 4.0 by tapping into the potential of artificial intelligence, deep learning, machine learning and computational linguistics.

Many learning theorists have argued that learning styles may be defined as the combination of cognitive, emotional and physiological factors that determine each individual's most effective process for learning. A variety of systems exist for categorising these factors into standardised classifications. Other researchers contend that since students have different learning styles, it is essential to provide a variety of instructional approaches, learning material and activities (Association for Quality and Participation [USA], 2003). Seemiller, Grace, Dal Bo Campagnolo, Da Rosa Alves and De Borba (2019) show that while a learning style refers to how learners take in and process information, learning methods are the skills and actions learners engage in to participate in learning. Seemiller and Grace (2016) examined the learning styles and motivators of Generation Z students, particularly how these students learn, engage and communicate. Academics and other key stakeholders in HE should make changes to optimise the educational impact on Generation Z students. Seemiller and Grace (2016:15) emphasise that the HE landscape has changed and that it is imperative that key stakeholders in HE embrace new models of education and support services, especially the physical environment: facilities, learning environments, libraries, and tools for learning that can accommodate current HE students.

Iftode (2019) indicates that establishing learning styles is a complicated process. He also emphasises that understanding and defining students' learning styles is an important process as it is the key to active involvement. He identifies Generation Z as having an "auto-didactic and independent learning type" and having a strong desire to choose what and how to study.

A technology-mediated, multimodal teaching and learning environment can include numerous "elements such as simulations, interactive diagrams, images, video and audio materials, interactive quizzes and crosswords, PowerPoint lectures with audio, and hyperlinked examples." (Gilakjani et al., 2011:1321). Shatto and Erwin (2017) indicate that using technology and mixed teaching methods will maximise the extent to which Generations Z students feel engaged. Innovative teaching using different forms of technology may be required to fully engage them. Methods such as flipped classrooms and active learning allow students to actively participate (e.g. case studies, group projects, use of clickers for voting, blogs, and critical thinking assignments). Narratives and storytelling are gaining popularity and can be especially useful when discussing varying viewpoints. They also indicate that allowing students to bring their own devices (cell phones, tablets and laptop computers) into the learning environment is an easy way to increase involvement.

Blended learning and/or online learning provides a multimodal teaching and learning environment which addresses the learning styles of the Generation Z student. This chapter will first discuss the concept of blended learning and thereafter discuss the concept of online learning.

The concept of blended learning

There are many varying definitions of blended learning offered in the literature. Graham (2004), drawing from numerous authors, defines blended learning as a combination of face-to-face instruction with computer-mediated instruction. Currently, this is the most widely used definition in the area of blended learning. However, Heinze and Proctor (2004) define blended learning as being "learning that is facilitated by the effective combination of different modes of delivery, models of teaching and styles of learning, founded on transparent communication amongst all parties involved with the course". Blended Learning (Figure 4.1) can be conceptualised as a wide variety of ICT integrated activities with conventional face-to-face classroom activities.

The outbreak of the Covid-19 pandemic and the subsequent lockdown has necessitated a rapid move to online learning. During this pandemic, online learning has been seen as an important means of access for students due to adhering to physical distancing. Educators, as well as students had to develop the skills to teach and learn online in a very short space of time. Many HE institutions are now seeing the benefits of online learning and that this could drastically change the way contact institutions operate in the future.

Expansions of online activities with a slow phase-in of face-to-face activities with the easing of lockdown rules are being implemented in South Africa. Most of the HE institutions have invested in eLearning management systems such as Moodle and have established support for staff and students to maintain the technological stability for their online activities. Synchronous online activities are being conducted using software packages such as Microsoft Teams and Zoom. Some educators are using social media platforms such as WhatsApp and Facebook. The current Covid-19 pandemic has forced HE institutions to confront issues dealing with access and success as they transition to new pedagogies.

Minimal Technology/Media

Student meet f2f
- teacher uses simple
  technology such as email,
  or web for e-lectures.

Students meet online
- teacher uses simple
  technology such as CMS,
  electronic bulletin boards.

Blended   **Blended**

Conventional
Face to Face
Classroom

Fully Online

Blended   **Blended**

Student meet f2f
- teacher uses technology
  in class such as interactive
  simulations, digitally
  controlled experiments.

Students meet online
- teacher uses more advanced
  technology such as interactive
  videoconferencing

Technology/Media Infused

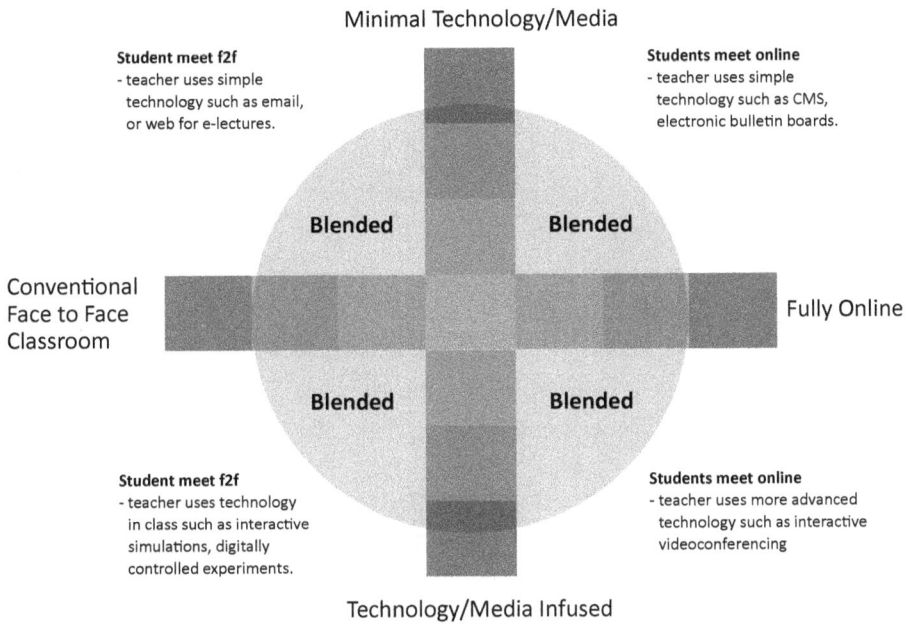

Figure 4.1   Blended Learning Conceptualisation
(Source Picciano, A.G.2009. Blending with Purpose: The Multimodal Model)

Educators are now compelled to review their taken-for-granted assumptions of teaching and learning as they construct the rationale for adopting or developing particular instructional strategies and use platforms in order to achieve the module outcomes. Knowing why a particular strategy works makes the exercise of teaching and learning more meaningful. A coherent framework avoids the "tyranny of adopting clever techniques" and the distortion that may arise from the separation of theory and practice (Garrison & Vaughan, 2008:13). Understanding how students acquire and develop knowledge in a blended learning environment is crucial. Therefore, a blended learning model/online model that addresses the needs of students that come from a diverse background and have a variety of needs is suggested. The Multimodal Model takes into account students that come from different backgrounds, different generations and with a variety of learning styles. Educators should therefore use multiple approaches to address the needs of a diverse student body.

Transition from "telling to partnering"

Covid-19 has necessitated shifts in pedagogies from "telling to partnering" (Prensky, 2010:14). In "partnering", educators do not just lecture to students, but provide students with scenarios, questions and tools that can be used. Prensky (2010) defines partnering as, "letting students focus on the part of the learning process that they can do best, and letting teachers focus on the part of the learning process that they can do best." (Prensky, 2010:13).

Students become partners in the learning and take responsibility for their learning. Teaching staff give students responsibility for the following (Prensky, 2010:13):

- Finding and following their passion
- Using whatever technology is available
- Researching and finding information
- Answering questions and sharing their thoughts and opinions
- Practicing when properly motivated (e.g. through games)
- Creating presentations in texts and multimedia

Prensky (2001) advises that the methodology and the content must change to include more future content. We would like to add that educators must also make pedagogical shifts in the type of assessments that they design as well. The shift must take place from traditional paper-based assessments to multimodal assessments.

Table 4.1   How partnering work is shared
            (Source Prensky (2010:16) How partnering works)

Teacher	Student
Doesn't tell, asks.	Doesn't take notes, finds out.
Suggests topics and tools.	Researches and creates output.
Learns about technology from students.	Learns about quality and rigor from teacher.
Evaluates students' output for rigor and quality; supplies context.	Refines and improves output, adding rigor, context and quality.

Assessment in a multimodal teaching and learning environment

Assessment serves multiple purposes whether it is conducted in a face-to-face or multimodal teaching and learning environment. Ramsden states that "... assessment is a way of teaching more effectively through understanding exactly what students know and do not know. Assessment is about several things at once. ... It is about reporting on students' achievements and about teaching them better through expressing more clearly the goals of our curricula" (Ramsden, 1992:182).

Ramsden (1992) asserts that "from our students' point of view, the assessment always defines the actual curriculum" (Ramsden, 1992:187). Although this view should shift our thinking in HE on assessment, especially during the Covid-19 pandemic, the opposite is true. Assessment, especially summative assessment, is generally considered the "last activity" in the learning and teaching process and staff across HE institutions need to restructure the teaching and learning in accordance with the newly structured assessments. Although researchers like Gibbs (1999) and Biggs (1999) have argued about the crucial role of assessment in learning and teaching this has not made much impact on the assessment practices in HE. Practices at HE institutions reveal that some teaching staff are still not reconsidering assessment as crucial when redesigning the academic programme (Boud, 2007).

Purposes of assessment

The four purposes of assessment as outlined by Luckett and Sutherland (2000:2-3) are diagnostic, formative, summative and quality assurance. We will briefly discuss these purposes of assessment.

Diagnostic Assessment is used for student placement in a specific learning programme and also identifies areas for remediation.

Formative Assessment provides feedback to students about their progress and this is useful in the learning process.

Summative assessment is used to promote students at the end of a semester/year and programme. Summative assessment is also used for quality assurance.

Assessment is thus viewed as Assessment of Learning (Gipps, 1994), Assessment for Learning (Gipps, 1994) and Assessment as Learning (Torrance, 2007). We will briefly discuss these three concepts.

Summative assessment **(Assessment *of* Learning)** is used to "sum up a person's achievement" (Knight, 2001:3) and provides "feedout" where students display particular competencies and are awarded an exit level certificate. Summative assessment is high-stakes in that the promotion of the student hinges on passing.

Most of the literature on formative assessment **(Assessment *for* Learning)** uses the definition provided by Black and Wiliam (1998) which is, "encompassing all those activities undertaken by teachers and/or by their students which provide information to be used as feedback to modify the teaching and learning activities in which they are engaged" (Black & Wiliam, 1998:7-8).

Formative assessment contributes to student learning through the provision of information about performance (Yorke, 2003) and Boud (2000) adds that it is "a fine-tuning mechanism for how and what we learn" (Boud, 2000:155).

Torrance (2007) argues that although assessment has shifted from assessment of learning to assessment for learning the focus on "procedures and practices come to completely to dominate the learning experience and "criteria compliance." He terms this shift in learning to assessment as learning (2007:282). The over-emphasis on "criteria compliance and award achievement" has resulted in students becoming more reliant on their assessors (Torrance, 2007:282). In order to improve throughput, the assessment objectives are transparent, and students receive coaching from tutors and practice (drafts and redrafts) to improve their grades. Torrance (2007) warns that in so doing we are "in danger of removing the challenge of learning and reducing the quality and validity of outcomes achieved" (Torrance, 2007:282). Boud (2007) offers an alternative which he terms sustainable assessment.

Sustainable assessment

Boud (2007) argues that the problem with the prevailing view of assessment in HE is that it "constructs the learners as passive subjects" (Boud, 2007:17) and this contradicts the view of the student as being an active, co-constructor of knowledge. He challenges the notion that feedback is the only process that impacts on learning. He advocates that a more "productive way to reframe assessment discourse [is] around the theme of informing judgement: that is informing the capacity to evaluate evidence, appraise situations and circumstances astutely, to draw conclusions and act in accordance with this analysis" (Boud, 2007:19). By placing "informing judgement centrally" lecturers will be able to assess graduate attributes as an integral part of assessment (Boud, 2007:20).

Assessment directs student learning, and it impacts on the methods of learning that students will take. Boud (2007) outlines the three features of assessment informing judgement as follows:

1. The first feature makes a direct connection between assessment and learning and how assessment equips students to engage in professional practice.

2. The second feature is that assessment develops reflexivity and self-regulation which is crucial in the development of the active learner. Students are able to monitor their own performance, to see one's own learning in the context in which it is deployed and to respond with awareness to the exigencies of the tasks in which one is engaged. Feedback from various sources is used to complete the feedback loop.

3. The third feature is the variety of contexts in which learning takes place. The context of assessment in HE is usually the course and not the world of work. In doing this, knowledge seems separated from the world of practice although this is where the knowledge will be applied. "Authentic assessment" (Wiggins, 1989:1) refers to assessment practices that are closely aligned with real work settings.

The assessment choices that lecturers make will impact on students adopting either a deep or surface approach to learning. Students are usually resistant to deep approaches to learning especially if they have obtained success using surface learning. According to Ramsden (1992:188), students adopt a "strategic approach" to learning where the objective is to achieve the highest marks possible.

Multimodal teaching, learning and assessment design

Emergency remote teaching has provided an ideal opportunity for educators who were reluctant to embrace online assessments to consider the various options available to meet the learning needs of the Generation Z student and find innovative ways of reaching every student. In this section, we discuss the multimodal teaching, learning and assessment design and the various options available for multimodal assessment.

There are many ways in which the content within a module can be delivered. The key factors that affect Generation Z students and their different learning styles can be provided for by using different ways of delivering the content. The model above (Figure 4.2) suggests that when providing and presenting content multiple technologies, media and visual simulation can be used to demonstrate processes and procedures. Rich digital images can be used for art, history and literature. Course management systems such as Moodle can provide basic content delivery for synchronous and asynchronous teaching.

Dialectic or questioning is an activity that allows teaching staff to probe what students know and to help them refine their knowledge. Discussions can be stimulated by asking the right questions. Threaded electronic discussion boards can be used on learning management systems such as Moodle.

Incorporating reflection can be a powerful pedagogical strategy. Activities that require students to reflect on what they have learnt and share these reflections with teaching staff and fellow students extend and enrich reflection. Blogs/blogging or individual reflective journaling activities are some of the tools that can be used to reflect on their learning practices. Learning journals require students to reflect on their learning during the course of a module. It provides insight to the instructor on how the student has linked the knowledge and learning with his/her life. Journals allow the educator "to look for growth over time – growth in knowledge, in critical thinking, in the development of comprehension or appreciation of a topic" (Conrad & Openo, 2018:79-80). Journals can be used in formative and summative assessments.

Pedagogical Objectives/Activities -> Approach/Technology

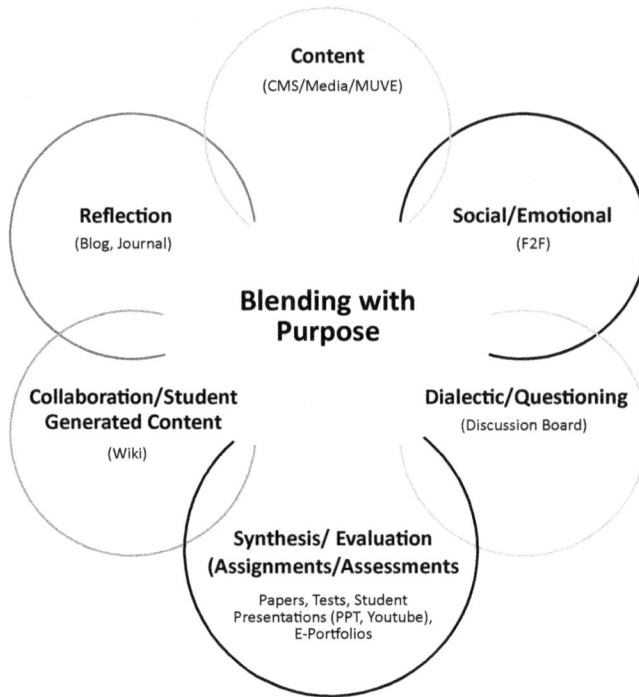

Content
(CMS/Media/MUVE)

Reflection
(Blog, Journal)

Social/Emotional
(F2F)

Blending with Purpose

Collaboration/Student
Generated Content
(Wiki)

Dialectic/Questioning
(Discussion Board)

Synthesis/ Evaluation
(Assignments/Assessments)
Papers, Tests, Student
Presentations (PPT, Youtube),
E-Portfolios

Figure 4.2   Blending with a Purpose - The Multimodal Model

(Source Picciano, A.G. 2009. Blending with Purpose: The Multimodal Model)

Collaborative learning is where students work in groups. Collaborative learning can be used as a technique for problem solving. Wikis allow students to generate content that can be shared with others.

The final component of the model (Figure 4.2) is synthesising, evaluating and assessing learning. Essays, tests, assignments, quizzes and e-portfolios are the major methods used in assessing students learning online. Oral class presentations can be done via Microsoft Teams, Zoom, YouTube videos and podcasts. The e-portfolios can be presentations of images, video and audio. E-portfolios are usually compiled by students to demonstrate their competency linked to a particular outcome. Conrad and Openo (2018) report that the e-portfolio "permits learners to accumulate, build on, and reflect on the shape of their learning experience throughout their programs, making cogent observations and connections amongst learning experiences over a period of time" (Conrad & Openo, 2018:74).

In a multimodal teaching and learning environment students need to be supported socially and emotionally. Educators, academic advisors and tutors should be available to consult with students to explain complex concepts or just for advice on academic issues. This can be done online via e-mail, social media or face-to-face.

Conclusion

The Covid-19 pandemic has created an ideal opportunity for HE to pause and reflect on their current teaching, learning and assessment philosophies and practices and its preparedness to teach the 21st century Generation Z student. The Covid-19 pandemic has highlighted the dire need for educators to utilise theories like connectivism to underpin their teaching and for students to become partners in the learning process. A multimodal model is recommended for the design and implementation of teaching, learning and assessment activities. Multimodal teaching and learning environments provide a dynamic and flexible learning space for students as it combines the use of multimedia and ICTs and can be presented in different modes and caters for the different learning styles. The multimodal design model encourages teaching staff to provide as many learning modalities as possible to supply Generation Z students with a variety of pathways to learning that corresponds to their skills and strengths.

References

Alexander, B., Ashford-Rowe, K., Barajas-Murphy, N., Dobbin, G., Knott, J., McCormack, M., Pomerantz, J., Seilhamer, R. & Weber, N. 2019. *EDUCAUSE Horizon Report: 2019 Higher Education Edition.* Louisville, CO: EDUCAUSE.

Alonso, F., López, G., Manrique, D. & Viñes, J.M. 2008. Learning objects, learning objectives and learning design. *Innovations in Education and Teaching International*, 45(4):389-400. https://doi.org/10.1080/14703290802377265

Association for Quality and Participation [USA]. 2003. Lingo bingo. *The Journal for Quality and Participation*, Winter:31-32.

Beyers, R.N. 2009. A five dimensional model for educating the Net generation. *Educational Technology and Society*, 12(4):218-227.

Biggs, J. 1999. *Teaching for quality learning at university.* Buckingham: Open University Press.

Black, P. & Wiliam, D. 1998. Assessment in classroom learning. *Assessment in Education*, 5(1):7-75. https://doi.org/10.1080/0969595980050102

Boud, D. 2007. Reframing assessment as if learning were important. In: D. Boud & N. Falchikov (eds.), *Rethinking Assessment in Higher Education: Learning for the Longer Term.* New York: Routledge, 25-35. https://doi.org/10.4324/9780203964309

Brown, C. & Czerniewicz, L. 2010. Debunking the 'digital native': Beyond digital apartheid, towards digital democracy. *Journal of Computer Assisted Learning*, 26(5):357-369. https://doi.org/10.1111/j.1365-2729.2010.00369.x

Conrad, D. & Openo, J. 2018. *Assessment strategies for online learning engagement and authenticity.* Edmonton: Athabasca University Press. https://doi.org/10.15215/aupress/9781771992329.01

Duffet, R.G. 2017. Influence of Facebook commercial communications on Generation Z's attitudes in South Africa. *The Electronic Journal of Information Systems in Developing Countries*, 81(8):1-22. https://doi.org/10.1002/j.1681-4835.2017.tb00600.x

Dunaway, M.K. 2011. Connectivism: Learning theory and pedagogical practice for networked information landscapes. *Reference Services Review*, 39(4):675-685. https://doi.org/10.1108/00907321111186686

Garrison, D.R & Vaughan, N.D. 2008. *Blended learning in higher education: framework, principles and guidelines.* San Francisco: Jossey-Bass.

Gazibara, S. 2018. Constructivist Active Learning Environments from the Students' Perspective. 5th International Multidisciplinary Scientific Conference on Social Sciences and Arts SGEM, SGEM. 2018 Conference Proceedings, 26 August-1 September, 5(3.4):183-190.

Gibbs, G. 1999. Using assessment strategically to change the way students learn. In: S. Brown & A. Glesner (eds.), *Assessment Matters in Higher Education.* Buckingham: SRHE and Open University Press, 41-53.

Gilakjani, A.P., Ismail, H.N. & Ahmadi, S.M. 2011. The effect of multimodal learning models on language teaching and learning. *Theory and Practice in Language Studies*, 1(10):1321-1327. https://doi.org/10.4304/tpls.1.10.1321-1327

Gipps, C. 1994. *Beyond testing: Towards a theory of educational assessment.* London: Farmer.

Gonzalez, C. 2004. *The role of blended learning in the world of technology.* Available: https://bit.ly/3laPTHP [Accessed 29 March 2012].

Graham, C.R. 2004. *Blended learning systems: definition, current trends, and future directions.* Available: https://bit.ly/3bFm3YK [Accessed 1 August 2020].

Hart, D. 2018. *Gen Z - training to unlock a generation's potential: Learning what makes Gen Z tick.* Available: http://bit.ly/3rlGwl4 [Accessed 2 September 2020].

Heinze & Practor. 2004. *Reflections on the use of blended learning.* Available: https://bit.ly/30BxZVh [Accessed 2 September 2020].

Hodges, D.Z. 2019. Use generational theory as a guide to understanding college students. *The Reflective Leader*, 21(3). https://doi.org/10.102/dap.30653.

Iftode, D. 2019. Generation Z and learning styles. *SEA: Practical Applications of Science*, VII(21):255-262. https://doi.org/10.2139/ssrn.3518722

Knight, P. 2001. A briefing on key concepts: Formative and summative, criterion and normreferenced assessment. *Assessment Series*, No.7. [s.l.]: LTSN Generic Centre.

Lester, S.W., Standifer, R.L., Schultz, N.J. & Windsor, J.M. 2012. Actual versus perceived generational differences at work: An empirical examination. *Journal of Leadership and Organisational Studies*, 19(3):341-354. https://doi.org/10.1177/1548051812442747

Luckett, K., & Sutherland, L. 2000. Assessment practices that improve teaching and learning. In: S. Makoni (ed.), *Teaching and Learning in higher education : A handbook for Southern Africa.* Johannesburg: Witwatersrand University Press, 98-130.

Lyons, S. & Kuron, L. 2014. Generational differences in the workplace: A review of the evidence and directions for future research. *Journal of Organisational Behaviour,* 35:139-158. https://doi.org/10.1002/job.1913

Marshall, A.L. & Wolanskyj-Spinner, A. 2020. Covid-19: Challenges and opportunities for educators and Generation Z learners. *Mayo Clinic Proceedings*, 95(6):1135-1137. https://doi.org/10.1016/j.mayocp.2020.04.015

Pikhart, M. & Klimova, B. 2020. eLearning 4.0 as a sustainability strategy for Generation Z language learners: Applied linguistics of second language acquisition in younger adults. *Societies*, 10(2):38. https://doi.org/10.3390/soc10020038

Prensky, M. 2001. Digital natives, digital immigrants. *On the Horizon*, 9(5):1-6. https://doi.org/10.1108/10748120110424816

Prensky, M. 2010. *Teaching digital natives: Partnering for real learning.* Thousand Oaks, CA: Corwin Press.

Ramsden, P. 1992. *Learning to teach in Higher Education.* London: Routledge.

Robson, A. 2015. Do nurses wish to continue working for the UK National Health Service? A comparative study of three generations. *Journal of Advanced Nursing*, 17(1):647-670. https://doi.org/10.1111/jan.12468

Scardamalia, M. & Bereiter, C. 2006. Knowledge building: Theory, pedagogy, and technology. In: R.K. Sawyer (ed.), *The Cambridge handbook of the learning sciences.* New York: Cambridge University Press. https://doi.org/10.1017/CBO9780511816833.008

Seemiller, C. & Grace, M. 2016. *Generation Z goes to college.* San Francisco, CA: Jossey-Bass.

Seemiller, C., Grace, M., Dal Bo Campagnolo, P., Da Rosa Alves, I.M. & De Borba, D.B. 2019. How Generation Z college students prefer to learn: A comparison of U.S. and Brazil students. *Journal of Educational Research and Practice*, 9(1):349-368. https://doi.org/10.5590/JERAP.2019.09.1.25

Shatto, B. & Erwin, K. 2017. Teaching millennials and Generation Z: Bridging the generational divide. *Creative Nursing,* 23(1):24-28. https://doi.org/10.1891/1078-4535.23.1.24

Siemens, G. 2004. *Connectivism: A learning theory for the digital age.* Available: https://bit. ly/3vfRcKd [Accessed 31 March 2011].

Starkey, T.J. 2015, The critical factors that influence faculty attitudes and perceptions of teaching English as Second Language nursing students: A grounded theory research study, *Nurse Education Today,* 35(5):718-725.

Strydom, F., Mentz, M. & Kuh, G. 2010. *Enhancing success in South Africa's higher education: Measuring student engagement.* Sabinet. Available: https://bit.ly/3vhKFPd [Accessed 1 September 2020].

Torrance, H. 2007. Assessment as learning? How the use of explicit learning objectives, assessment criteria and feedback in post-secondary education and training can come to dominate learning. *Assessment in Education,* 14(3):281-294. https://doi.org/10.1080/09695940701591867

Trevino, N.G. 2018. *The arrival of Generation Z on college campuses.* PhD thesis. San Antonio, TX: University of the Incarnate Word.

Wiggins, G. 1989. Teaching to the authentic test. *Educational Leadership,* 46(7):41-47.

Yorke, M. 2003. Formative assessment in higher education: Move towards theory and the enhancement of pedagogic practice. *Higher Education,* 45:477-501. https://doi.org/10.1023/A:1023967026413

5

Creating safe spaces for critical class dialogue and reflection

Lize-Mari Mitchell

Introduction

> Thinking leads man to knowledge. He may see and hear and read and learn whatever he pleases, and as much as he pleases; he will never know anything of it, except that which he has thought over, that which by thinking he has made the property of his own mind (Pestalozzi, 1843).

As the development of Covid-19 necessitated social distancing, higher education institutions (HEI) have been in a race against time to salvage the academic year by ensuring course content reaches students virtually (Dipa, 2020; Universities South Africa, 2020). Virtual learning is not a new phenomenon in the South African context, in fact, most universities have some version of digitalised education (Letseka, Letseka & Pitsoe, 2018:121; Phakeng, 2020). There also exists a significant body of literature covering e-learning within the South African context (Bharuthram & Kies, 2013; Letseka et al., 2018; Meier, 2017; Njenga & Fourie, 2010). Although, it is not possible to give herein an exhaustive list of these works, so prolific are they.

Despite this, the process of migrating to online education has been plagued with issues ranging from technological needs, poor network coverage to data costs (Macupe, 2020; Van Rooi, 2020), as well as the late adaption to technology (Letseka et al., 2018; Mahlangu, 2018:17-21; Universities South Africa, 2020). Evidently, many of these challenges had been noted prior to the pandemic by South African scholars (Bharauthram & Kies, 2013:412; Letseka et al., 2018:121-123; Mahlangu, 2018:17-21). Due to these longstanding issues, many educators used to contact learning experience migrating to fully online teaching as unchartered territory. For these educators, the primary concern has been mastering the new technology. The pandemic situation is still novel, therefore the research on the adoption, quality of online learning and student engagement in South Africa, is limited. However, it is concerning that the actual critical engagement with course content seem to be neglected (Cleophas, 2020; Seepe, 2020; Vilakasi, 2020). By prioritising delivery of the material in an electronic format, educators might be falling trap to what Paul and Elder (2019:8) described as the flawed educational assumption that "lecture content can be absorbed with minimal intellectual engagement" and that "memorisation is the key to learning" (Paul & Elder, 2019:8).

The traditional method of teaching, where the teacher as authoritative figure simply transfers information to students, has become obsolete (Ashoori, Kajbaf, Manshee & Talebi, 2020:34; Mbembe, 2015:9). Educators must take command of their curriculum and not only teach students the content they need to master, but also how to engage with it in a meaningful way (Paul & Elder, 2019:8). Educators must therefore create circumstances where students must contextualise new information within the paradigm of existing knowledge, think themselves to new conclusions and ultimately become lifelong, self-directed learners. These skills are generally referred to as critical thinking and the development thereof is central to all tertiary institutional aims.

Critical thinking skills are especially essential for law students who, after all, will become the shapers of the South African legal future. The ideal is that law students should ostensibly be taught the discipline's version of critical thinking which includes a moral, political and social consciousness (Quinot, 2015:432; Van den Berg, 2013:4). These deeper understandings advance it from critical thinking skills to the related concept of critical citizenship skills. A critical law student would, for example, not memorise the definition of the rule of law, but rather take ownership of it and internalise the ideals found within it (Burbules & Berk, 1999:46). One of the central ways through which this is facilitated, is by creating, in class, a safe space for students to engage in continuous dialogue, debate and critical reflection (Ali, 2017:4; Arao & Clemens, 2013:143; Brown, 2011:7). Within a conventional physical classroom, open engagement can freely be encouraged as discussion has little permanence and there is a higher level of social responsibility as anonymity is almost impossible. Covid-19 has forced both students and lecturers out of the conventional safe space and moved class engagement into the infamous terrain of online spaces. The virtual sphere is one of contradiction in which students can enjoy a higher level of anonymity, but still have evidence of their every reaction virtually documented.

This chapter provides a theoretical investigation of selected adverse effects that an online environment may have on the provision of a safe space for critical dialogue. This will be done by defining and emphasising the importance of critical thinking, critical citizenship and describing how active student engagement relates to these concepts. This will be followed by a more general exploration of virtual classrooms, the notion of a safe space and the threats of cyberbullying and digital footprints.

Data was chiefly obtained from secondary sources, mainly newspaper articles, magazines and peer-reviewed journals. The conceptual nature of the paper therefore presents a particular limit due to the restricted data and the fact that Covid-19 is an unfolding event.

Developing critical citizens

One of the products of a liberal undergraduate education is the ability to think critically (Burbules & Berk, 1999:46). Correspondent to this, the Department of Higher Education prioritises it in most, if not all, curriculum mandates (Council of Higher Education, 2018). Whether HEI are achieving this aim, is a debate too lengthy to discuss here, but educators should heed this call and design their classes and course content to prioritise and foster critical thinking skills. Higher education educators must not teach students what to think, but simply to think, and most importantly, to think about their own thinking. For law students, as the future members of the judiciary, this implies a strive towards social justice, a commitment to constitutional values and the critical analysis of their own understandings and ingrained beliefs regarding race, class, politics and socio-economic issues (Quinot, 2015:432; Van den Berg, 2013:4).

Related to critical thinking and holistically developed students, is critical citizenship, based on the seminal work of John Dewey (1916), which entails stimulating critical social and political consciousness in students. Two question arise which are addressed in this section: firstly, how are critical thinking and critical citizenship distinct? And secondly, what impact does class discussions and safe spaces have on the promotion of these skills?

In answering the first question, critical thinking, as a term familiar to most academics, will be defined briefly while focusing on the comparison between critical thinking and critical citizenship. The second question will be addressed by investigating class engagement within a critical pedagogy. It should be noted that the length of this chapter does not allow for in depth discussions of the relevant concepts. Multifaceted ideas are reduced to single paragraphs which serve the purpose of providing a theoretical framework. However, for more in depth understanding, further reading is highly recommended.

Critical thinking

Cottrell (2017:2) lists the following dispositions and abilities associated with the process of critical thinking:

> identifying other people's positions ... evaluating the evidence ... weighing up opposing arguments ... reading between the lines ... reflecting on issues in a structured way ... drawing conclusions about the validity of arguments ... synthesising information and presenting a point of view in a structured, clear and well-reasoned way.

Developing critical thinking in students is in essence emphasising the importance of arguments that appeal to one's critical faculties, in other words, the need for proper justifications for actions or beliefs (Bowell & Kemp, 20024). It is the ability to think logically (Johnson & Morris, 2010:4), identify the flaws in the thinking of others (Cottrell, 2017:2) and detect rhetoric, coercion, threats and bribes (Bowell & Kemp, 2002:7). It is the development of the metacognitive ability (Moon, 2008:56). This critical self-reflection allows one to detect errors in one's own reasoning and develop more logical patterns of argument. As Moon (2008:61) describes it, "the more sophisticated the critical thinker is, the more she will be aware of ... the essential subjectivity of her reasoning". Ultimately, a critical thinker will display intellectual courage and autonomy, whilst still being intellectually humble and empathetic (Paul & Elder, 2019:7). The development of critical thinking inherently links to communication and dialogue (Paul & Elder, 2019:7). A critical educator would therefore use a dialectical approach to teaching.

Critical citizenship and critical pedagogy

Critical citizenship is related to and dependent on critical thinking, but entails developing skills that transcends the logical element of critical thinking. The aims of critical citizenship include individual, holistic student transformation while emphasising a multi-disciplinary approach to course content (Constandius & Bitzer, 2015:3). This transformation is facilitated by the promotion of a shared set of values (Constandius & Odiboh, 2016:1). For example, within a South African law course, these values would be reflective of constitutional values like freedom, equality, tolerance and dignity. These are also the shared values emphasised in the 1997 White Paper on the Transformation of Higher Education (Department of Education, 1997) and in the later 2018 Council of Higher Education report on the Bachelors of

Laws Qualification (Council of Higher Education, 2018). Critical citizenship focuses on developing responsible and accommodating citizens on social, emotional and cognitive levels. It functions from the understanding that the individual and society are inextricably interwoven (McLaren, 2003:69; Mitchell, 2020:11). It is of specific relevance in South Africa as a reaction to the colonial stigmatising, historical exclusion and marginalisation, but also addressing the current inequalities and societal problems (Mitchell, 2020:6).

As explained above critical thinking aims to address unjustified, unmethodical and potentially prejudiced perceptions and to replace it with "thinking based upon reliable procedures of inquiry" (Burbules & Berk, 1999:81). The distinction between critical thinking and critical citizenship can be found in the moral component of the latter. There are various pedagogies capable of developing critical thinking (Greenlaw & DeLoach, 2003:41), however the competencies associated with critical citizenship require that an active learning pedagogy be followed, of which the best suited is a critical pedagogy (Johnson & Morris, 2010:4-6). Critical citizenship must be taught within a critical pedagogy as it addresses both moralistic and ideological concerns in students, which is missing in most conceptions of critical thinking (Mitchell, 2020:13). In other words, whilst critical thinking focuses on the development of logical thinking, critical citizenship and critical pedagogy transcend this and introduce political thinking (Johnson & Morris, 2010:2). Within a law class, this implies the merging of law and politics and teaches students to be critical of both, whilst striving to attain social justice. Critical citizenship education is therefore fundamentally tied to the ideal of establishing a society based on social justice and nonexploitative relations (McLaren, 2003:3).

Linking critical pedagogy and class engagement

Various scholars have made a compelling case for using class discussions to develop high-order cognitive skills (Afify, 2019; Brown, Worth & Boylan, 2017; Greenlaw & DeLoach, 2003; Hansen & Salemi,1990). A well-managed, constructive class dialogue has a sustained and dynamic nature which has been proven to stimulate the transfer of ideas and development of individual thinking skills (Greenlaw & DeLoach, 2003:41). Class discussions are specifically well suited to assist law students in becoming critical thinkers and citizens, as it creates a structure in which, firstly, students must individually form an opinion and then secondly, they are immediately faced with a multiplicity of perspectives. Every opinion they are exposed to forces a response from them, whether it be on metacognitive level or more openly (Anderson, 2017).

Similarly, Freire (1972) in his seminal work on critical pedagogy, emphasises the importance of developing context specific pedagogical methods to promote dialogue between students and educators to unlock critical consciousness (Freire, 1972:41). Similar sentiments were later given by Garrison, Anderson and Archer (1999) in their seminal work on the community of enquiry model, wherein a worthwhile educational experience is described as an interaction between teachers and learners in the presence of three essential elements: cognitive, social and teaching. The cognitive presence is based on a generalised model of critical thinking (Anderson, 2017) and will be enhanced by striving towards the aims of critical thinking. The social presence is described to be present when learners "project themselves socially and emotionally, in all aspects of their personality, through the communication media that they use" (Garrison et al., 1999:94). This is most notable in critical class discussions. The teaching presence will be illustrated in establishing both individual and collaborative learning activities that will support the aims of critical pedagogy (Anderson, 2017). Jezegou (2010:4) later refined the understanding of a community of enquiry, by defining it as a group of knowledgeable people who are jointly involved in a collaborative learning process that "facilitate[s] the individual and collective construction of knowledge".

The irrefutable link between critical pedagogy, a community of enquiry and continuous class discussion was confirmed by later scholars Johnson and Morris (2010). Freire (1976:15) also underscored the importance of open discourse founded on mutual respect, faith and humility, which directly relates to the idea of a safe discussion space.

The aim of critical pedagogy is to guide students to take all that they know, have learnt and accept as moral and political truths and place it under a critical lens. It assists both students and educators to "see the limitations and lacunae in our own understandings" of socio-political issues (Burbules & Berk, 1999:61). An open dialogue, within a safe space, provides an opportunity for students to learn that blind consensus and amalgamation of other's perceptions would rarely, if ever, lead to an informed, critical citizen. Increased exposure and response to different opinions leads to a realisation that truth is both objective and relative (Bowell & Kemp, 2002:57).

Therefore, class discussions in, for example, a philosophical law course, should do more than guide students to logical patterns of thinking. Rather, as a critical pedagogy requires, the focus of dialogue should be on social justice, oppression, democracy, corruption and the various rights and responsibilities constitutionally given to us.

These topics must be taught, discussed, debated and continuously critically reflected upon within moral, political and ideological levels. In this respect, there needs to exist a safe, open and controlled space in which these crucial discussions can take place.

Virtual classrooms as safe spaces for critical discussion

As set out above, HEIs should by their very definition be free and open spaces in which students and staff alike can explore ideas and critically converse. However, Fain (2004:11) reminds us that a school is still a constructed, public space and that a safe and free intellectual space only exists when it is intentionally created (Ruthotto, Kreth, Stevens, Trively & Melkers, 2020:2). It is the responsibility of the educator to create this space within a dialectical understanding of HEIs as a site of both domination and liberation. Complicating the matter is that the creation of such a space must now take place in the infamously unsafe terrain of online domains.

In the investigation of virtual classrooms as safe spaces, both these terms need to be defined and then the relevance between them can be explored.

Safe spaces

The concept of a safe space is a symbolically powerful declaration, but it has been critiqued for being a potential threat to academic freedom and an excuse for students to retreat from perspectives at odds with their own (Leonardo & Porter, 2010:147; Shulevitz, 2015; Whitten, 2018). It is therefore important to define the concept within the context of the discussion. A safe space is an educational metaphor for creating a classroom that is both open enough to include a myriad of perspectives (Gayle, Cortez & Preiss, 2013:4; Redmond, 2010:5), but also structured by rules to make the exchange of these perspectives safe for both students and teachers (Flensner & Von der Lippe, 2019:276). It is a challenging space where students can express and communicate ideas, and find their voices without fear of silencing, intimidation, retribution, marginalisation or undue psychological harm (Ali, 2017:4; Arao & Clemens, 2013:143; Brown, 2011:7). The critical educator should therefore stimulate critical dialogue (Gayle et al., 2013:4; Leonardo & Porter, 2010:154) and the exploration of diversity and experiences, but also provide ground rules that all participants agree to (Flensner & Von der Lippe, 2019:276).

The term "safe" has been criticised for its ambiguity (Iversen, 2018:1) and the unrealistic expectations of creating a space that is perceived as psychologically safe by all students (Barrett, 2010:7; Boostrom, 1998:407). Callan (2016:65) states that a safe class should be one that ensures students' dignity is safe, but they are still "intellectually unsafe". In this regard, it is important for educators to redefine the classrooms as a "place of risk" (Leonardo & Porter, 2010:153), a safe space that does not imply a stress-free space without contention, disagreement or discomfort (Boostrom, 1998:405; Gayle et al., 2013:4; Redmond, 2010:4) and trying to create this would defeat the purpose of critical engagement. There must be challenging, continuous dialectical processes in which reaching consensus should never be the aim. A safe space is still a space in which educators and students do place themselves at risk (Arao & Clemens, 2013:14; Leonardo & Porter, 2010:153). In a racially diverse society like South Africa, this idea of an unsafe-safe space is especially vital, educators should strive towards "creating risk" in their classes as the "antidote to safety" as it leads to more transformative learning opportunities that will challenge existing power relations and ideologies (Leonardo & Porter, 2010:154). Boostrom (1998:407) states that teachers "need to manage conflict, not prohibit it". A safe space should rather imply a place where expression is encouraged, but with the knowledge that there are limits on what is acceptable expression (Ali, 2017:6; Redmund, 2010:8). This is especially true for a student body and course content as potentially contentious as those of a law degree.

Within a traditional classroom there exists numerous methods to create a safe space. The question is how to create a similar space in an online environment?

Virtual classrooms

In an attempt to answer the above question, we first need to delve into the definition of an online class. A virtual classroom can be described as:

> ... an online synchronous session to support student learning delivered via a Web-conferencing technology which potentially incorporates voice, text, images and video. (Terry, Taylor & Davies, 2019:212)

It should firstly be noted that within the context of this chapter, virtual classes refer exclusively to classes that take place on formal, licenced teaching and Web conferencing platforms, for example Blackboard, Google classroom and Zoom. All research reported are limited to studies done within these parameters and excludes findings of unorganised chatrooms or informal platforms.

Secondly, it is important to note that with regard to a safe virtual space, the discussion will be centred around synchronous learning, as opposed to traditional asynchronous learning where students can download pre-recorded lessons. Asynchronous classes, although useful in conjunction with a synchronous classroom, leave no room for purposeful and immediate engagement, which greatly neglects the aims of critical thinking, knowledge transmission and the co-creation of knowledge (Terry et al., 2019:213). With the technology at lecturers' disposal, asynchronous classrooms should never be used as the sole or primary method of teaching. Studies have also shown that synchronous classes have significantly higher success rates, student interaction and student satisfaction (Martin & Parker, 2014:193; Ruthotto, Kreth, Stevens, Trively & Melkers, 2020:2).

As stated above it is required that a community of enquiry be established to promote the development of critical thinking and critical citizenship (Anderson, 2017; Freire, 1972). In the case of synchronous online learning, the potential exists for all three of the the described elements to be present, and therefore the creation of a community of enquiry, which will facilitate critical thinking and higher-order discussion (Anderson, 2017). The social presence can be seen in the emphasis on two-way communication (Terry et al., 2019:212) and active student participation. This engagement will be both among students and between students and instructors (Ruthotto et al., 2020:1). It implies real time interaction (Martin & Parker, 2014:192), for example breakout rooms, text chat, white boards and audio chat. The experience is also significantly more socio-emotional (Chou, 2002) with increased interaction and immediate feedback (Park & Bonk, 2007), exploration and integration, allowing for participants to project their "personal characteristics into the community", another key feature of the social presence (Garrison et al., 1999). Both students and lecturers are able to share their screen; webcams are used (dependant on stable bandwidth) and the use of emoticons during live chat (Cornelius, 2014:266). Synchronous discussions allow for reactions to other students' contributions which increases interpersonal connections (Martin & Parker, 2014), critical discussions and challenging perspectives and ideologies. The teaching presence, as described by Garrison et al. (1999:90), can be found predominantly in the educator, as designer and facilitator of the educational experience. The discussed virtual tools enrich the educator presence as it provides an opportunity for the facilitator to establish both individual and collaborative learning activities (Anderson, 2017) that support the development of critical citizens.

Virtual tools

Virtual classrooms can take place on various platforms, for example Zoom, Google Classroom, Microsoft Teams, Moodle, Schoology etc. or as in the authors' case, Blackboard collaborate.

The technology can be engaged to strengthen the learning and instructional design (Anderson, 2017), as well as the proposed critical pedagogy. Educators need to capitalise on the available tools to stimulate class engagement. A brief summary is provided of some of the main tools that the author has found useful when facilitating class discussions between law students. These tools, or similar functions, are available on most educational and conferencing platforms.

- Polling

Polling systems have various functions, for example it can be used to determine the level of student understanding (Theroux & Kilbane, 2005), getting them to think about the content (Mollborn & Hoekstra, 2010:18) and determining the general opinion on a contentious issue. Polling questions can be written prior to the class engagement. The development of effective questions has been shown as a key element in enhancing cognitive presence (Anderson, 2017; Richardson, Sadaf & Ertmer, 2012). Polling is anonymous and it is possibly the most non-threatening way for students to engage (Brady, Seli & Rosenthal, 2013:886). When the poll is done, the facilitator can share the overview of the responses with the class, but only the facilitator can determine individual participants' responses. Polling can activate the cognitive presence in the educational experience (Mollborn & Hoekstra, 2010:18). Recent studies have shown that experimental systems that force students to interact with short responses, for example polling or like buttons, increase at least the social presence of the community of inquiry model, in most cases it showed an increase in all three elements (Anderson, 2017; Makos, Oztok, Zingaro & Hewitt, 2013; Schellens, Van Keer, De Wever & Valcke, 2009).

- Live chat and emoticons

Garrison (1999:91) described text-based communication as ideal for higher education purposes when the aim is higher-cognitive learning, as it provides time for reflection and careful and critical thinking about complex issues (Anderson, 2017). The majority of students might be hesitant to speak up during class, but most of the students are comfortable with text-based communication (Fry, 2017:59). The chat function of the class can be activated during class discussion and students can, in real time, react with a text response, again supporting both a social and cognitive presence in the community of enquiry (Anderson, 2017). To support this non-verbal communication most platforms will have a range of emoticons for participants to use to communicate, to assist in reflecting the tone of their reactions and to reduce ambiguity in their written cues (Ganster, Eimler & Krämer, 2012:227). This immediately increases the feeling of coherence in class (Grieve, Moffitt & Padgett, 2019:232-238) and gives autonomy to students.

- Breakout groups

Breakout rooms have the potential of creating a platform for critical reflection, discourse reasoning, questioning, connecting and deliberating. All which are key features of a community of enquiry (Garrison, 1999:91). All attendees start in the main classroom and if the instructor wants to facilitate engagements within smaller groups, participants are assigned (randomly by the platform or the facilitator can do custom assignments) to what is known as a 'breakout group' for an allotted time. These groups function completely separately from each other and have their own private functions, for example audio, video, chat and whiteboard. An added benefit is that facilitators can monitor students by seamlessly entering and exiting the groups. This type of online presence and analysis assist in the teaching presence as teachers can monitor the groups and identify emergent problems (Anderson & Dron, 2012). This tool is especially helpful for large classes in which a need exists to maximise student engagement (Loughleed, Kirkland & Newton, 2012:17). For most of the students contributing to a conversation with 5 people is a lot less daunting than contributing to a room of 200. Studies have shown that the majority of students feel that breakout groups enhance the learning experience (Loughleed et al., 2012; Saltz & Heckman, 2020). Breakout groups provide a sheltered and informal opportunity for students to apply learnt knowledge, again allowing for a cognitive presence (Anderson, 2017).

These tools can open a whole new way of engaging with students and creating a safe and accessible environment for them to voice their opinions. However, the virtual space is infamous for the many threats it poses to its users and has to be properly managed. The next section addresses these barriers.

Barriers to creating an online safe space

This chapter analyses two of the major hurdles to creating a safe online space, firstly managing students' digital footprints, and secondly, dealing with the threat of cyberbullying. Although the discussion is limited to these barriers, the chapter acknowledges that they form part of a myriad of issues, for example technological disruptions, substandard equipment, social inequalities and poor training.

Digital footprints

The aim of creating a safe space is effective student engagement (Redmond, 2010:5). Encouraging students to speak their minds is not an easy feat even in a traditional classroom, but at least in face-to-face engagement there is an additional sense of safety in the non-permanence of statements. The audience is limited to those attending class and either one's statement or one's identity, or both, will most likely be forgotten.

However, in most synchronous online classes the entire session can be archived for later use. Every class contribution is a traceable online action. In fact, engagement in any online activity leaves a unique data trail, known as a digital footprint (Rogers,

2020:68). Communication experts regularly heed warnings that statements and information shared online, even when deleted, is never fully retractable (Aswani, 2020:108; Rogers, 2020:66). Any action, no matter how mundane, is now perdurable, ubiquitous and instantly available world-wide (Fertik & Thompson, 2015:2). For example, a live chat history is automatically stored by most of the popular teaching and communication platforms (Blackboard, 2019; Microsoft, 2019; Zoom, 2020) and even when deleted, can easily be screenshotted and be posted to social media, thus creating a new chain of permanence. Although it can be argued that this knowledge will increase students' accountability for their class conduct, it can also severely hinder the openness and willingness of participation (Anderson & Dron, 2012:9).

This threat of a digital footprint is especially worrisome within critical discussion. Educators encourage students to test the limits of their own ingrained ideologies and in this endeavour, they will explore and support notions and concepts that they might find later in life they no longer identify with. Many students impetuously speak up in class simply to be provocative or to express underlying hostility. As an intellectual space, this must be allowed as it is all part of the process of developing critical thinking, but the consequences could be harmful. Although it is evident that there must be a sense of accountability for one's statements, human nature must be kept in mind. Various statements are made in the heat of the moment or simply out of ignorance. One can also not lose sight of the fact that without these debate-igniting comments, there would be little ideological change.

The option of not recording classes is in most cases unfeasible. However, in a bid to protect students, one can attempt to control when class debates take place and have allocated, unrecorded portions of the class for this. These segments can also be cut from class recordings before uploading and distributing. There will have to be consistency in this, as to not create the impression that an educator is trying to sensor their classes. Live chats can also be excluded from saved, uploaded content. However, this is a precarious situation as the facilitator cannot control what students choose to record on their own. Anderson and Dron (2012:9) also recommended that students be given the option of choosing their access level, they can then determine to what extent personal information and content is made public.

Cyberbullying

Bullying within traditional, on-campus higher education is not a new concept, although the bullying can predominantly be found between staff members (Keashly & Neuman, 2013:1-8; King & Piotrowski, 2015:257-261), student to faculty in the form of threats and blackmailing (Keashly & Neuman, 2010:48-51; Kolonko et al., 2006) and out of class bullying between students. Direct attacks in a traditional class are a far less frequent occurrence. This is mostly due to the fact that in a traditional classroom, any student that speaks up is immediately identifiable. This recognition brings accountability and a sense of social responsibility and makes action against a bully a significantly easier process to initiate compared to a cyberbully. A significant concern of any online environment is the ease with which users can hide behind the anonymity provided by the platform (Watts, Wagner, Velasquez & Behrens, 2017:269). A switched off webcam and pseudonym guarantees anonymity and creates a breeding ground for cyberbullying. Perpetrators feel physically separated from their victims, which has also shown to heighten disinhibition and decreased levels of empathy (Brody & Vangelisit, 2014; Heirman, Angelopoulos, Wegge, Vandebosch, Eggermont & Walrave, 2015; Watts et al., 2017:271). Although cyberbullying is more prominent within schools, recent studies have identified the growing presence of cyberbullying in higher education (Eskey & Eskey, 2014; Elçi & Seçkin, 2019; Minor, Smith & Branshen, 2013; Ndiege, Okello & Wamuyu, 2020; Vaill, Campbell & Whiteford, 2020; Washington, 2015; Watts et al., 2017). These studies have identified examples of student-to-student interaction, but also student-to-instructor.

Cyberbullying in HEI's manifests in various forms, but within a synchronous classroom environment, it would be primarily found in live chat comments (Elçi & Seçkin, 2019:949; Ndiege et al., 2020:4; Washington, 2015:25) and anonymous verbal contributions (Watts et al., 2017). Inappropriate comments can either be related to class content or simply be personal attacks against the current speaker or the lecturer (Elçi & Seçkin, 2019:950; Washington, 2015:25). Personal attacks include defamation, threats, verbal abuse, aggressive language, intimidation and degrading comments (Minor et al., 2013:16). These comments, because they are given on a live feed and can be read or heard by all participants, can cause class division, psychosocial distress (Elçi & Seçkin, 2019:951), significant damage to a lecturer's reputation (Eskey & Eskey, 2014:37) and learners' self-confidence to engage in class (Vaill et al., 2020) and completely destroy the notion of a safe environment.

Cyberbullying is difficult to regulate and in many cases this leads to a permissive attitude from management (Minor et al., 2013:25). Although a new phenomenon within the South African HEI sphere, there will be a subsequent rise as we become more cemented in the online environment. HEIs need to be pre-emptive by laying the foundations for a bully-free culture (Vaill et al., 2020:11), before it becomes a fixture in online class environments. A lenient climate towards cyberbullying has shown to lead to a significant increase in abusive behaviour (Eskey & Eskey, 2014:38; Heirman et al., 2015:263). Studies have shown that many actions of cyberbullying in HEIs go unpunished, not only due to the absence of a code of conduct, but also due to lecturers being uncertain of the existence of a code of conduct, or the code being rarely enforced (Minor et al., 2013:15). Awareness is the key (Eskey & Eskey, 2014:39). HEIs should ensure that the following is in place: clear procedure (Vaill et al., 2020:10-11), proper student and teacher training (Cornelius, 2014:261), a zero-tolerance policy and a code of conduct that addresses cyberbullying (Elçi & Seçkin, 2019:956; Vaill et al., 2020:11). In that respect, defining what constitutes cyberbullying should also not be vague or left to interpretation. Students should not have the opportunity to claim ignorance, free speech or academic freedom as a defence for abusive behaviour.

Recommendations

Digital footprints

Dealing with this issue is not as clear-cut as with cyberbullying, as the extent to which HEIs can exert control over class recordings is limited. The methods with which students can document others' contributions are endless and can vary from sophisticated recording programmes to the taking of screenshots during class. The following suggestions may address a digital footprint concern:

- Keep class discussions unrecorded.
- Make use of breakout groups, which limits the exposure students have within the larger group.
- Educate students on the importance of a safe space and their role in the success of such a space.
- Allow students to control the access to their digital actions.

Cyberbullying

- As discussed above, on an institutional level a zero-tolerance cyberbullying policy should be developed and properly communicated.
- Faculty staff should be trained to identify and address cyberbullying from students and also their own behaviour that could constitute bullying. They should be aware of and be able to master a clear process.
- Students should receive training on how to conduct themselves in an online environment and be able to distinguish between appropriate and inappropriate behaviours.
- A clear code of conduct should be communicated to all participants and any behaviour in violation of this conduct should be punishment in a timely, coherent, fair and consequent manner.
- Students should not be given the option to use an online username that makes them unidentifiable, but rather all students should have a uniform identification system.

Conclusion

With the introduction of Covid-19 regulations, South Africa has seen an unprecedented migration to online platforms. The transition, in many cases, has not been smooth with institutional under preparedness and the gross inequalities within higher education being emphasised by the desperate situation. In an attempt to save the academic year by converting to online learning, the critical engagement with course content seems to be lost among more pressing concerns. This chapter explores the importance of active, critical engagement with course content and lays out a conceptual framework that identifies the elements that are crucial prerequisites for achieving proper engagement, whilst recommending virtual tools that can enrich the virtual class experience.

Critical engagement and reflection are shown to be especially crucial for law students as the shapers of the South African legal future. A holistically developed law student is one that has been taught to think critically and has a well-developed moral and social consciousness. Critical pedagogy is identified as being the best-suited to these aims and central to this is class discussions to develop high-order cognitive skills. It is worth noting that critical pedagogy is also flawed as some scholars have provided in-depth critique of the approach. In spite of these critiques, the study still finds it valuable. To enhance the educational experience to one where effective class dialogue can take place, a community of enquiry must be established in the educational setting. Within this community a well-managed, constructive class dialogue gives students an opportunity to critically engage with course content.

The chapter identifies the creation of a virtual safe space as vital to facilitate and encourage establishment of the community of enquiry and encourage students to engage in debates, negotiations and critical reflections. A virtual safe space is an online space that allows a myriad of perspectives, where students can express and communicate ideas without fear of silencing, intimidation, retribution, marginalisation or undue psychological harm. It is illustrated that such a safe space can be created on various, widely used platforms, for example Blackboard Collaborate, Zoom, Google Classroom, etc. These platforms contain on board tools that can enrich class discussions and engagement for example: polling, live chat, emoticons and breakout groups. Educators need to capitalise on the available tools to stimulate class engagement. In addition, the two major barriers to open virtual discourse, namely cyberbullying and the everlasting digital footprint, were explored and best practice recommended. To maximise the benefits and minimise the threats, the focus should be on preparation, proper training and instructions to staff and students. However, further research is necessary to fully understand the complex issues that will affect developing critical skills in a virtual classroom.

References

Afify, M.K. 2019. The influence of group size in the asynchronous online discussions on the development of critical thinking skills, and on improving students' performance in online discussion forum. *International Journal of Emerging Technologies in Learning*, 14(5):132-152. https://doi.org/10.3991/ijet.v14i05.9351

Ali, D. 2017. Safe spaces and brave spaces. *NASPA Policy and Practice Series*, (5):1-13.

Anderson, T. 2017. *How communities of inquiry drive teaching and learning in the digital age.* North Online Learning. Available at: https://bit.ly/3rsblcO [Accessed 13 August 2020].

Anderson, T. & Dron, J. 2012. Learning technology through three generations of technology enhanced distance education pedagogy. *European Journal of Open, Distance and E-Learning*, 1-15.

Arao, B. & Clemens, K. 2013. From safe spaces to brave spaces: A new way to frame dialogue around diversity and social justice. In: L.M. Landreman (ed.), *The art of effective facilitation: Reflections from social justice educators*. Sterling, VA: Stylus, 135-151.

Ashoori, J., Kajbaf, M.B., Manshee, G. & Talebi, H. 2020. Comparison of the effectiveness of webbased, cooperative learning and traditional teaching methods in achievement motivation and academic achievement in the biology course interdisciplinary. *Journal of Virtual Learning in Medical Sciences*, 25-34.

Aswani, N. 2020. The right to be forgotten and its enforcement in India. *International Journal of Legal Developments and Allied Issues*, 6(3):107-123.

Barrett, B.J. 2010. Is "Safety" Dangerous? A Critical Examination of the Classroom as Safe Space. *Canadian Journal for the Scholarship of Teaching and Learning*, 1(1):1-12. https://doi.org/10.5206/cjsotl-rcacea.2010.1.9.

Bharuthram, S. & Kies, C. 2013. Introducing e-learning in a South African Higher Education Institution: Challenges arising from an intervention and possible responses. *British Journal of Educational Technology*, 44(3):410-420. https://doi.org/10.1111/j.1467-8535.2012.01307.x

Blackboard. 2019. *Chat history.* Available at: https://bit.ly/2QB3wVr [Accessed 11 June 2020].

Boostrom, R. 1998. 'Safe spaces': Reflections on an educational metaphor. *Journal of Curriculum Studies*, 30(4):397-408. https://doi.org/10.1080/002202798183549

Bowell, T. & Kemp, G. 2002. *Critical thinking: A concise guide.* London: Routledge. https://doi.org/10.4324/9780203193754

Brady, M., Seli, H. & Rosenthal, J. 2013. Metacognition and the influence of polling systems: How do clickers compare with low technology systems. *Educational Technology Research and Development*, (61):885-902. https://doi.org/10.1007/s11423-013-9318-1

Brown, E.K. 2011. *Safe spaces in online learning: The role of faculty perceptions in design and practice.* PhD thesis. Georgia: University of Georgia.

Brown, M., Worth, M. & Boylan, D. 2017. Improving critical thinking skills: Augmented feedback and post-exam debate. *Business Education & Accreditation*, 9(1):55-63.

Burbules, N.C. & Berk, R. 1999. Critical thinking and critical pedagogy: Relations, differences, and limits. In: T. Popkewitz & L. Lender (eds.), *Critical theories in education: Changing terrains of knowledge and politics*. New York: Routledge, 45-67.

Callan, E. 2016. Education in safe and unsafe spaces. *Philosophical Inquiry in Education*, 24(1):64-78. https://doi.org/10.7202/1070555ar

Cleophas, F. 2020. *Covid-19 pandemic highlights challenges of online teaching and learning.* Available at: https://bit.ly/3u2s1tn [Accessed 12 August 2020].

Chou, C. 2002. A comparative content analysis of student interaction in synchronous and asynchronous learning networks. Proceedings of the 35th Hawaii International Conference on System Sciences. Available at: https://bit.ly/3ssdoip

Constandius, E. & Bitzer, E. 2015. *Engaging higher education curricula: A critical citizenship perspective.* Stellenbosch: African Sun Media. https://doi.org/10.18820/9781920689698

Costandius, E. & Odiboh, F. 2016. *The relevance of critical citizenship education in an African context.* Stellenbosch: African Sun Media. https://doi.org/10.18820/9781928314080

Cornelius, S. 2014. Facilitating in a demanding environment: Experiences of teaching in virtual classrooms using web conferencing. *British Journal of Educational Technology,* 45(2):260-271. https://doi.org/10.1111/bjet.12016

Cottrell, S. 2017. *Critical thinking skills: Effective analysis, argument and reflection.* London: Palgrave. https://doi.org/10.1057/978-1-137-55052-1

Council of Higher Education. 2018. *The state of the provision of the Bachelors of Laws qualification in South Africa Report.* Available at: https://bit.ly/3coAp0j [Accessed 11 April 2020].

Dewy, J. 1916. *Democracy and education: An introduction to the philosophy of education.* New York: The Macmillan Company.

Department of Higher Education. 1997. *White Paper on the Transformation of Higher Education.* Available at: https://bit.ly/3tVxEJx [Accessed 27 May 2020].

Dipa, K. 2020. *Covid-19 presents curricula crunch for SA's universities.* Available at: https://bit.ly/31nstG1 [Accessed 5 May 2020].

Elçi, A. & Seçkin, Z. 2019. Cyberbullying awareness for mitigating consequences in higher education. *Journal of Interpersonal Violence,* 34(5):946-960. https://doi.org/10.1177/0886260516646095

Eskey, M.T. & Eskey, M.T. 2014. *Cyberbullying in the online classroom: Faculty as the targets.* Proceedings of TCC Worldwide Online Conference 2014. Hawaii: TCC. Available at: https://bit.ly/32guxAh

Fain, S.M. 2004. The construction of public space. In: D.M. Callejo-Pérez, J.J. Slater, S.M. Fain & P. Lang (eds.), *Pedagogy of place: Seeing space as cultural education.* New York: Peter Lang, 9-33

Fertik, M. & Thompson, D. 2015. *The reputation economy: How to optimise your digital footprint in a world where your reputation is your most valuable asset.* London: Hachette.

Flenser, K. & Von der Lippe, M. 2019. Being safe from what and safe for whom? A critical discussion of the conceptual metaphor of 'safe space'. *Intercultural Education,* 30(3):275-288. https://doi.org/10.1080/14675986.2019.1540102

Freire, P. 1972. *Pedagogy of the oppressed.* Harmondsworth: Penguin.

Freire, P. 1976. *Education, the practice of freedom.* London: Writers and Readers Publishing Cooperative.

Fry, R. 2017. Young adult household economic well-being: Comparing millennials to earlier generations in the United States. In: M. Moos, D. Pfeiffer & T. Vinodrai (eds.), *The millennial city: Trends, implications, and prospects for urban planning and policy.* London: Routledge, 57-66. https://doi.org/10.4324/9781315295657-4

Ganster, T., Eimler, S.C. & Krämer, N. C. 2012. Same same but different!? The differential influence of smilies and emoticons on person perception. *Cyberpsychology, Behavior, and Social Networking,* 15(4):226-230. https://doi.org/10.1089/cyber.2011.0179.

Garrison, D.R., Anderson, T. & Archer, W. 1999. Critical inquiry in a text-based environment: Computer conferencing in higher education. *The Internet and Higher Education,* 2(2-3):87-105. https://doi.org/10.1016/S1096-7516(00)00016-6

Gayle, B.M., Cortez, D. & Preiss, R.W. 2013. Safe spaces, difficult dialogues, and critical thinking. *International Journal for the Scholarship of Teaching and Learning,* 7(2):1-10. https://doi.org/10.20429/ijsotl.2013.070205

Greenlaw, S.A. & DeLoach, S.B. 2003. Teaching critical thinking with electronic discussion. *Journal of Economic Education,* 34(1):36-52. https://doi.org/10.1080/00220480309595199

Grieve, R., Moffitt, R. & Padgett, C.R. 2019. Student perceptions of marker personality and intelligence: The effect of emoticons in online assignment feedback. *Learning and Individual Differences,* 69:232-238. https://doi.org/10.1016/j.lindif.2018.02.008

Hansen, W.L. & Salemi, M.K. 1990. Improving classroom discussion in economics courses. In: P. Saunders & W.B. Wal-stad (eds.), *The principles of economics course: A handbook for instructors.* New York: McGraw-Hill, 96-110.

Heirman, W., Angelopoulos, S., Wegge, D., Vandebosch, H., Eggermont, S. & Walrave, M. 2015. Cyberbullying-entrenched or Cyberbully-free classrooms? A class network and class composition approach. *Journal of Computer-Mediated Communication,* (20):260-277. https://doi.org/10.1111/jcc4.12111

Iversen, L.L. 2018. From Safe Spaces to Communities of Disagreement. *British Journal of Religious Education,* 1-12. https://doi.org/10.1080/01416200.2018.1445617.

Jézégou, A. 2010. Community of inquiry in E-learning: A critical analysis of Garrison and Anderson model. *Journal of Distance Education,* 24(3):1-18.

Johnson, L. & Morris, P. 2010. Towards a framework for critical citizenship education. *The Curriculum Journal,* 21(1):77-96. https://doi.org/10.1080/09585170903560444

Keashly, L. & Neuman, J.H. 2010. Faculty experiences with bullying in higher education: Causes, consequences, and management. *Administrative Theory & Praxis,* 32(1):48-70. https://doi.org/10.2753/ATP1084-1806320103

Keashly, L. & Neuman, J.H. 2013. Bullying in higher education. *Workplace Bullying in Higher Education,* 1-22.

King, C. & Piotrowski, C. 2015. Bullying of educators by educators: Incivility in higher education. *Contemporary Issues in Education Research (CIER),* 8(4):257-262. https://doi.org/10.19030/cier.v8i4.9434

Leonardo, Z. & Porter, R.K. 2010. Pedagogy of fear: Toward a Fanonian theory of 'safety' in race dialogue. *Race Ethnicity and Education,* 13(2):139-157. https://doi.org/10.1080/13613324.2010.482898

Letseka, M., Letseka, M.M. & Pitsoe, V. 2018. The challenges of e-Learning in South Africa. In: M. Sinecen (ed.), *Trends in E-learning.* London: Intech Open, 121-138. https://doi.org/10.5772/intechopen.74843

Lougheed, J., Kirkland, J.B. & Newton, G. 2012. The use of breakout groups as an active learning strategy in a large undergraduate nutrition classroom. *Teaching and Learning Innovations,* 15:1-30. https://doi.org/10.5206/cjsotl-rcacea.2012.2.6

Macupe, B. 2020. *Online push sets us up for failure*. Available at: https://bit.ly/3tXgnjm [Accessed 10 August 2020].

Mahlangu, V.P. 2018. The good, the bad and the ugly of distance learning in higher education. In: M. Sinecen (ed.), *Trends in E-learning*. London: Intech Open, 17-31. https://doi.org/10.5772/intechopen.75702

Makos, A., Oztok, M., Zingaro, D. & Hewitt, J. 2013. *Use of a "Like" Button in a Collaborative Online Learning Environment*. Available at: https://bit.ly/3d6FgSV [Accessed 19 April 2020].

Martin, F. & Parker, M.A. 2014. Use of synchronous virtual classrooms: Why, who, and how? *Merlot Journal of Online Learning and Teaching*, 10(2):192-210.

Mbembe, A. 2015. *Decolonizing knowledge and the question of the archive*. Available at: https://bit.ly/31lcvw9 [Accessed 18 March 2020].

McLaren, P. 2003. Critical pedagogy: A look at the major concepts. In: A. Darder, M. Baltondo & D. Torres (eds.), *The Critical Pedagogy Reader*. New York: Routledge Falmer, 69-96.

Meier, C. 2007. Enhancing intercultural understanding using e-learning strategies. *South African Journal of Education*, 27(4):655-672.

Microsoft. 2019. *Conversations inside MS Teams*. https://bit.ly/3fhfY72 [Accessed 11 June 2020].

Minor, M.A., Smith, G.S. & Brashen, H. 2013. Cyberbullying in higher education. *Journal of Educational Research and Practice*, 3(1):15-29.

Mitchell, L. n.d. Developing critical citizenship in LLB students: The role of a decolonised legal history course. Manuscript submitted for publication.

Mollborn, S. & Hoekstra, A. 2010. A meeting of minds': Using clickers for critical thinking and discussion in large sociology classes. *Teaching Sociology*, 38(1):18-27. https://doi.org/10.1177/0092055X09353890

Moon, J.A. 2008. *Critical thinking: An exploration of theory and practice*. London: Routledge. https://doi.org/10.4324/9780203944882

Ndiege, J.R., Okello, G. & Wamuyu, P.K. 2020. Cyberbullying among university students: The Kenyan experience. *The African Journal of Information Systems*, 12(1):2.

Njenga, J.K. & Fourie, L.C.H. 2010. The myths about e-learning in higher education. *British Journal of Educational Technology*, 41(2):199-212. https://doi.org/10.1111/j.1467-8535.2008.00910.x

Park, Y.J. & Bonk, C.J. 2007. Is online life a breeze? A case study for promoting synchronous learning in a blended graduate course. *MERLOT Journal of Online Learning and Teaching*, 3(3):307-323.

Paul, R. & Elder, L. 2019. *A guide for educators to critical thinking competency standards: Standards, principles, performance indicators, and outcomes with a critical thinking master rubric*. Maryland: Rowman & Littlefield.

Phakeng, M. 2020. *Live Covid-19 discussion with Mamokgethi Phakeng*. Available at: https://bit.ly/3w1Xqh9 [Accessed 18 April 2020].

Quinot, G. 2015. Transformative legal education. *South African Law Journal*, 129:411-433.

Redmond, M. 2010. Safe space oddity: Revisiting critical pedagogy. *Journal of Teaching in Social Work*, 30(1):1-14. https://doi.org/10.1080/08841230903249729

Richardson, J.C., Sadaf, A. & Ertmer, P.A. 2012. Relationship between types of question prompts and critical thinking in online discussions. In: Z. Akyol & D.R. Garrison (eds.), *Educational communities of inquiry: Theoretical framework, research and practice*, 197-222. https://doi.org/10.4018/978-1-4666-2110-7.ch011

Rogers, S.A. 2020. Curation of your online persona through self-care and responsible citizenship: Participatory digital citizenship for secondary education. In: S.P. Huffman, S. Loyless, S. Albritton & C. Green (eds.), *Leveraging technology to improve school safety and student wellbeing*. Hershey: IGI Global, 65-84. https://doi.org/10.4018/978-1-7998-1766-6.ch005

Ruthotto, I., Kreth, Q., Stevens, J., Trively,C. & Melkers, J. 2020. Lurking and participation in the virtual classroom: The effects of gender, race, and age among graduate students in computer science. *Computers and Education*, 151:1-15. https://doi.org/10.1016/j.compedu.2020.103854

Saltz, J. & Heckman, R. 2020. Using structured pair activities in a distributed online breakout room. *Online Learning*, 24(1):227-244. https://doi.org/10.24059/olj.v24i1.1632

Schellens, T., Van Keer, H., De Wever, B. & Valcke, M. 2009. Tagging thinking types in asynchronous discussion groups: Effects on critical thinking. *Interactive Learning Environments*, 17(1):77-94. https://doi.org/10.1080/10494820701651757

Seepe, S. 2020. *Covid-19: Why is higher education silent?* Available at: https://bit.ly/3foyLxg [Accessed 12 August 2020].

Shulevitz, J. 2015. *In college and hiding from scary ideas*. Available at: https://nyti.ms/3rnrL6s [Accessed 17 June 2020].

Terry, R., Taylor, J. & Davies, M. 2019. Successful teaching in virtual classrooms. In: K. Daniels, C. Elliott, S. Finley & C. Chapmen (eds.), *Learning and Teaching in Higher Education*. London: Edward Elgar Publishing, 211-221. https://doi.org/10.4337/9781788975087.00035

Theroux, J.T. & Kilbane, C. The real-time case method: The internet creates the potential for new pedagogy. In: J. Bourne & J.C. Moore (eds.), *Elements of Quality Online Education: Engaging Communities*. Needham: The Sloan consortium.

Universities South Africa. 2020. *Public universities have either embraced emergency teaching/learning, or are getting ready for the inevitable, in the Covid-19 era.* Available at: https://bit.ly/31l0cjp/ [Accessed 8 June 2020].

Van Den Bergh, R. 2013. Legal Education in South Africa with Specific Reference to the Uncertain Future of Roman Law and Legal History. *Osaka University Law Review*, 60:13-24.

Van Rooi, L. 2020. *Covid-19 could spell the end of the residential university*. Available at: https://bit.ly/3srIfMb [Accessed 19 June 2020].

Vaill, Z., Campbell, M. & Whiteford, C. 2020. Analysing the quality of Australian universities' student anti-bullying policies. *Higher Education Research and Development*, 34(3):1-15. https://doi.org/10.1080/07294360.2020.1721440

Vangelisti, A.L., Pennebaker, J.W., Brody, N. & Guinn, T.D. 2014. Reducing social pain: Sex differences in the impact of physical pain relievers. *Personal Relationships*, 21(2):349-363. https://doi.org/10.1111/pere.12036

Vilakazi, Z. 2020. *Education is more than receiving content. It is about interaction*. Available at: https://bit.ly/31kdvR4 [Accessed 7 June 2020].

Watts, L.K., Wagner, J., Velasquez, B. & Behrens, I.P. 2017. Cyberbullying in higher education: A literature review. *Computers in Human Behavior*, 69:268-274. https://doi.org/10.1016/j.chb.2016.12.038

Washington, E.T. 2015. An overview of cyberbullying in higher education. *Adult Learning*, 26(1):21-27. https://doi.org/10.1177/1045159514558412

Whitten, S. 2018. *Why 'safe spaces' at universities are a threat to free speech*. Available at: https://bit.ly/3rvYHd6 [Accessed 11 June 2020].

Zoom. 2020. *Storing chat message history*. https://bit.ly/3swihqY [Accessed 11 June 2020].

6

A case analysis of higher education contexts during the Covid-19 pandemic in South Africa

Amile Olwethu Mavundla and Tennyson Mgutshini

Introduction

The year 2020 will be remembered as the chronological venue for the most catastrophic societal and public health emergency that the globe and humankind have been faced with since the flu pandemic 100 years ago. First reported in January 2020, the coronavirus, Covid-19 or SARS-COV-2 had, in 6 months, established itself as the deadliest global virus infecting over 11 million people and causing 532 340 deaths globally in 180 days (WHO Coronavirus Disease (Covid-19) Dashboard). The statistical magnitude of infections and the associated mortality depict only one facet of the catastrophre. Infection predictions and the lack of a cure for the virus signal a bleak future in which social and physical distancing will be primal social behaviours. Beyond its well specified and much heralded health impact, the pandemic has caused serious disruptions in the provision of education globally and as such, all aspects of educational provision have been altered dramatically. This is primarily because the practice of proximal human-contact based teaching is one of the most high risk activities that require complete re-conceptualisation to comply with Covid-19 risk management practices and the ever-dynamic social distancing protocols.

Online learning options: Are they the true panacea to Covid-19 challenges within higher education?

Guided by these uncontested assertions, minimising contact has become the single universal educational priority that all teaching contexts aspire to. For the most part, successful transition has been described in terms of how well different educational providers are able to reimagine their teaching and learning towards total reliance on online learning alternatives. This transitional emphasis has been so widespread that within four months of the pandemic, there is evidence that up to 90% of all teaching and learning (primary, secondary and tertiary) has relocated from traditional face-to-face modalities to variants of online, blended or multimodal learning (Hodges, Moore, Lockee, Trust & Bond, 2020). This transition has received such widespread support that even governments have touted it as the gold standard option that educational institutes should aim to provide. This transition has not been without its difficulties, as noted by Bao (2020) and Hodges et al., (2020) who show widespread problems of inequality that exist between the materially advantaged and their disadvantaged counterparts when it comes to accessing the educational provisions that are availed to them through these online options. Even so, much of the contestation has focused entirely on issues to do with access, with limited (and almost absent) attention being devoted to issues to do with the quality of these alternative provisions.

Assessment of learning: A forgotten educational priority within the Covid-19 crisis

It is particularly notable that certain aspects of the educational journey have received little or no critical attention. The domain of "student assessment" or "the assessment of learning" arguably represents one such sphere, where the absence of formal questions about prospective challenges is particularly striking. Questions about the veracity, validity, authenticity and credibility of non-venue based assessments must be posed to ensure informed engagement with this new educational vade mecum. Similarly, publicised concerns relating to the comparative quality of non-venue based assessment options and issues relating to whether assessments are being completed by the intended learner(s), represent a few of the many questions that learners, educators, potential employers and society at large could rightfully expect to have answered.

Guided by these initial clarity-seeking imperatives, the current chapter offers an introspective analysis of the implications for the assessment of students' learning that may arise from the global transition towards online and multimodal learning options, particularly within South Africa. More specifically, the chapter begins with an initial consideration of why assessment of learning is important, followed by an articulation of the various challenges that have emerged as a result of the pandemic. To ensure a contextualised exploration of this aspect, the challenges that will be focused on will specifically be those that are related to the consequences of the pandemic and in particular how this impacts the South African higher education context. Finally, the chapter explores some of the contemporary solutions to pre-identified issues and in so doing we focus specifically on how these solutions have applicable relevance to South Africa's higher education environment.

Why assess? Revisiting the tenets for this do-or-die educational requirement

In higher education, student assessment serves a number of functions. The two most referred to functions are firstly, as the means for facilitating learning and secondly, as a vehicle by which formal records of achievement can be kept (Charyton, Ivcevic, Plucker & Kaufman, 2010). Educationalists, including Arjomandi, Kestell and Grimshaw (2009), have suggested that assessment serves more deeply ingrained functions, including being an avenue by which student satisfaction and general institutional reputation can be harnessed or tarnished (Evans, 2013; Wilson & Scalise, 2006). Therefore, it is argued by many, including Dunn and Mulvenon (2009) and Gikandi, Morrow and Davis (2011), that assessment or the measurement of learner achievement represents one of the most critical activities within any institute of learning. Even though the lens and context through which assesments are currently being viewed is brand new and uncharted, it is important to recognise that, where possible, explorations of the viability of pre-existing theory on assessment are necessary for guidance and operationalisation within the current challenging environment.

Archer (2017) offers one such possibility via his suggested assessment purpose triangle which illustrates the critical factors that are required for successful educational assessments. The triangle posits that assessment has three fundamental purposes which are: (i) assessment to support learning; (ii) assessment for accountability; and (iii) assessment for certification, progress, and transfer. These need to enjoy appropriate attention to support quality education. Archer's (2017) triangle can be operationalised within the Covid-19 context to highlight the range of resulting impacts on assessment functions. The Critical Incident-Moderated Assessment framework, in Figure 6.1 below, offers a diagrammatic representation of how traditional assessment purposes in higher education have been affected by Covid-19.

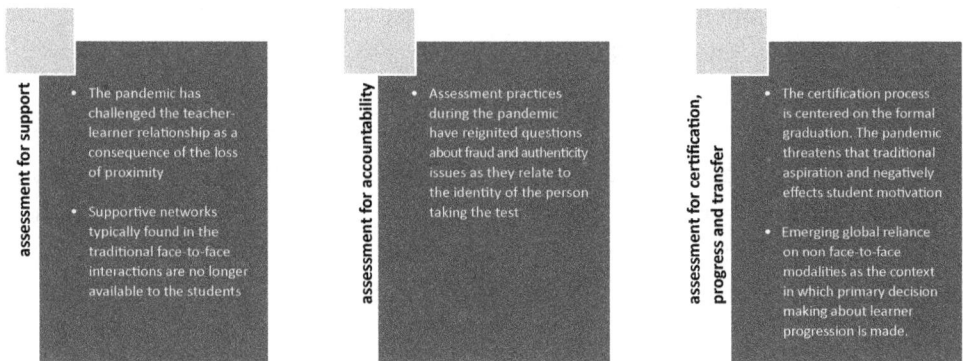

Figure 6.1   Critical Incident-Moderated Assessment framework.

The path of discourse-development in issues related to assessment within education has transitioned over time with initial debates focusing on the value that assessment offers with respect to long-term learning (Demuyakor, 2020), followed by the debates on the validity of assessment approaches (Beebe, Vonderwell & Boboc, 2010). More recent considerations have focused on issues related to the locus of control as it pertains to assessment i.e. whether assessment must always be instructor led or whether it could be more meaningfully conceptualised as a continuous process in which the learner can meaningfully assess their own progress or that of peer learners (Evans, 2013; Wilson & Scalise, 2006).

This identification of the discourse offers a brief "pit-stop" review of the development of more sophisticated interrogations of assessment. The Covid-19 pandemic has resulted in a reversal within the discourse to a point where previously resolved contestations have suddenly become the subject of current questions. For example, the re-imagining of assessment within the era of the pandemic has directed educators to ask foundational questions about whether or not assessments have any value as a tool for long-term learning, whether or not assessments should be instructor or learner led and also whether the assessment modalities available have the ability to meaningfully assess the progress of students. This regression in the discourse, in essence, requires a total re-evaluation of assessment of learning and its value within the post-Covid-19 environment. Driven by this and in spite of the fact that a differently focused discourse on assessment exists, it is acknowledged here that a more substantial role exists in which assessment processes impact the student experience, student development, learning and other pedagogical entities related to the university.

Online assessments: Friend or foe to the learning journey?

The sudden shift from face-to-face contact lectures to online and remote learning platforms uniquely challenges the higher education system and forces stakeholders into an unfamiliar path of assessment and challenges standard teaching and learning norms. It is worth noting that online assessment options are not new and have existed in very specialised contexts. The challenges specified in this section relate specifically to the post-Covid-19 roll-out of multimodal learning to universities that are traditionally contact based. Both students and lecturers in traditional contact higher education institutions have had to embrace this new phenomena, irrespective of their level of competence and/or preparedness to engage in teaching and learning. Similarly, the facilitation of assessments via online platforms presents a new, uncharted challenge, not least because learners and education providers have had to consider the alignment of module outcomes to the new assessment strategies, but have also had to take into consideration the change in context where learning is taking place.

Whilst a number of studies have been conducted on teaching and learning on online learning platforms, there appears to be a greater silence around online assessment practices post-Covid-19. Within this, very few studies have reported on the types and distribution of assessments that are used by instructors to contribute to students' overall grades in online courses (Castle, Author & Mcguire, 2010). Notably, there also appears to be evidence of a number of strategies that have been adopted for online assessments, which include but are not limited to: online discussions, exams, written assignments, experimental assignments, quizzes, journals, projects and presentations (Castle et al., 2010). Critically, Covid-19 has posed a challenge to the implementation of each of the above mentioned aspects, because both teachers and learners have little training on how to deliver and learn within these new conditions.

Post-Covid-19: Challenges with online assessments

Prior to Covid-19, the area of online assessment represented ongoing challenges for online educaters and content developers. However, this has been magnified significantly by the fact that all education providers, regardless of readiness, find themselves suddenly required, without negotiation, to totally rely on this format of assessment. In order to be effective in online learning platforms, there are a number of challenges that need to be mitigated that may pose a threat to the academic integrity of the assessments, as well as the educational programme as a whole. Moore (2013) and Beebe et al, (2010) identify and allude to a range of challenges (presented in Figure 6.2) in the implementation of online assessments:

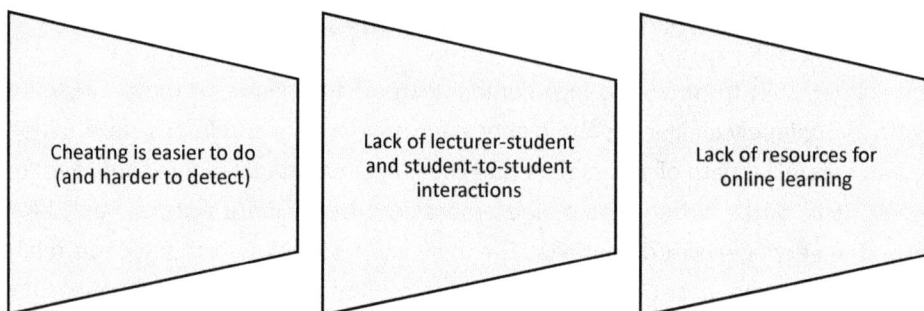

Figure 6.2   Implementation challenges related to online assessments

Cheating is easier to do (and harder to detect)

The physical distance between the lecturer and the students that comes with online learning, limits the potential for monitoring. Additionally, the medium compromises the extent to which the lecturer can authenticate that the specified student is indeed the one who undertakes the assessment. Academic dishonesty is nothing new, but online testing environments require varied strategies to those used within traditional face-to-face testing scenarios. The current Covid-19 challenge is not only a consequence of platform weaknesses related to online work, but it also reflects the consequence of a global desperation to seek alternative teaching and learning methods which minimise the risks related to students seeing themselves as vulnerable, thus increasing unacceptable academic behaviours. Murphy (2020) further acknowledges that whilst cheating and plagiarism in education are not new phenomena, technology is widely seen as having facilitated their explosive increase.

When taking into account the distance between the lecturer and the student, lecturers need to find methods to detect and mitigate both planned and panic cheating, be it through plagiarism or the sharing of answers in online texts. A trawl of the literature reveals opposing viewpoints regarding cheating on online assessments with some, including Kennedy, Nowak, Raghuraman, Thomas, and Davis (2000) and Watson and Scottile (2010), reporting that students admitted to higher rates of cheating on face-to-face courses compared to those on online classes. Strikingly, King, Guyette, and Piotrowski (2009) reveal that almost 75% of the students in their study sample (n=354), thought it is easier to cheat on online assessments. Following on from this, Michael and Williams (2013) identified various forms of cheating that are worsened within online environments, including taking tests together, ordering pairs, covertly using the internet during examinations and the outsourcing or "ghost writing" of assignments.

To navigate through cheating for online assessments, Mellar, Peytcheva-Forsyth, Kocdar, Karadeniz and Yovkova (2018), proposed the implementation of authentication and authorship systems. Even so, many of these strategies need time for planning and preparation – a luxury that was not afforded to many educational providers during the Covid-19 crisis. There is evidence that even the most basic of interventions, such as authentication of authorship mechanisms, have often been overlooked in the haste to implement online teaching and learning in order to respond to the sudden emergence of Covid-19 (Wang, Cheng & Yue, 2020). All of the above cited concerns around academic cheating have themselves been modified by the context that we are in, primarily because everyone within the lecturer-learner relationship is faced more openly with having to deal with not just mastering the content, but the context which the content is delivered in. Unfortunately, online options allow for more continued and unsupervised cross engagement between students in ways that have been associated with increased cheating behaviours. So different is the challenge, that there is a need for re-thinking the way in which we identify the potential challenges related to cheating and the methods used to manage cheating.

Lack of lecturer-student and student-to-student interactions

Prior literature has established that skills development for lecturers is critical to promote flexible and responsive approaches to teaching and learning and for students. For example, the ability to navigate the technology and interact with the learning environment in meaningful ways, were associated with positive interactions between students and lecturers. This is particularly important because the absence of physical infrastructure and opportunities for face-to-face interactions in online environments places a greater emphasis on alternate forms of communication (Roddy, Amiet, Chung, Holt, Shaw, McKenzie, Garivaldis, Lodge & Mundy, 2017). For the smooth transition from face-to-face classroom interaction to online learning platforms, there needs to be substantial mental preparation on the part of the student. It becomes necessary for the student to motivate themselves and become proactive in the absence of the supportive networks of their classmates and peers, that were more commonplace during contact-learning.

Johnson (2015) and Khiat (2015) show that self-regulated learning, where students use metacognitive skills to plan, implement and reflect on their learning, have been increasingly associated with better academic achievements. In the absence of motivation, support and preparation for distance learning, efforts for effective teaching and learning may fail. Roddy et al. (2017) found that the lack of social interaction was the largest single barrier to student success online. Furthermore, meaningful connections with the institution were found to be a key ingredient in student engagement, specifically in the area of discussions. The abrupt move onto online learning platforms without prior planning may deprive students the benefits inherent in discussions. Castaneda and Rentz (2020) give a more specified articulation of these benefits and identifies that: (i) discussions require students to articulate what they are learning, (ii) discussions create active participation in meaning-making, and (iii) discussions generate social interaction; all of which play an integral part of a student's academic journey.

The Covid-19 pandemic, by virtue of its life threatening nature, has forced people to re-think life priorities. Physical and physiological needs have become so much more intrenched in people's lives, that their ability to focus on the learning journey has been, in some instances, eroded. For example, it is not uncommon for many university students to have a dual role as parents and learners and these roles offer competing priorities that now play out within the same home environment. Therefore, apart from the normal challenges that come with online learning, students find themselves simultenuously trying to balance the competing demands of their domestic and academic priorities.

The consequence of using their domicile as the venue for learning has been shown to have inherent challenges. Similarly, physical distancing from academic peers and lecturers who may provide support is no longer a product of individual choice, but a mandated behaviour across all elements of life. To that end, physical separation has been dictated and enforced onto the lecturer-student relationship. The physical separation between the lecturer and student necessitates that all communication must be mediated by some kind of technology, which is not always available to both parties. By that account, access to the varied e-learning content types such as the internet, intranets, extranets, satellite broadcast, audio/video tape, interactive TV and CD-ROM, can prove inaccessible to a substantial number of students. Notably, where there is no face-to-face interaction, instructors are particularly challenged to convey their intentions accurately and provide appropriate feedback to help students achieve the targeted learning objectives.

Worthy of noting is the fact that any form of online teaching and learning is a costly exercise for both the lecturer and the students and as such, it requires financial preparation and extensive budgeting for its success. In the face of minimal and/or adhoc preparation, necessitated by the Covid-19 pandemic, no such planning or budgeting occured and as such, disrupted teaching and learning immensely. Furthermore, the unintended consequence of this transition is the reinforcement and exposure to the vast socio-economic inequalities that continue to mask South

Africa, particularly to the students who have had to return to their rural homesteads for the duration of the nationwide lockdown. The spoken aspirations to facilitate online teaching and learning have not, to this point, been delivered, in actual fact the very opposite has happened. Promises of internet connectivity, data and devices for teaching and learning have not been met and have ultimately become a stumbling block for the continuation of online learning.

The tradition of university existence has portrayed universities as having four areas of scholarship that it should promote: (i) the scholarship of discovery, that which is related to research, (ii) the scholarship of teaching and learning, (iii) the scholarship of integration, and (iv) the scholarship of application. Each of these areas have in some shape or form been affected by the way the pandemic has played out. For example, within the scholarship of research, all the processes that required face-to-face engagement have now needed to be reconsidered, particularly for students registered for post-graduate degrees whose assessment formats relate to the completion of dissertations or research thesis.

The new mode of operation requires that they focus their data collection options on methodologies that minimise person-to-person contact. From this emanates a number of challenges, because traditionally this is not how some disciplines operate and similarly, the assessment processes of how well students are doing in relation to their research activity have assumed the possibility of face-to-face engagement. Another area that represents a core function of the university is that which relates to transferring all intellectual property into community engagement possibilities, which generally reside in local communities, but the fear and threat of spreading Covid-19 requires re-thinking of how communities are accessed. Innovative and new ways of assessing students are needed so that they can reduce or totally avoid working in community contexts that may pose a risk of infection. The observations made here may appear premature, but nonetheless they are important future considerations for the academic community and they are considerations that cannot be solved by being ignored, because the world of being cautious of our proximity to others seems to be a world that will remain until some curative intervention is found for Covid-19.

Summative appreciation of challenges and directions for corrective actions

The universal roll-out of multimodal learning options, within the short timeline of three months for many of the countries, has thrust the whole higher education fraternity into an area of curriculum implementation that has been the purview of a few selected online and distance education providers. As acknowledged earlier, many of the challenges that have resulted from this are not in themselves brand new, but their presentation and the scale at which we see them makes for new and previously less-appreciated challenges for education providers, curriculum developers and the students themselves. For example, the identification of the increased threat of cheating and assessment fraud is one that presents "an age-old problem dressed in new clothes".

The online environment poses very particular challenges with regards to managing the growing incidents of cheating and in fact, detecting it in ways that protect the credibility of educational processes. The posited view is that this new level of reliance on technology offers the potential for many more breaches in security than is typically possible in environments where assessments can be conducted on the basis of single, hard copy exam papers, only accessible to the examiner themselves. Critical explorations of the challenge relating to assessment fraud and lack of academic integrity suggest a number of important and alternative ways of addressing the issue of cheating. Each of the corrective interventions are guided by a number of principles which have arguable relevance to the current range of challenges. Provided below is a summative outline of some of the important measures that represent viable approaches to reducing the scourge of cheating that appears to be growing exponentially within higher education assessment practices:

- The transactional, rather than the transformational, engagement relationships between educational insitutes and learners have progressively eroded the commitment to academic integrity as a result of a number of changes over time, such as the assessment-driven emphasis of learning where students have been conditioned that they learn to be assessed rather than for the purposes of expanding their knowledge base. This change in culture is largely within the control of education providers and is something that could be systematically addressed so that traditional principles could be selectively re-adopted to ensure a much more responsible relationship between students.

- Some, including Graff (2003) and Baleni (2015), identify the obsession with secrecy as one of the key shortcomings of current assessment culture. This viewpoint is supported by wide ranging studies that have shown how open, non-secretive assessment formats, such as open-book examinations and seen examinations, deliver the same benefits and are as challenging as traditional, secrecy-based alternatives. Adopting the former approach would devalue the benefits of academic theft related to assessment fraud and this has been shown to drastically reduce the motivation and resulting existence of these undesirable behaviours.

- Much of the work on cheating and plagiarism-related student behaviours has been premised on the belief that all students who engage in cheating do so with prior knowledge of how improper this behaviour may be. By contrast, there is a substantial body of evidence that shows that "generalized lack of appreciation of issues related to academic integrity" may be at the heart of some of the observed cheating and fraudulent behaviours (Farley, Jain & Thomson, 2011; Ghilay, 2013). Accepting this may compel education providers towards being more conscientious and aware of the need to provide training on academic integrity to all their learners as a means of ensuring that unintentional cheaters can be re-directed to more positive academic behaviours.

Importantly, a lack of meaningful lecturer-to-student and peer-student interactions have been reported as one of the key challenges that threaten the veracity of assessment, particularly within online learning environments. This challenge has far-reaching implications for the learning experience and some of these implications may include, but are not limited to:

- Generalised feelings of being isolated among some of the students.
- A lack of sensitisation to academic norms due to being unable to model one's behaviour on examplary peers and/or teachers.
- Adoption of inappropriate learning behaviours in isolation and without moderation from others.

Efforts to identify and propose corrective interventions consistently cite possibilities for educational socialisation theory and put forward the argument that the genesis of isolative tendencies among learners are a result of a complex interplay between generic societal patterns, the existence of social media as an alternative to traditional human-to-human contact and the high pressure nature of contemporary learning.

Jaggars (2011) and Kearns (2012) attribute the erosion of meaningful student-to-student and teacher-to-student interactions as resulting from any of the above identified changes within society. This viewpoint calls for education providers to develop new, diverse engagement methodologies that go beyond just providing a venue for students to discuss assignment tasks but rather, these social media platforms should provide opportunities for individuals to have collegial and non-academic conversations with each other in much the same way that the traditional university social club would allow. Chen, Wei, Wu and Uden (2009) and Kearns (2012) present findings from a range of academic culture studies and from studies that they conducted with learners and within this, they provide clear evidence of a need for more socialisation opportunities that bring students and their peers together beyond just attending to classroom activities.

As with all areas of educational provision, the introduction of online learning modalities impacted on by both the socio-economic and material status of the educational provider, the educators themselves and also the learners. This observation represents an intractable source of inequality that has long required attention well before the recent emergence and total reliance on online options that has been necessitated by Covid-19. To that end, there is clear evidence of the fact that those who study within well-resourced educational contexts and are themselves materially advantaged, are less likely to find the transition towards online learning a severe drawback, primarily because they have more reliable access to supportive resources, such as up-to-date gadgets, adequate data and pre-existing competence in information technology.

Addressing issues of resources should be a primal point of focus for all education providers from the onset and ideally, all education providers should have conducted readiness assessments of all their learners as part of the initiation and transition to multimodal learning options. Notably, many of the current interventions by higher education institutes have tended to treat the student population as a homogeneous entity in which all students have the same needs and preferences. As a result, any efforts to meaningfully address the issue of inadequate resourcing would need to promote a much more individualistic engagement with students so that their particular range of needs can be addressed as part of resource readiness-planning efforts. Acceptance of this proposition ultimately means that current university efforts need to be modified and customised for the different contexts in which they will be pursued.

Finally, the urgent transition towards a total reliance on online learning options had very specific impacts on universities in their ability to deliver to their three core areas of research and innovation, teaching and learning, and community engagement, as far as they relate to the fulfillment of postgraduate activities that would ordinarily be assessed. Responding to this emergent challenge requires innovative and out-of-the-box thinking, for example in terms of community engagement activities, it may be a worthwhile to consider exploring engaging with communities via online video options. This, of course, has implications that emanate from the fact that many of the communities that are in receipt of community engagement interventions do not ordinarily have resources to engage in information technology dependent activities. This is likely to require that universities and other education providers find ways to provide resources, such as gadgets and data, to support the range of remote interventions that are likely to be necessary as part of socially distanced engagement with communities.

Conclusive thoughts

Assessment of learning within the higher education context represents an age old challenge for education providers and the learners themselves. It is unsurprising that within the context of Covid-19, it continues to be a challenge that raises more questions than there are answers. Even so, it represents such a critical aspect of the learning continuum that there is no basis upon which theorists within higher education can overlook the serious implications that arise from a total reliance on online learning modalities. The chapter offers an initial foray into this discourse and in so doing, intends to open up prospective debates about how this critical aspect can be improved substantially to ensure, at the least, equal credibility between new forms of assessment and the traditional methodologies that have been utilised.

Within the chapter, there is acknowledgment that even though the challenges to assessment practices exist as specific items, the likely solutions are likely to be better articulated by ensuring the protection of certain principles that relate to academic integrity. It is important to note that, in spite of the Covid-19 era representing new challenges, it also provides opportunities for academia to attend to longstanding, unresolved practice contentions.

References

Archer, E. 2017. The assessment purpose triangle: Balancing the purposes of educational assessment. *Front. Edu.*, 2:41. https://doi.org/10.3389/feduc.2017.00041

Arjomandi, M., Kestell, C. & Grimshaw, P. 2009. An EFQM Excellence Model for higher education quality assessment. *Engineering Education*, 1015-1020. Available at: https://bit.ly/31nYTAl

Baleni, Z.G. 2015. Online formative assessment in higher education: Its pros and cons. *Electronic Journal of e-Learning*, 13(4):228-236.

Bao, W. 2020. Covid-19 and online teaching in higher education: A case study of Peking University. *Human Behavior and Emerging Technologies*, April, 113-115. https://doi.org/10.1002/hbe2.191

Beebe, R., Vonderwell, S. & Boboc, M. 2010. Emerging patterns in transferring assessment practices from F2f to online environments. *Electronic Journal of E-Learning*, 8(1):1-12.

Castaneda, D. & Rentz, S. 2020. *The power of discussion: Activating learning online (and in person).* Available at: https://bit.ly/39l2inN

Castle, S.R., Author,C. & Mcguire, C.J. 2010. An analysis of student self-assessment of online, blended, and face-to-face learning environments. *Implications for Sustainable Education Delivery*, 3(3):36-40. https://doi.org/10.5539/ies.v3n3p36

Charyton, C., Ivcevic, Z., Plucker, J.A. & Kaufman. 2010. Creativity assessment in higher education. *Learning*, 249-255. https://doi.org/10.1016/B978-0-08-044894-7.00336-5

Chen, N., Wei, C., Wu, K. & Uden. 2009. Effects of high level prompts and peer assessment on online learners' reflection levels. *Computers & Education*, 52(2):283-291. https://doi.org/10.1016/j.compedu.2008.08.007

Demuyakor, J. 2020. Coronavirus (Covid-19) and online learning in higher institutions of education: A survey of the perceptions of Ghanaian international students in China. *Online Journal of Communication and Media Technologies*, 10(3):1-9. https://doi.org/10.29333/ojcmt/8286

Dunn, K.E. & Mulvenon, S.W. 2009. A critical review of research on formative assessment: The limited scientific evidence of the impact of formative assessment in education. *Practical Assessment, Research & Evaluation*, 14(7):1-11.

Evans, C. 2013. Making sense of assessment feedback in higher education. *Review of Educational Research*, 83:70-120. https://doi.org/10.3102/0034654312474350

Farley, A., Jain, A. & Thomson, D. 2011. Blended learning in finance: Comparing student perceptions of lectures, tutorials and online learning environments across different year levels. *Economic Papers*, 30(1):99-108. https://doi.org/10.1111/j.1759-3441.2010.00094.x

Ghilay, R. 2013. ROTLA: A new model for online teaching, learning and assessment in higer education. *Journal of Educational Technology*, 10(1):10-21. https://doi.org/10.26634/jet.10.1.2300

Gikandi, J.W., Morrow, D. & Davis, N.E. 2011. Online formative assessment in higher education: A review of the literature. *Computers & Education*, 57(4):2333-2351. https://doi.org/10.1016/j.compedu.2011.06.004

Graff, M. 2003. Cognitive style and attitudes towards using online learning and assessment methods. *Electronic Journal of e-Learning*, 1(1):21-28.

Hodges, A.C., Moore, S., Lockee, B., Trust, T. & Bond, A. 2020. *The difference between emergency remote teaching and online learning*. Educase Review. Available at: https://bit.ly/3stoLqt

Jaggars, S.S. 2011. *Online learning: Does it help low-income and underprepared students?* Community College Research centre. Available at: https://bit.ly/3lUEj3S

Kearns, L.R. 2012. Student assessment in online learning: Challenges and effective practices. *MERLOT Journal of Online Learning and Teaching*, 8(3):198-208.

Kennedy K., Nowak, S., Raghuraman, R., Thomas, J. & Davis, S.F. 2000. Academic dishonesty and distance learning: Student and faculty views. *College Student Journal*, 34:309-331.

Khiat, H. 2015. Measuring Self-Directed Learning: A Diagnostic Tool for Adult Learners. *University Teaching and Learning Practice*, 12(2):1-15. Available at: https://bit.ly/3d9f4ah

King, C.G., Guyette, R.W. & Piotrowski, C. 2009. Online exams and cheating: An empirical analysis of business students' views. *Journal of Educators Online*, 6(1):1-11. https://doi.org/10.9743/JEO.2009.1.5

Mellar, H., Peytcheva-Forsyth, H., Kocdar, S., Karadeniz, A. & Yovkova, B. 2018. Addressing cheating in e-assessment using student authentication and authorship checking systems: Teachers' perspectives. *International Journal for Educational Integrity*, 14(2):1-21. https://doi.org/10.1007/s40979-018-0025-x

Michael, T.B. & Williams, M.A. 2013. Student equity: Discouraging cheating in online courses. *Administrative Issues Journal: Education, Practice and Research*, 3(2):30. https://doi.org/10.5929/2013.3.2.8

Moore, E.A. 2013. *7 Assessment challenges of moving. your course online (and a dozen solutions)*. Faculty Focus. Available at: https://bit.ly/2PftpK9

Murphy, M.P.A. 2020. Covid-19 and emergency eLearning: Consequences of the securitization of higher education for post-pandemic pedagogy. *Contemporary Security Policy*, 41(3):492-505. https://doi.org/10.1080/13523260.2020.1761749

Roddy, C., Amiet, D.L., Chung, J., Holt, C., Shaw, L., McKenzie, S., Garivaldis, F., Lodge, J.M. & Mundy, M.E. 2017. Applying best practice online learning, teaching, and support to intensive online environments: An integrative review. *Front. Educ.*, 2(59):1-10. https://doi.org/10.3389/feduc.2017.00059

Wang, C., Cheng, Z. & Yue, X. 2020. Risk management of Covid-19 by universities in China. *Journal of Risk and Financial Management*, 13(2):36. https://doi.org/10.3390/jrfm13020036

Watson, G.R. & Sottile, J. 2010. Cheating in the digital age: Do students cheat more in online courses? *Online Journal of Distance Learning Administration*, 13(1):1-9.

Wilson, M. & Scalise, K. 2006. Assessment to improve learning in higher education: The BEAR Assessment System. *Higher Education*, 52:635-663. https://doi.org/10.1007/s10734-004-7263-y

7

Applying Constructivism Theories to Online Teaching at the Durban University of Technology

T.P. Govender and O.O. Olugbara

Introduction

The influx of the coronavirus 2019 (Covid-19) disease that originated from Wuhan in China has compelled millions of people into undesirable lockdown, created infelicitous hiatus and untimely deaths worldwide. The World Health Organisation (WHO) declared the disease a pandemic. In an attempt to curb the spread of the infectious disease, institutions of higher learning across the globe have moved swiftly into the realm of emergency remote teaching (ERT), learning and research (Gewin, 2020; Sahu, 2020). Conventional face-to-face teaching has now been replaced with equivalent online teaching. Students, academics, researchers and managements have been struggling with the transition to online teaching. In a short span of time, the Covid-19 pandemic has highlighted the need for educational institutions to strengthen their practices in the design of curriculum and use of technology for innovative practices of education (Toquero, 2020).

Durban University of Technology (DUT) went into the highest level of lockdown declared by President Cyril Ramaphosa of South Africa on 27 March 2020. Students at the university were released from their lectures and requested to return to their homes. The movement of students out of university premises, residences and back to rural settlements has brought about a set of intrinsic challenges. Students had limited or no internet access or no suitable devices to access ERT resources. DUT has tended to focus on resolving the issues associated with network connectivity, given the wide disparity between the connected urban students and unconnected rural students. A strong emphasis has been on providing students and staff with data bundles and computer devices to seamlessly shift to online teaching. It is understandable that a small number of students and staff are resistant to the measures of online teaching. However, there was a consensus that academics from institutions of higher learning cannot return to the full lecture halls because of the seriousness of the Covid-19 pandemic. This implies that higher education institutions in South Africa were confronted with the intrinsic challenge of ensuring the successful completion of the 2020 academic year in a sustainable way.

South Africa cannot afford to forfeit the 2020 academic year to Covid-19 as the country is ranked one of the most unequal societies in the world (Webster, 2019; World Bank, 2019). Whilst the national planning commission (NPC, 2012) for the country is ambitious with its 2030 vision for post-school education, the higher education landscape of the country mimics the historic past of the apartheid regime that has created wide inequality in all spheres. This inequality, as posited by Graven (2013) and Letseka and Maile (2008), has contributed to unequal educational opportunities for students from different socio-economic backgrounds. The Covid-19 pandemic has reinforced, strengthened, and exacerbated the chauvinism of unequal educational opportunities for students, which is more so of the existing bigotry between rural and urban students. The remnants of the country reinforce the notion of students in rural communities having disproportionate access to basic internet connectivity and access to quality education.

The purpose of this study was to explicate the application of constructivism theories with synchronous software application (SSA) for online teaching. The application is demonstrated with a case study of students from the departments of information systems and information technology at DUT. The methodological approach of this study draws primarily on desktop examination of theories of constructivism. In addition, qualitative research methods have been utilised to reflect on the experiences of the authors. This study contributes uniquely to the relatively new body of knowledge of a higher education institution adapting to the intrinsic challenges created by the Covid-19 pandemic by applying the fundamental theories of constructivism for online teaching. The authors undertook to reflect on the micro perspective within the context of the institution to reflect on the dynamics of transforming the higher education sector. The theories of constructivism by Piaget (1977), Vygotsky (1980) and Von Glasersfeld (1974) have been successfully applied to online teaching at DUT. This chapter contains four main sections that are succinctly summarised as follows: the first section gives the introductory message, followed by explicating learning theories of constructivism for ease of lucidity. Thereafter, the application of the learning theories of constructivism is delineated for online teaching and the last section gives a concluding remark.

Learning theories of constructivism

Learning constructivism is an educational philosophy, which holds that people actively construct or build new knowledge upon previous experiences and foundations (Elliot, Kratochwill, Littlefield Cook & Travers, 1999). Constructivism postulates that students are not passive vessels, but they actively participate to construct own learning that can be influenced by their prior knowledge (Phillips, 1995). The passivity of teaching views a student as an empty vessel, sponge, or liability to be filled with knowledge. However, constructivism explicates that students construct meaning through active engagement with the world. The concept fosters a sense of personal agency because students have ownership of their learning (McLeod, 2017). Bada and Olusegun (2015) indicate that central to the tenet of constructivism is that learning is an active process. Constructivists advocate that learning is interactive and it is constructed on what students already know. Consequently, information may be imposed on students, but understanding cannot be imposed, because it must come from the inner mind. The literature on educational psychology has documented the continuum of constructivism into three broad categories. These are cognitive constructivism, social constructivism and radical constructivism that are succinctly ventilated in this section of the chapter.

Cognitive constructivism

The notion of cognitive constructivism states that knowledge is something that is actively constructed by students based on their existing cognitive structures. The purpose of cognitivist teaching methods, tools and environments is to assist students in assimilating new information upon their existing knowledge. In addition, it is to enable them to make appropriate modifications to their existing intellectual framework to accommodate that information. Cognitive constructivism is propagated through the theory of Piaget (1977) that advocates learning as constructive. It addresses how learning occurs but does not focus on factors that influence learning. Piaget (1977) believed in operative knowledge that postulates change and transformation as producing operative knowledge, which is a form of acquired learning that aids someone to perform functions. The operative knowledge is much related to skill, which Piaget said cannot be taught, but acquired through practice that makes perfect. It is a more basic knowledge when compared to figurative knowledge that focuses on relating accurate information about entities.

Theory of cognitive constructivism argues further that people produce knowledge and form meaning based upon their previous experiences. It covers learning theories, teaching methods and education reforms. The foundation of the theory of Piaget is adaptation of individuals to environment through assimilation and accommodation. Assimilation means that a person applies an already learned schema to understand or interact with an object (Barrouillet, 2015). Assimilation causes an individual to incorporate new experiences into the old experiences and thereby develop new outlooks, rethink previous misunderstandings, and evaluate what is important to ultimately alter perceptions. The concept of accommodation reframes new experiences into the mental capacity already present. Individuals conceive ideas in which the world operates and when things do not operate within that context, they must accommodate and reframe expectations with the resulting outcomes.

Social constructivism

Social constructivism refers to a learning theory that is built and socially negotiated through interactions with others (Hodson & Hodson, 1998). Learning is generally not an abstract concept, but a collaborative social activity that develops from interaction of individuals with culture and society (Dewey, 1986). Social constructivism was developed by Vygotsky (1980) who suggested that cognitive development stems from social interactions from guided learning within the zone of proximal development (ZPD) as people construct knowledge cooperatively. In addition, Vygotsky (1980) suggested that learning is first through interpersonal interactions and then individually through an internationalisation process that can lead to deep understanding of the phenomenon being studied. The environment in which people are developed will influence their beliefs, knowledge, skills, experiences, how they think, what they think about and how they behave. This is because social knowledge is about societal conventions, norms, ethos, believes and behaviours.

Social constructivism is a theory of knowledge in sociology and communication theory that examines knowledge and understanding of the world that are developed cooperatively by individuals (Amineh & Asl, 2015). The theory assumes that understanding, significance and meaning are developed in coordination with people of a society. In the social constructivist approach, instructors are introduced as facilitators, inspirators, mentors, coaches, or promoters of knowledge and not as teachers or lords. A teacher who is the lord of a module gives a didactic lecture that covers the entire topic whimsically. However, a facilitator helps the students to get to their own understanding of the content being studied by providing an inspiration. Students play a passive role when an instructor teaches without providing inspiration.

However, they play an active role when the instructor inspires the learning process and helps the students learn the right knowledge. Hence, the teaching and learning process is about sharing experiences and negotiating socially constituted knowledge.

Radical constructivism

The tenet of the theory of radical constructivism is that any architype of knowledge is constructed rather than perceived through senses (Von Glasersfeld, 1974). It is the theory of knowing, which states unequivocally that knowledge constructed by individuals does not tell anything about reality, but only helps to function in an environment. The theory does not deny the existence of objective reality, but it posits the non-existence of methods of attaining objective knowledge (Hardy, 1997). This hypothesis implies that knowledge is invented, not discovered, and that humanly constructed reality is constantly being modified and attempts to fit an ontological reality, but can never give a true picture of it (Von Glasersfeld, 1974).

The interactions of individuals with external structures coupled with their interpretations of those interactions are important components for constructing knowledge in radical constructivism (Steffe & Thompson, 2000). In the context of radical constructivism, knowledge consists of mental constructs that have satisfied the conditions of objective reality and it is used in the sense of adaptation by Piaget (1977). Knowledge refers to the sensory motor actions and conceptual operations that have proven to be viable in the experience of a knower. It is the idea of viability that makes radical constructivism an instrumentalist theory of knowledge. A viable construction is a mental or physical action that is consistent with experiences of individuals and fulfils an intended purpose (Hardy, 1997).

The theory of radical constructivism extends the concept of equilibration credited to Piaget (1977). Equilibration contends the existence of interactions between the parts of knowledge of individuals and their total body of knowledge at any given moment. The theory posits that "there is a constant differentiation of the totality of knowledge into the parts and an integration of the parts back into the whole" (Piaget, 1977:839). Radical constructivism elaborates on this conception of equilibration by arguing that these constructions are not interpretations or approximations of an external objective reality that the knower came to know, but rather constitute reality for the knower (Lerman, 1989). The theory puts the interactions, interpretations and equilibrations of an individual with all externalities at the centre of knowledge construction. This learning theory has direct implications for the nature of reality, but an objective reality cannot come to be known, so positivist and post-positivist positions are untenable. The knowledge theory is based on principles that knowledge is not passively received, but actively constructed by cognising subject. Cognition is adaptive and serves an organisation of the experiential world, not the discovery of ontological reality (Husen & Postlethwaite, 1989).

Constructivism theories for online teaching

Literature on developmental psychology has suggested the benefits of agglutinating several learning theories in the classrooms. However, there is no clear understanding of how such agglutination will facilitate learning in a virtual environment. Previous authors have argued that computer mediated peer learning within a virtual environment can help promote student development and create positive outcomes (Khalili & Olugbara, 2011) as in the case of digital media archive systems (Ochieng, Olugbara & Marks, 2017).

However, previous studies have rarely discussed how the theories of constructivism can be applied to online teaching scenarios. Teaching in a virtual environment presents unique challenges such as high cost of data bundles, network connectivity bottlenecks in deep rural society, lack of appropriate devices for accessing learning content and inconstant availability of facilitators to mediate learning interactions. According to Ng'ambi, Brown, Bozalek, Gachago and Wood (2016), all students now own mobile devices and are socially interconnected. Anecdotal evidence, in 2020, at DUT supports the afore mentioned assertion. Students are able to actively interact with the presented content, academics and fellow students to ultimately aptly construct and co-construct their understanding of the curriculum.

This assertion applies to the constructivist notion of teaching and learning, however, the implementation of constructivism for online teaching generally presents a unique challenge for first year students who are frequently regarded as "undecided students". The lack of "tertiary student maturity" and capability to easily acclimatise to the university environment to co-construct knowledge and actively participate in learning, presents an apparent challenge for constructivist online teaching.

In addition, students are expected to swiftly cope with the sudden change from face-to-face lectures to an online teaching mode, which may not be realistic. Bao (2020) supported this belief by stating that the challenges for students did not come from technical operational obstacles, instead, they have difficulties because of lack of a good behaviour to learning. Students often have inherent problems such as lack of self-discipline, suitable learning materials or good learning environments when they are self-isolated at home as in the case of the current lockdown worldwide. Students require social interactions with peers and instructors and require the right knowledge and comprehension of theories of constructivism.

In this study, we have exploited the notion of reinforcement learning to investigate theories of cognitive constructivism (Piaget, 1977), social constructivism (Vygotsky, 1980) and radical constructivism (Von Glasersfeld, 1974) for online teaching. It is hoped that reinforcement would encourage consistent participation of students in constructivist online teaching. Reinforcement learning is a potent tool in machine learning where the adaptability of algorithms to an environment is determined by evaluating the environmental feedback to action. The algorithm adapts to the environment for a positive incentive and strategy of positive incentive is strengthened continuously. However, the algorithm does not adapt to the environment for a negative incentive. The maximum cumulative return is obtained by the algorithm through incessant interaction with the environment and the strategy can be updated according to a reward penalty function (Zhou, 2018). In the context of constructivist online teaching, a reward function for students is not necessarily monetary. It could be as simple as sharing the idea of a well-performing student, giving praise for a good response to a question, asking a student to explain his/her idea to everyone in the network, allocating a certain percentage of the final score to online class attendance, providing free data bundles and internet access devices to students. The choice of an appropriate reward function will depend heavily on an institution and the context.

Case study of online teaching

A detailed case study of online classes was undertaken at the Faculty of Accounting and Informatics (FAI) at DUT. Moving instructions to online can enable flexibility, accessibility, cost effective education and personalised learning. However, the speed with which this movement to online instructions is expected to happen is unprecedented and staggering (Hodges, Moore, Lockee, Trust & Bond, 2020). The regime of the Covid-19 pandemic has resulted in an abrupt and almost overnight complete migration to online teaching. Bao (2020) states that it is a massive and disruptive shift to move all the existing courses online in a matter of days. In general, a complete online course requires an elaborate design of lesson plans, teaching materials and technology support teams. All these requirements present a strong ramification for changing education (Robinson & Aronica, 2015).

Neither students nor academics at DUT had a mental model of what to expect from the lockdown regime. Their schema of teaching and learning embraced traditional lecture venues and laboratories coupled with deep face-to-face interactions. This includes having dialogue with academics and students, asking questions and expecting answers, as well as verbal and non-verbal cues. In constructivism, learning is socially mediated and interaction is essential for negotiation of meaningful learning. Students and staff could no longer partake in this, because of the physical disconnection caused by the Covid-19 hiatus.

119

This disconnectedness has reduced interaction significantly and placed undue anxiety on students and staff. Problem-based learning or more creative project-based learning in a social setting became obsolete overnight. Students and instructors had to adapt to a new mental model and a schema against a new reality. They had to adapt to course materials and education pedagogies that fit into a new normality of online teaching and adjust the model when it is not viable. Moreover, students and instructors had to ultimately adjust the concept of online teaching. This new reality of a new schema coupled with the concept of adaptation correlates positively with the theory of Piaget (1977). In this context, the already learned schema is the conventional pedagogies associated with deep face-to-face teaching. The pedagogies must now be applied to the new online teaching environment.

The original idea of DUT was to implement the concept of frugal technology (Olugbara & Ndhlovu, 2014) based multimodal learning that would alleviate the burden of technology costs for students and staff. The university then embraced low cost technology such as smartphones, universal service bus (USB) and transporting of printed learning materials to students through Globeflight shipping services. The university is providing data bundles for staff and students monthly. In addition, staff were provided with mobile Mi-Fi hotspot routers, laptop computers, or desktop computers to alleviate high costs of technology. The reward function has proved to be highly effective because students and staff are participating regularly in online activities.

Synchronous software application (SSA)

The overarching objective of SSA is to replace physical face-to-face teaching with sustainable online teaching. This objective was achieved at DUT using different technology platforms that support internet connectivity, synchronous and asynchronous interactions. The synchronous platforms, including Microsoft Teams (MS Teams) and WhatsApp, have been used to demonstrate the application of constructivism theories to online teaching. In a constructivist online teaching environment, certain strategies must be implemented for empowering instructors to deconstruct conventional objectivist perceptions of teaching in the sense of radical constructivism by Von Glaserfeld (1974), promote social interaction with meaningful instructions as emphasised by social constructivism of Vygotsky (1980) and advocate learning as construction through teaching activities that see learning as appropriation as suggested by cognitive constructivism (Piaget, 1977). Tam (2000) identified certain basic characteristics of a constructivist environment for implementing constructivist teaching strategies. This includes sharing of knowledge by instructors and students. Instructors and students must share and delegate authority. The prime role of an instructor is one of a facilitator or guide using guided practices in the teaching environment. Learning groups should consist of small numbers of students with a heterogeneous background.

Teaching activities that promote autonomy of students, higher-order thinking, critical reasoning, dialogue with negotiation and the use of interactive materials should be encouraged strongly in a constructivist online teaching environment. The nature of questions that an instructor asks the students, the kind of examples that the instructor uses to explain concepts and methods for solving a problem must be real, and not fictitious. Instructors must allow students to reflect because reflection can help students build a strong understanding of the hard concepts. Reflection is germane to learning; there can be no understanding without it and it is induced by verbalisation (Von Glasersfeld, 2001). It should be encouraged by fostering conversation. The theories of constructivism impact curriculum because instructors must design a curriculum plan that enhances the logical and conceptual growth of students. Learning is an active process in constructivism, where students create mental models that are constructs of the real world and test those models through experience. The resources and lesson plans that must be initiated for constructivist learning usually take a different approach from the traditional learning. Table 7.1 highlights the dimensional characteristics and implications of constructivism theories for online teaching.

Table 7.1   Dimensional characteristics and implications of constructivism theories for online teaching (adapted from Sadeghi, 2015)

Dimension	Constructivism	Implication
Educational paradigm	Constructivist approaches unfocused goals based on knowledge transfer	Knowledge transfer is a key factor in online lectures. Goals must be highly focused and instructors should use technology tools to communicate online lessons.
Experimental values	Learning practices based on real world examples	Students must be afforded maximal opportunities to practice on real world problems. The opportunities can be in the form of their participation in a global project, crowdsourcing or global software that engages a group of students and experts to cooperatively solve challenging problems.
Role of instructor	Student-centred teaching	Pursuit of student ideas, questions, interests, use of familiar examples and build on existing knowledge of students.

Value of errors	Mistakes as part of the learning process	Instructors should not aim for perfect lessons where there is no error. Errors in computer programming, for example, are part of the learning process that can help students acquire programming skills and develop a deep understanding of the necessary logics.
Origin of motivation	Internal motivation and true desire	Motivation must be constantly reinforced to ensure online students stay actively engaged. Students must be encouraged to engage with academics through online platforms. In addition, students should be inspired to share their challenges with peers through appropriate online discussion forums.
Individual differences	Multi-faceted consideration on the needs and preferences of students based on affective and physiological differences	Online teaching should accommodate the needs of individual students to promote personalised learning. Designers of online content and instructors should understand that students have heterogeneous backgrounds and learn differently.
Student control	Students have power to choose what section or what learning paths to follow	Instructors should allow for flexible and reflective teaching in terms of class schedules, alternate sections in the course and ruminating on previous lessons. Students must be able to recall previous lessons and access learning materials ubiquitously.
User activity	Students engage in the learning process for constructing knowledge	Instructors need to inspire students to conduct their own learning and collaborate in the knowledge construction process.
Collaborative learning	Provisioning of a variety of different technological facilities and support for collaborative learning	Instructors should encourage collaborative learning amongst students. For instance, through Microsoft Teams to setup groups for collaboration or using other online collaborative platforms like collaborative online international learning (COIL) and discussion forums.

Microsoft teams synchronous learning platform

The implementation of constructivist learning methods can be complemented using a synchronous technology platform that fosters a high level of interactivity. Constructivism is a philosophy that asserts learning occurs in contexts, but technology refers to the environment for contexture learning to occur. Technology in a nutshell provides an interactive platform and diverse tools for constructivist teaching and learning. The first SSA considered in this study for constructivist online teaching is the MS Teams medium. The platform is an enhanced technology for communication and collaboration in modern organisations. It is an upgrade of the Skype platform for working at home, learning remotely and for scheduling meetings. The tool was adopted by DUT for synchronous teaching, working from home and holding distance meetings. The new content that DUT academics had to learn at the commencement of the lockdown regime was the synchronous methodology for online teaching. DUT academics had to learn to implement both synchronous and asynchronous strategies for online teaching. Moodle open source software is the conventional asynchronous learning management system (LMS) being used at DUT to supplement face-to-face teaching. MS Teams in conjunction with Moodle LMS ensure synchronous and asynchronous teaching and learning within all faculties at DUT. However, SSA based on MS Teams has conveniently replaced the conventional face-to-face lecture at the university.

The university has attempted to implement a blended multimodal teaching approach, but most of the staff and students preferred the SSA teaching because of fear and stigma associated with contracting the Covid-19 virus. Students and staff have found that MS Teams is simple to use and effective in the transition to synchronous online teaching. The MS Teams platform has the interface to depict a timetable of venues, class times and modules in a virtual learning space that can mimic the real learning space. Consequently, the faculty of Accounting and Informatics (FAI) at DUT has implemented MS Teams in a novel way to be utilised as a managed synchronous virtual learning classroom that simulates the physical lecture venue. In MS Teams, the departments within FAI are represented as teams with instructors represented as owners and organisers of meetings (online lecturers) and students are represented as team members (participants) for a module. Moreover, the concept of channels in MS Teams has been used by the faculty to represent the official venue timetable.

In a typical example, the department of Information System (IS) in FAI can have three channels, which are DB0001, DB0002 and DB0003. These are code names of physical lecture venues within FAI. The calendar scheduling option within Microsoft Outlook was used to set the lecture times in lecture venues represented as channels. Students are invited as participants to a venue through the e-mail facility in Microsoft Outlook. This would be presented in the general announcement area of a group in MS Teams. Students automatically become a part of a synchronous virtual lecture when they accept an e-mail request for that time in the group that is linked to a venue channel. All venue timetables are linked to channels within a department. MS Teams group such as modules and venues for a department can be loaded onto the system. The virtual lectures scheduled for instructors are linked to channel venues. The Executive Dean, Heads of Departments and/or Programme Coordinators can now report on the virtual allocation of the timetable through the channel facility of MS Teams. This mechanism enforces control, auditing, and accountability of online teaching.

Moreover, it assists both instructors and students in scheduling and attending virtual lectures. Figure 7.1 below shows an example of how the physical lecture venues in the Information Systems department have been mapped to virtual lecture venues using MS Teams.

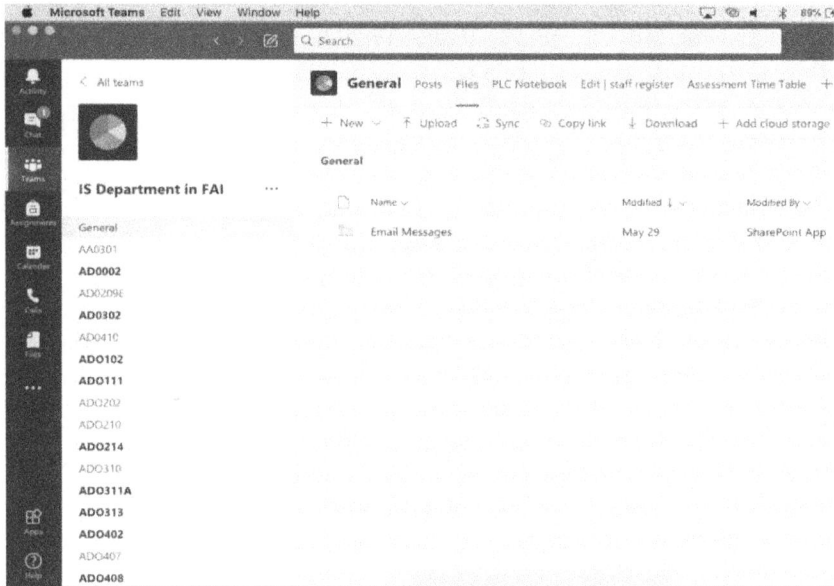

Figure 7.1   MS Teams depicting physical timetable for IS department

The instructors from FAI have adapted to the MS Teams SSA based on the theories of constructivism. Figure 7.2 below shows the online layout of timetabling within the framework of MS Teams. In this instance, the already learned schema by an instructor is the physical delivery of timetabling associated with physical lecture venues. This lecture mode must now be applied to the new lecture modality of an online lecture venue created using MS Teams. Moreover, with respect to students, the already learned schema was receiving face-to-face instructions in the physical venues on campus. Students must now adapt to the methodology of online teaching venues for ubiquitous learning. One attractive feature of MS Teams is the support for a portable and "storable" whiteboard that differs from the static whiteboard in face-to-face classrooms for note taking. Online lecture notes can be taken and shared interactively within the online teaching environment by anyone using any kind of productivity enhancement tools such as Word processor, PowerPoint and Excel spreadsheet. Lecture notes that are taken using any of these productivity tools can be shared and stored for future references.

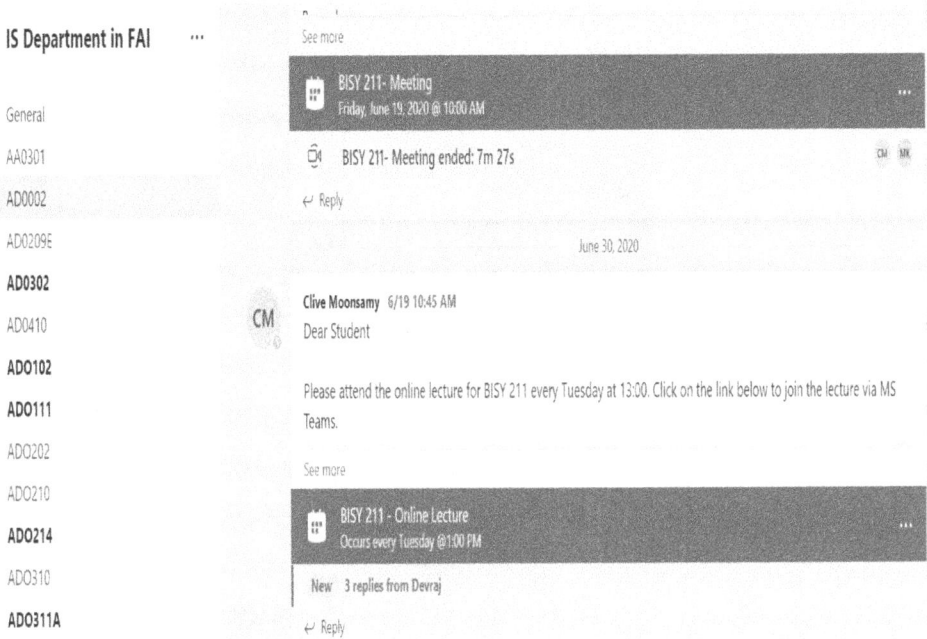

| IS Department in FAI | ... |
| General |
| AA0301 |
| AD0002 |
| AD0209E |
| **AD0302** |
| AD0410 |
| **ADO102** |
| **ADO111** |
| ADO202 |
| ADO210 |
| **ADO214** |
| ADO310 |
| **ADO311A** |

Figure 7.2   Module business information systems 2 depicted on logical timetable in MS Teams

WhatsApp synchronous learning platform

Since the inception of multimodal ERT, the first author of this chapter has been successfully using the WhatsApp instant messaging smartphone application in conjunction with Moodle LMS and MS Teams. WhatsApp is a cross-platform instant messaging and voice over internet protocol service of Facebook that allows the users to communicate using text, voice, image, and location. This technology platform was accepted by DUT to complement Moodle LMS and MS Teams for implementing multimodal ERT. WhatsApp is being used by all students in the computer programming (COMP 201) module because of their familiarity with the platform. Students had to adapt to using the WhatsApp environment for online learning besides using it for social communication. In addition, students had to apply their already learned WhatsApp schema to understand module content and online teaching delivery. Figure 7.3 below shows a screenshot of a WhatsApp group for synchronous communication of COMP201. There are 99 participants in the new online learning classroom who shared knowledge and engaged in active learning.

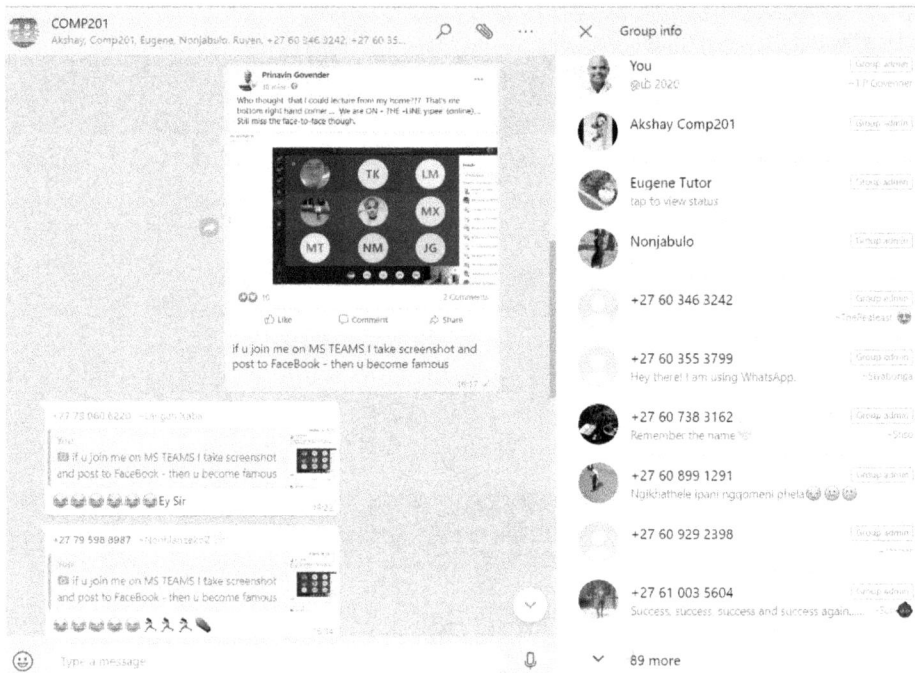

Figure 7.3   WhatsApp group for synchronous communication of COMP201

WhatsApp provides the intrinsic merits of improved communication amongst students and instructors. It supports the reach of students and facilitates their availability for consultations. It allows for the simulation of instances where instructors make announcements in a lecture venue, or where students and staff post all kinds of notices on physical noticeboards. It allows for full participation of students in interactivity and encourages the use of visual and audio aids for communications. It supports real-time feedback where for instance, an instructor posts a portable data format (PDF) document with screenshots of C++ codes. Students were able to access and execute the instructions given and provided instant feedback, especially when they encountered errors in the computer codes and they wanted instant answers. However, the application presents several inherent deficiencies that need to be emphasised in this chapter. There is the blurring of personal space because students would post messages at bizarre hours with no consideration for the personal space of the instructors. This is one useful application area for a bot or a web robot application that can engage with students to automatically respond to questions or queries raised by students at any time.

DUT is considering the implementation of such a bot system to support real-time responses to student queries. Sometimes, students claim that they do not own smartphones and could not access resources posted by an instructor. In addition, there are regular complaints from certain students of lack of data and internet connectivity. Moreover, some students are posting messages in mother languages such as isiZulu. However, not all students in a group are isiZulu speakers and the Google Translate application does not always translate the information correctly. This is another useful application area for language immersion research to develop a robot that can efficiently translate local South Africa languages in an online teaching environment. This application will facilitate unrestricted interactions that can be caused by language hegemony. Language is an important factor that can inhibit seamless interactions in an online teaching environment. Figure 7.4 shows the number of media or document files in the WhatsApp group of consisting of 156 members, for instance.

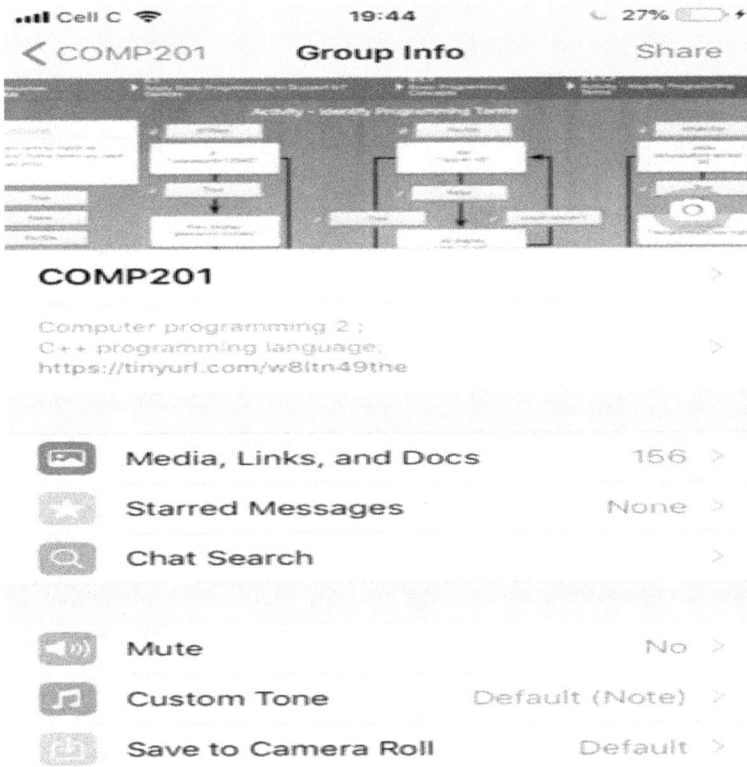

Figure 7.4   Number of media or document files in the WhatsApp group of 156 members

The DUT experience has generally indicated the acceptance of SSA for online teaching. DUT staff and students are using several technology tools such as Google Documents for collaborative authoring, Dropbox for file sharing, email for enquiry, phone calls for communication, MS Teams for online teaching and WhatsApp for instant messaging. Figure 7.5 shows a screenshot of a conversation between an instructor and students regarding the date and time of a synchronous lecture in MS Teams.

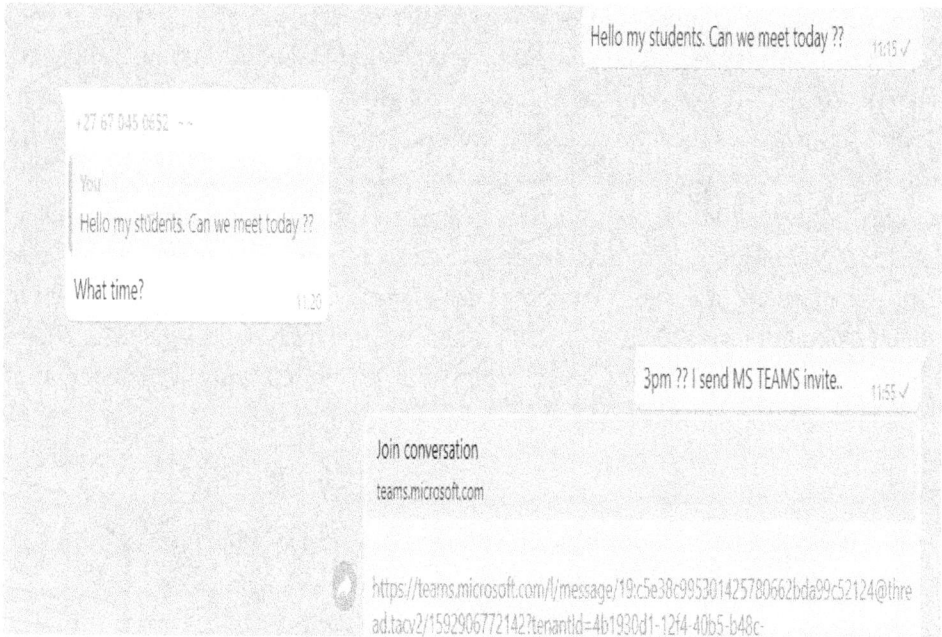

Figure 7.5   Screenshot of a conversation between an instructor and students

Conclusion

In this chapter, we explicate the application of constructivism theories with synchronous software application for online teaching at the Durban University of Technology. This transition from conventional teaching to synchronous online teaching has been successful. The practical experiences of the authors indicate that constructivist online teaching processes foster collaborative learning and simplify the teaching of computer programming in a way that fosters interactivity. However, in most cases, academics are experiencing challenges with the sudden transition to constructivist online teaching. The shortage of adequate online infrastructure, lack of devices for students and issues of network connectivity can hinder the transition to complete constructivist online teaching. Academics had to make the transition from the conventional face-to-face lectures to online teaching almost overnight when emergency remote teaching was introduced swiftly at the commencement of the lockdown regime in April 2020. This process was considered too cumbersome for inexperienced online instructors. There is the need to introduce the resources of constructivism to academics and students for transforming the culture of teaching with the associated pedagogies. This will provide the means for empowering instructors with a moral imperative for deconstructing anarchistic perceptions of education as a service and reconstructing personal epistemologies, associations with students and education practices.

References

Amineh, R.J. & Asl, H.D. 2015. Review of constructivism and social constructivism. *Journal of Social Sciences, Literature and Languages*, 1(1):9-16.

Bada, S.O. & Olusegun, S. 2015. Constructivism learning theory: A paradigm for teaching and learning. *Journal of Research & Method in Education*, 5(6):66-70.

Bao, W. 2020. Covid-19 and online teaching in higher education: A case study of Peking University. *Human Behavior and Emerging Technologies*, 2(2):113-115. https://doi.org/10.1002/hbe2.191

Barrouillet, P. 2015. Theories of cognitive development: From Piaget to today. *Developmental Review*, 38:1-12. https://doi.org/10.1016/j.dr.2015.07.004

Dewey, J. 1986. Experience and education. In: *The educational forum*, 50(3):241-252. https://doi.org/10.1080/00131728609335764

Elliott, S.N., Kratochwill, T.R.L. & Travers, J.F. 1999. *Educational psychology: Effective teaching effective learning*. Pennsylvania: McGraw-Hill College.

Gewin, V. 2020. Five tips for moving teaching online as Covid-19 takes hold. *Nature*, 580(7802):295-296. https://doi.org/10.1038/d41586-020-00896-7

Graven, M., Hewana, D. & Stott, D. 2013. The evolution of an instrument for researching young mathematical dispositions. *African Journal of Research in Mathematics, Science and Technology Education*, 17(1-2):26-37. https://doi.org/10.1080/10288457.2013.826968

Habermas, J. 1984. *The Theory of Communicative Action: Jurgen Habermas*. Trans. by Thomas McCarthy. Portsmouth: Heinemann.

Hardy, M.D. 1997. Von Glaserfeld's radical constructivism: A critical review. *Science & Education*, 6(1):135-150. https://doi.org/10.1023/A:1008664626705

Hodges, C., Moore, S., Lockee, B., Trust, T. & Bond, A. 2020. The difference between emergency remote teaching and online learning. *Educause review*, 27:1-12.

Hodson, D. & Hodson, J. 1998. From constructivism to social constructivism: A Vygotskian perspective on teaching and learning science. *School science review*, 79(289):33-41.

Husen, T. & Postlethwaite, T.N. 1985. *International encyclopedia of education*. Oxford: Pergamon Press.

Khalili, P. & Olugbara, O.O. 2011. Positive youth development in mobile dynamic virtual environment. In: P. Kommers & P. Isaías (eds.), *Proceedings of the IADIS International Conference e-Society*. Available at: https://bit.ly/32kFi4B [Accessed 30 July 2020].

Lerman, S. 1989. Constructivism, mathematics and mathematics education. *Educational Studies in Mathematics*, 20(2):211-223. https://doi.org/10.1007/BF00579463

Letseka, M. & Maile, S. 2008. *High university drop-out rates: A threat to South Africa's future*. Pretoria: Human Sciences Research Council.

McLeod, S.A. 2017. *Kolb - learning styles and experiential learning cycle*. Available at: https://bit.ly/3dhOpJK (Accessed 10 January 2021).

National Planning Commission. 2012. *National Development Plan 2030: Our future-make it work*. Available at: https://bit.ly/3dqVXJ1 [Accessed 30 July 2020].

Ng'ambi, D., Brown, C., Bozalek, V., Gachago, D. & Wood, D. 2016. Technology enhanced teaching and learning in South African higher education – A rearview of a 20 year journey. *British Journal of Educational Technology*, 47(5):843-858. https://doi.org/10.1111/bjet.12485

Ochieng, D.M., Olugbara, O.O. & Marks, M.M. 2017. Exploring Digital Archive System to Develop Digitally Resilient Youths in Marginalised Communities in South Africa. *The Electronic Journal of Information Systems in Developing Countries*, 80(1):1-22. https://doi.org/10.1002/j.1681-4835.2017.tb00588.x

Olugbara, O.O. & Ndhlovu, B.N. 2014. Constructing frugal sales system for small enterprises. *The African Journal of Information Systems*, 6(4):1.

Phillips, D.C. 1995. The good, the bad, and the ugly: The many faces of constructivism. *Educational researcher*, 24(7):5-12. https://doi.org/10.3102/0013189X024007005

Piaget, J. 1977. Problems of equilibration. In: M.H. Appel & L.S. Goldberg (eds.), *Topics in cognitive development*. Boston, MA: Springer, 3-13. https://doi.org/10.1007/978-1-4613-4175-8_1

Piaget, J. 2008. Developmental psychology: Incorporating Piaget's and Vygotsky's theories in classrooms. *Journal of cross-disciplinary perspectives in education*, 1(1):59-67.

Robinson, K.& Aronica, L. 2015. *Creative schools: Revolutionizing education from the ground up*. UK: Penguin.

Sadeghi, S.H. 2015. Cultural context and e-practice: an assessment on USA institutions. *International Journal of Advanced and Applied Sciences,* 2(9):32-36.

Sahu, P. 2020. Closure of universities due to coronavirus disease 2019 (Covid-19): impact on education and mental health of students and academic staff. *Cureus*, 12(4). https://doi.org/10.7759/cureus.7541

Steffe, L.P. & Thompson, P.W. 2000. Interaction or intersubjectivity? A reply to Lerman. *Journal for Research in Mathematics Education*, 31(2):191-209. https://doi.org/10.2307/749751

Tam, M. 2000. Constructivism, instructional design, and technology: Implications for transforming distance learning. *Journal of Educational Technology & Society*, 3(2):50-60.

Toquero, C.M. 2020. Challenges and Opportunities for Higher Education Amid the Covid-19 Pandemic: The Philippine Context. *Pedagogical Research*, 5(4). https://doi.org/10.29333/pr/7947

Von Glasersfeld, E. 1974. Piaget and the radical constructivist epistemology. *Epistemology and education,* 1:24. https://doi.org/10.1007/BF03220058

Von Glasersfeld, E. 2001. Radical constructivism and teaching. *Prospects*, 31(2):161-173.

Vygotsky, L.S. 1980. *Mind in society: The development of higher psychological processes*. Cambridge: Harvard University Press. https://doi.org/10.2307/j.ctvjf9vz4

Webster, D. 2019. Why South Africa is the world's most unequal society. *Mail & Guardian*, 19.

WHO. 2020. *Coronavirus disease (Covid-19) pandemic*. Available at: https://bit.ly/3cpFHIE [Accessed 20 March 2020].

World Bank. 2019. *South African Overview*. Available at: https://bit.ly/31qqAIE [Accessed February 2021].

Zhou, Z. 2018. *Machine learning*. Beijing: Tsinghua University.

POSTGRADUATE TRAINING AND SUPERVISION DURING AND POST THE COVID-19 CRISIS IN SOUTH AFRICA

Have universities addressed challenges and seized opportunities?

Urmilla Bob, Suveshnee Munien, Amanda Gumede and Rivoni Gounden

Introduction

Postgraduate education is critical for the training of the next generation of researchers, as outlined by Cloete, Mouton and Sheppard (2015) and Manyike (2017). Several concerns have been raised nationally and within higher education institutions about the state of postgraduate training in South Africa with the quality of graduates, throughput rates, supervision capacity, the preparedness of students to undertake postgraduate degrees, state of research infrastructure, etc. (Academy of Science of South Africa, 2018; Cloete et al., 2015; National Planning Commission [NPC], 2013). Research is vital to inform evidence-based practices and responses. The Covid-19 pandemic has, in several ways, further exposed the challenges that universities face in relation to postgraduate training and supervision, which this chapter examines. Additionally, the pandemic has reinforced inequalities and inefficiencies that characterise South Africa's higher education landscape. Thus, it is imperative that research examines Covid-19's impacts on postgraduate training and supervision. In the context of this study, postgraduate training and supervision are widespread global occurrences in the higher education sector. While numerous challenges with postgraduate education have been identified as indicated in the South African context, the Covid-19 pandemic is a type of disruption that has not been experienced previously in terms of the scope and nature of the impacts, intensity and unpredictability. Social constructivism is, in this context, a useful framework to reflect on observations and experiences. It is a theoretical lens which is embedded in adopting a critical stance to examine taken-for-granted or common phenomena that challenges the notion of objective knowledge construction and focuses on experiences and differences. Two of the authors are supervisors, and two of the authors are doctoral students. The experiences and reflective stance of the authors also provide insights pertinent to the focus of this study.

Social constructivism, according to Dreyer (2017) and McKenzie and Roodenburg (2017), is a theory of knowing that is suspicious of categorisation and assuming that phenomena are experienced or results in similar impacts across a populace, in this instance postgraduate students and supervisors. They specifically underscore the importance of reflective practice, which the authors undertake in this study. Social constructivism also adopts the position that knowledge is socially constructed or sustained by social processes and interactions (Aitken, 2019; Mariguddi, 2020). Mariguddi (2020:8) states that social constructivism is a theory that "acknowledges that social interactions influence how an individual interprets various pieces of information and experiences", which in the context of this study includes the views and experiences of the authors in their respective roles as academics/supervisors and postgraduate students. Additionally, social constructivism, as indicated by Mertkan and Bayrakli (2018), notes the importance of considering power dynamics and specific contexts associated with social interactions. The manner in which individuals perceive and view the world are influenced by their social lenses, which include socio-cultural attributes including gender, population group, educational level and class. In the postgraduate context, disciplinary background, supervisor, etc. are influential. Thus, for the purposes of this research, institutional responses, student and supervisor capacity to deal with change, as well as student-supervisor interactions, are among the aspects examined pertaining to postgraduate training and supervision during the Covid-19 pandemic and how these reflections can inform future practices.

This chapter primarily adopts a desktop study approach. The key secondary information sourced relate to postgraduate statistics that reflect trends and critical issues in the South African context. Specifically, information from the Department of Higher Education and Training (DHET) is used in this regard. Additionally, an advanced Google Scholar search was used with various filters including 'postgraduate education and Covid-19', 'postgraduate education in South Africa' and 'challenges faced by postgraduate students'. Relevant and the most current publications were used to inform the discussions. Thus, a purposive sampling approach was adopted to undertake the desktop study.

The next section contextualises the higher education landscape in South Africa, focusing on postgraduate education and supervision. Thereafter, shifts in postgraduate training and supervision in response to the Covid-19 pandemic disruptions are discussed, followed by reflections on undertaking research and supervision when home-based. Recommendations to improve postgraduate supervision and training post-pandemic are then presented, which is a main contribution of the study. Finally, concluding remarks are forwarded.

Contextualising the higher education landscape in South Africa: Focus on postgraduate considerations

The higher education landscape is highly differentiated and, more than two decades on, continues to reflect apartheid constructions of advantaged and disadvantaged universities, with the former being historically white (including those that have been recently merged) and urban-based institutions (Cloete et al., 2015; NPC, 2013). The NPC (2013) further states that despite these differences, the entire system has been bogged down with administrative challenges, quality concerns and the inability to transform. Lessing and Schulze's (2002) assessment of postgraduate supervision and academic support in South Africa reveals that close to two decades later, the system remains mostly unchanged today. They assert that universities faced challenges of transformation, increasing numbers of disadvantaged students, low completion rates, and concerns pertaining to the quality of postgraduate education (including inadequate/ineffective supervision). Similar assertions are noted by ASSAf (2018), Cloete et al. (2015) and Pillay (2019), with the South African government itself in the NPC (2013) characterising the quality of universities in the country as being mid-level performers in terms of knowledge production, low throughput and high dropout rates, and insufficient capacity (including supervision capacity) to produce the required levels of skills. The NPC (2013) further notes that the sector continues to reflect historical inequities and distortions, and is under considerable strain with enrolments increasing without concomitant increases in funding, insufficient numbers and underprepared academics, inadequate infrastructure and facilities, equipment shortages, and administrative challenges. Furthermore, ASSAf (2018) and Rogan and Reynolds (2016) state that a major concern in South Africa is the unemployability of South African graduates. Resource constraints are likely to worsen as funding is shifting to curb the spread of the virus and address direct Covid-19 related health and economic impacts, which will further constrain the higher education system in South Africa.

The DHET's (2020a) latest research outputs report (based on 2018 publications) indicates that out of the 1 085 568 students enrolled in public higher education institutions in South Africa, 61 096 (5.6%) were registered for masters degrees and 23 650 (2.2%) for doctoral studies. Statistics South Africa (2019) states that a large and increasing proportion of students at South African public universities are foreigners from Africa, from 4.3% (25 039) in 2000 to 5.8% (56 074) in 2016. Additionally, DHET (2020a) shows that 63.1% of the 2019 enrolments were through contact mode with the rest enrolled through the distance mode of learning. These statistics reveal that most students are acclimatised to contact-based learning while, as a result of the Covid-19 pandemic, universities are forced to transition to online/virtual/remote learning, including postgraduate training and supervision, with many students and supervisors not being previously exposed to this approach to teaching and supervision. DHET (2020b) also indicates that in 2018, among the South African public universities, only 48% of academics had doctoral degrees ranging from 13.2% at Walter Sisulu University to 69.6% at the University of Pretoria. This has severe implications for postgraduate supervision and also reflects the inadequacies of supervisory capacity in South Africa and inequalities in the higher education system. It is important to note that most academics with doctoral degrees are emerging and black (at lecturer and senior lecturer levels) with lower levels of research productivity in relation to both publications, as well as the graduation of masters and doctoral students (DHET, 2015; Sadiq, Barnes, Price, Gumedze & Morrell, 2019).

Teferra (2020) asserts that South African higher education institutions are deemed to be more stable, diverse, well-endowed, and comprehensive than their counterparts on the continent, noting that some South African institutions dominate the rankings lists. Teferra (2020:239) indicates, however, that South African universities reflect the racist and systematic discriminatory practices of the past, with legacies continuing "to be felt and manifested in the higher education system in a number of ways" with the system facing "multiple systemic challenges, structural shortcomings and frequent strikes and crises - largely around issues of access, quality, funding, race and decolonisation". Mohamedbhai (2020) cautions that the impacts of the Covid-19 pandemic will destabilise higher education in Africa with serious consequences at a time when the continent is investing substantial efforts to transform and improve this sector.

Cloete et al. (2015), Manyike (2017), Mutula (2011) and Sadiq et al. (2019) note that effective postgraduate supervision is a concern at universities globally, which are even more disconcerting in development contexts such as South Africa where many students study part-time (even if registered as full-time students), resource constraints are evident, supervisory capacity is lacking (primarily because of younger academics who lack the necessary experience) and where there is increasing demands by universities (as a result of government pressure linked to subsidies) to increase postgraduate student numbers (although throughput challenges are straining the system). Mutala (2011) asserts explicitly that some South African universities are characterised by inexperienced supervisors, supervisors training in research areas that varied from their specialisations, and the lack of research expertise.

Cloete et al. (2015) highlight a range of strategies from various sources (including government, universities, academics, and agencies/organisations involved in the higher education sector) being advocated to improve postgraduate education in South Africa. These include the need for increased synergies and collaboration, quality considerations, adequate resourcing of students and research activities, developing supervisory capacity, and embracing alternative modes of delivery (including online learning which has now become the norm).

Shifts in postgraduate training and supervision in response to the Covid-19 pandemic

The initial lockdown caused significant changes within university communities. In relation to postgraduate research, most studies have been postponed, and others modified to desktop-based research; however, there is a need to carefully examine the quality of research that is being conducted under these conditions. Laboratory and field-based research came to an abrupt halt with the restrictions limiting these types of research, with only Covid-19 approved studies permitted. The focus for many students and supervisors shifted to undertaking literature reviews and data analysis, if some or all of the primary data was collected. Master's students still in the process of formulating their proposals were advised (by supervisors and in some cases university ethics committees) to consider desktop studies, given the shorter length of master's compared to doctoral studies, and that key components of doctoral level research are to contribute to knowledge in a specific field/area and demonstrate methodological competence. The varied responses reinforce the importance of being sensitive to differences, as noted in relation to adopting social constructivism. Four months on, and in the current context of the rise in the number of infections and deaths associated with the virus; universities, supervisors, and postgraduate students are realising that the disruptions are unlikely to end in the near future. Foreign students will not be allowed to re-enter the country, domestic travel restrictions and social distancing protocols will continue, and although some level of re-opening universities has started at Risk Level 3, the requirements of the number of staff and students that are permitted on campuses will result in prioritisation of who should be allowed to be at universities physically. For example, students undertaking laboratory-based research are groups that have been prioritised.

The restrictions on the number of researchers permitted in the laboratory and other social distancing protocols, however, will impact on the time taken to complete the research, which is already a significant challenge in South Africa as noted by Cloete et al. (2015) and Manyike (2017). Additionally, concerns are raised that the challenges experienced to procure laboratory materials and equipment, often sourced from other countries, may delay research. Because of the disruptions and restrictions, some students may need to change their research topics altogether. The changes in topics, research design and data collection approaches all require ethical approval. Students and supervisors are required to understand processes that need to be followed for ethical approval and amendments during this time, which can be a difficult and time-consuming process at many universities that still rely on paper-based ethical approval processes and do not have online application systems. Navigating these administrative procedures (together with registration, accessing funding, getting the necessary support to go online, etc.) can be extremely frustrating for both students and supervisors since, as indicated earlier, administrative inefficiencies and challenges characterise many South African universities. Dealing with bureaucratic, administrative processes that have not adapted to the "new normal" are likely to be even more overwhelming for students who are not based near or at universities (when partial re-opening commences), including students who are foreign and are residing in rural areas, which reinforce the importance of considering differing contexts as outlined in relation to the theoretical framework used.

Covid-19 restrictions have brought to the fore the ability of postgraduate students to conduct and carry out research remotely and independently, emphasising their theoretical knowledge and analytical research skills. It has long been identified that postgraduate students in South African higher education institutions are poorly prepared in comparison to other countries, which instigated country-level upskilling of master's and doctoral students; a department of higher education initiative to increase postgraduate throughput and quality (Cloete et al., 2015; Mutula, 2011). The limited understanding, displayed by some, around the relevant epistemological and ontological underpinnings of their research can give rise to the surge in the use of ghostwriters and statisticians at exorbitant costs to students, and long-term legacy impacts associated with persons with the qualifications but not having the skills. Worryingly, under Covid-related restrictions with limited face-to-face contact with supervisors and peers, this could increase.

The gaps between different socio-economic and geographic groupings emerge quite poignantly amidst Covid-19, which reflect that the postgraduate experiences are influenced by social attributes as noted earlier. Limited connectivity could limit the number of online searches for current and relevant literature, jeopardising the quality of the meta-analyses and systematic reviews, an essential undertaking in the current context. More importantly, postgraduates who have limited access to the internet, relevant hardware and software are further disadvantaged. This is particularly true in the case of shifting to online data collection tools and the use of virtual laboratories for experimental research. Friederici, Ojanperä and Graham (2017) and Manyike (2017) stress the importance of internet connectivity to promote online interactions, stating that internet access enables postgraduate students to interact more regularly with each other and their supervisors.

A positive trend among some universities, that have the technological infrastructure to do so, is the increase in online training for supervisors and students covering various aspects including proposal writing, research design, statistical and qualitative software packages, academic/scientific writing skills, etc. Some students and supervisors (especially those with no or limited internet connectivity and technical know-how) are not well-positioned to benefit from this training. Additionally, there are challenges when undertaking online training which often focus on content and technical aspects rather than critical, context-specific disciplinary skills; which is important at postgraduate levels as noted by Mutala (2011), but tends to be undermined. This type and level of training also require facilitation expertise. Aitken (2019) notes the importance of examining the experiences of academic staff (and students) to online postgraduate education, mostly since this platform will remain even post the pandemic. Aitken (2019) indicates the importance of focusing on variations (which is advocated when adopting social constructivism) in relation to the perceived role of the educator, evolving awareness of the social aspects of online learning, and engagement.

For students undertaking field-based social research, the disruptions are dire since face-to-face contact is restricted. Increasingly, these students are opting to shift their research to desktop studies and/or online or electronic (emails and telephone calls) platforms for primary data collection, which is understandable since it is unclear when the disruptions will cease. These data collection approaches have several limitations in relation to quantitative research including generalisability, even if large response rates are achieved, because of the targeted approach to encourage participation and the fact that only those persons with internet connectivity can participate in the study. In terms of qualitative research, online engagements (for example, focus group discussions and key informant interviews) can undermine the nuances of observing context, body language, and reactions. Thus, quality issues need to be considered when using online platforms and telephonic interviews to undertake research. Supervisors and students need to be aware of these limitations. Specific methodological training is required that encompasses issues pertaining to research limitations, sampling approaches, data collection challenges (for example, many online surveys are plagued with lower response rates, especially if surveys are longer which doctoral studies tend to be) and how to interpret results.

Manyike's (2017) assessment of postgraduate supervision in an Open Distance E-learning environment in South Africa reveals difficulties associated with training and supervising students in contexts where face-to-face communication between supervisor and student is restricted or totally non-existent. This, as a result of the Covid-19 pandemic, has become the norm. Yet, as Manyike (2017) indicates, there is a need to train students and supervisors on how to supervise and engage with each other online. Supervisors who are not competent to teach/supervise online revert to a mechanistic approach to supervision which is primarily based on students submitting written drafts and receiving feedback from supervisors in writing, usually using track changes. This negates the add-on value of supervision which places emphasis on critically working through ideas, embracing contestation and debates, and formulating and defending arguments. This happens through engagement, not only between a student and supervisor/s, but between peers and communities of practices (usually via conferences, workshops, seminars, etc.).

Challenges with co-supervision can also be confusing and overwhelming for students under these conditions, especially if the main engagement with students is written feedback on drafts. Olmos-López and Sunderland (2017) assert that co-supervision can be time-consuming and challenging, especially if approaches and viewpoints among supervisors differ. Co-supervision challenges are likely to be exacerbated as a result of the Covid-19 disruptions. If supervisors have not agreed on processes to follow, feedback that differs can be difficult for a student to resolve, especially given student-supervisor power dynamics with students generally hesitant to challenge or disagree with their supervisors. Agreeing on processes could entail, for example, providing one set of comments after resolving differences of opinion. A more academically robust approach would be to discuss the differing points of view with the student to resolve differences so that the student can be trained to disagree academically, which is the cornerstone of academic freedom. It is imperative that the student is a part of and central to making decisions about his/her dissertation/ thesis. For doctoral students, this becomes more important since the focus is on the student's contribution to knowledge and demonstrating expertise in a particular field/area of research.

As indicated earlier, a large proportion of South Africa's postgraduate students are foreigners, mainly from Africa. Yet, in dealing with the pandemic (from closing universities to moving online) very little attention has been paid to this cohort of postgraduate students. In terms of internet connectivity, discussed earlier, the challenges experienced in South Africa are even worse in many parts of Africa with connectivity in many places being non-existent, unreliable and expensive (Friederici et al., 2017; Mohamedbhai, 2020). Friederici et al. (2017) refer to the mirage of inclusive digital development in Africa. Many foreign students are, therefore, unlikely to benefit from existing training efforts using online platforms. Students may also experience difficulties in accessing and downloading internet-based resources.

Undertaking research and supervising when home-based

The shift to remote teaching and learning came almost instantaneously; however, there was limited consideration of the following aspects:

- Increased assumption that both students and supervisors are able to work independently.
- Changes in the number of hours spent on work-related activities given that most would now juggle home and family responsibilities while attempting to meet their daily 8-hour work obligation.
- The need to establish home offices, ensure connectivity, access to suitable hardware and software, all during a Level 5 lockdown. During these restrictions, only essential items could be purchased.
- The ability to multi-task across sectors while working from home and the resultant impacts on the mental and psychological well-being of employees.
- The risks posed to people living in abusive relationships.

These aspects are discussed in this section.

It is important to note that in relation to supervisors, these are academics who generally also have undergraduate teaching responsibilities and are themselves learning new teaching tools and approaches. Furthermore, many academics in South Africa are themselves students completing their doctoral studies, as indicated earlier. These academics have the triple burden of balancing family life, their work, and their student commitments; experiencing many of the challenges outlined in this chapter as students. Furthermore, key issues that need to be better understood are whether experienced supervisors are better able to cope and guide students during periods of severe disruptions. Furthermore, are the workloads of some of the supervisors an issue? Unequitable workload distribution among academics has been noted by Sadiq et al. (2019). In the South African context, more established researchers who are a part of the professoriate tend to have lower undergraduate teaching loads. This has major impacts on the morale of emerging academics, as well as their research productivity, including their ability to successfully supervise postgraduate students to completion since preparing for and teaching online can be extremely time consuming and demanding, especially if the necessary skills, software and hardware

are not in place. Additionally, given that many students are unable to participate in online classes, it is possible that academics are repeating classes and assessments to accommodate students. An interesting, potential student-supervisor dynamic that is likely to be experienced is that some students may be more competent with using online platforms than their supervisors as a result of the generational gap.

Reliance on technology in relation to studying and supervising from home is a major feature of the current response to cope with the pandemic disruptions. However, as discussed earlier, access to technology and internet connectivity can disadvantage certain groups, especially those in rural areas and poorer students (if universities are not providing adequate data bundles and internet connectivity). Additionally, research quality and training issues need to be considered.

Students (and supervisors) are and can experience high levels of anxiety and stress to cope and adapt to these dramatic and unpredictable changes, which can impact on their psychological well-being and impact on their ability to focus on their studies and roles as supervisors, respectively. As Albertyn and Bennett (2020) state, postgraduate students often experience uncertainties when planning and conducting research. They further assert that uncertainties are critical for good research; however, if not appropriately managed could negatively impact on the quality of the research, completion rates and the well-being of students. They note the importance of supervisors to support students to understand and cope with anxieties and advocate for the need for supervisors to be trained to assist students to cope. In the South African context, this situation is worse with many supervisors themselves experiencing these stressors because they are also completing doctoral studies. During this time of heightened uncertainties, dealing with anxiety and stress becomes more pronounced.

In addition to academic apprehensions, anxieties can also be associated with juggling personal and professional lives, other stressors at home (such as being in abusive relationships), anxiety about employment prospects or continued employment (in the case of supervisors), restrictions students face, and fear of the virus (for self and loved ones). In addition to the stress, fear, anxiety and uncertainty that often characterise postgraduate studies; these emotions could be enhanced as a consequence of the lockdown. Sood (2020) asserts the need for interventions to prevent long-term psychological morbidity associated with the Covid-19 pandemic. The impacts of Covid-19 are escalating, with some studies citing increases in suicide and suicidal tendencies, depression, stress, fatigue and overall stress (Karnon, 2020; Kazmi, Hasan, Talib & Saxena, 2020).

Studying from home poses additional burdens for women in particular. Female students based at home have the triple burden of studying, taking care of the bulk of the domestic responsibilities (cleaning and cooking) and being caregivers (especially if members of the household include children and elderly persons). Additionally, gender-based violence is experienced worldwide and the President of South Africa, Cyril Ramaphosa, in his speech to the nation on 17 June 2020 apologises to girls and women as they are subjected to the additional pandemic of gender-based violence in the country:

> It is with the heaviest of hearts that I stand before the women and girls of South Africa this evening to talk about another pandemic that is raging in our country – the killing of women and children by the men of our country.

Thus, many female students are at a substantial disadvantage compared to their male counterparts.

Some supervisors and students could be more productive and focused during this period. These are generally persons who may have help at home, have the necessary infrastructure and space to work effectively from home, are undertaking desktop-based research, and/or have data.

Cloete et al. (2015) indicate that doctoral students are allocated to supervisors mainly via administrative processes or students engaging with supervisors before being registered. Students and supervisors who 'choose' each other are more likely to have better relationships compared to supervisors who have been allocated students who they deem to not be undertaking research in their area of research or perceive to be under-prepared. Students allocated in the former manner are also more likely to successfully graduate and have more productive and collegial student-supervisor relationships.

Recommendations to improve postgraduate supervision and training post-pandemic

A key contribution of this chapter is its forward-looking stance to reflect on recommendations emanating from the Covid-19 response experiences and the challenges exposed. As indicated earlier, it is imperative to underscore that most (if not all, given that protests have persistently led to the closure of universities) of the postgraduate training and supervision challenges that universities are grappling with are not the result of the pandemic, but have been reinforced by the current crisis and has exposed the under-preparedness to manage and adequately supervise postgraduate students. Pillay (2019) highlights that inclusion and equity remain elusive in the South Africa context. The Covid-19 pandemic has reinforced and further exposed glaring inequalities in the higher education sector.

Universities (and society more generally) need to tackle discriminatory practices head-on in relation to how and which students are recruited for postgraduate studies, how students are supported during and after completion of their degrees, and sensitivity to the differing lived realities of students. This includes addressing persistent imbalances and inequities in relation to gender, sexual orientation, population group, disability status and other forms of discriminatory practices. Shifts in teaching, learning, and supervision modalities (such as online learning as discussed earlier) need to consider implications for different groups. As this chapter has highlighted, these changes can reinforce existing inequalities and have consequences that universities should anticipate. Targeted assistance should be provided for students who are further disadvantaged.

A key issue as the research world shifts to online and electronic platforms is what is the plight of students without internet connectivity? What are their research options? Some research options include identifying data sources where collection has been completed. Several disciplines use these data sources, which can include survey results from national or municipal studies, spatial data, data embedded in publicly available reports, etc. Supervisors unfamiliar with these sources need to engage with colleagues who know how to access and use the data in the context of peer learning and mentoring so that they are better positioned to support students who cannot do any form of primary data collection. Since much of this data is publicly available for free, library ervices at universities need to focus on creating data portals with these types of information for researchers and students. Again, however, as discussed earlier, it is important to reiterate the need for training on how to source and use this data, which also has limitations.

There is a need to develop and embrace innovative approaches to foster research and collaboration for improved data collection rather than have students attempt to collect data under current conditions that could undermine standards of validity and reliability. Additionally, students and supervisors (if applicable) need to be trained on the limitations of undertaking online research or switching to research designs that they are not trained to fully understand.

The student-supervisor relationship is the cornerstone of successful postgraduate education. Capacitating supervisors with the necessary skills to have the expertise to uphold rigorous academic standards and research integrity will ensure that future generations of researchers and supervisors will break the legacy of inadequate supervision and poorly trained graduates (if they complete their studies). Additionally, training needs to focus on softer skills as well to create a culture of mentoring and coaching that assists in developing graduates that are knowledgeable in their field, are research competent, and understand issues of empathy, embracing flexibility and change, adaptability, being self-motivated and disciplined, conducting themselves ethically, taking responsibility, and having the necessary social skills to interact with others.

Collaboration, as well as sharing of expertise and resources, will strengthen universities in South Africa. Specifically, public universities in South Africa need to be seen as part of one system and mechanisms need to be put in place where students can access laboratories, library facilities, and attend practicals and training sessions at universities close to where they reside, although they may be registered at other universities. This will require comprehensive databases of current students and supervisors, as well as appropriate administrative processes that support these efforts. It is also important to note that more students and supervisors are becoming aware of the multitude of resources available (including videos, presentations, guidelines, etc.) to assist them to develop the skills needed for successful postgraduate studies. There are also freely available packages and programmes to develop online surveys, assist with academic writing and editing, and undertake additional training. Universities need to share this information with both students and supervisors.

Conclusion

The discussion reveals that universities across South Africa have responded to the Covid-19 pandemic, particularly in relation to embracing online learning. However, the range of socio-economic conditions that different groups of students face in different locations (during the lockdown being home-based and as restrictions ease, most will continue their studies from home); supervisor experience, capacity and workloads; disciplinary and methodological differences; and persistent unresolved inequalities and challenges within South Africa's higher education sector and specific universities; pose several challenges for many postgraduate students and supervisors. Despite the current conditions faced, key recommendations are emerging to transition universities to change modalities of supervision and rethinking institutional boundaries. The key question is whether universities, supervisors and students will seize the opportunity to utilise these recommendations to radically rethink what constitutes postgraduate studies and how we change processes and systems to address the systemic structural, administrative, supervisory, and quality issues that burden South Africa's higher education system?

References

Aitken, G. 2019. Experiences of staff new to teaching postgraduate students online: Implications for academic staff development. *Journal of Perspectives in Applied Academic Practice*, 7(1):37-46.

Albertyn, R. & Bennett, K. 2020. Containing and harnessing uncertainty during postgraduate research supervision. *Higher Education Research and Development*, 1-15. https://doi.org/1 0.1080/07294360.2020.1775559

ASSAf. 2018. *Status of postgraduate research training in engineering in South Africa*. Available at: http://doi.org/10.17159/assaf.2018/0032. [Accessed 18 June 2020].

Cloete, N., Mouton, J. & Sheppard, C. 2015. *Doctoral education in South Africa: Policy, discourse and data. African Minds*. Available at: https://bit.ly/3lYH1oZ [Accessed 20 June 2020]. https://doi.org/10.47622/9781928331001

DHET. 2015. *Staffing South Africa's universities framework*. Pretoria: DHET.

DHET, 2020a. *Statistics on post-school education and training in South Africa: 2018*. Pretoria: DHET.

DHET, 2020b. *Report on the evaluation of the 2018 universities' research outputs*. Pretoria: DHET.

Dreyer, L.M. 2017. Digital storytelling to engage postgraduates in reflective practice in an emerging economy. *South African Journal of Education*, 37(4):1-10. https://doi.org/10.15700/saje.v37n4a1475

Friederici, N., Ojanperä, S. & Graham, M. 2017. The impact of connectivity in Africa: Grand visions and the mirage of inclusive digital development. *The Electronic Journal of Information Systems in Developing Countries*, 79(1):1-20. https://doi.org/10.1002/j.1681-4835.2017.tb00578.x

Karnon, J. 2020. A simple decision analysis of a mandatory lockdown response to the Covid-19 pandemic. *Applied Health Economics and Health Policy*, 18:329-331. https://doi.org/10.1007/s40258-020-00581-w

Kazmi, S.S.H., Hasan, K., Talib, S. & Saxena, S. 2020. Covid-19 and lockdown: A study on the impact on mental health. *SSRN*, 1-13. https://doi.org/10.2139/ssrn.3577515

Lessing, A.C. & Schulze, S. 2002. Postgraduate supervision and academic support: Students' perceptions. *South African Journal of Higher Education*, 16(2):139-149. https://doi.org/10.4314/sajhe.v16i2.25253

Manyike, T.V. 2017. Postgraduate supervision at an open distance e-learning institution in South Africa. *South African Journal of Education*, 37(2):1-11. https://doi.org/10.15700/saje. v37n2a1354

Mariguddi, A. 2020. Perceptions of the research–practice nexus: A case study of a secondary postgraduate certificate in education course. *Practice*, 2(1):4-20. https://doi.org/10.1080/25 783858.2020.1732636

McKenzie, W. & Roodenburg, J. 2017. Using PeerWise to develop a contributing student pedagogy for postgraduate psychology. *Australasian Journal of Educational Technology*, 33(1):32-47. https://doi.org/10.14742/ajet.3169

Mertkan, S. & Bayrakli, H. 2018. Re-inventing researcher identity: When the individual interacts with the contextual power dynamics. *Higher Education Research and Development*, 37(2):316-327. https://doi.org/10.1080/07294360.2017.1355891

Mohamedbhai, G. 2020. *Covid-19: What Consequences for Higher Education?* University World News: Africa Edition. Available at: https://bit.ly/39lzH1F [Accessed 3 May 2020].

Mutula, S.M. 2011. Challenges of postgraduate research: Case of developing countries. *South African Journal of Libraries and Information Science*, 77(2):184-190. https://doi.org/10.7553/77-2-60

NPC. 2013. *National Development Plan 2030: Our Future – Make it Work.* Pretoria: Ministry of the Presidency. Available at: https://bit.ly/2NZgTOv [Accessed 28 April 2020].

Olmos-López, P. & Sunderland, J. 2017. Doctoral supervisors' and supervisees' responses to co-supervision. *Journal of Further and Higher Education*, 41(6):727-740. https://doi.org/10.1080/0309877X.2016.1177166

Pillay, V. 2019. Displaced margins and misplaced equity: Challenges for South African higher education. *South African Journal of Higher Education*, 33(2):142-162. https://doi.org/10.20853/33-2-2692

Rogan, M. & Reynolds, J. 2016. Schooling inequality, higher education and the labour market: Evidence from a graduate tracer study in the Eastern Cape, South Africa. *Development Southern Africa*, 33(3):343-360. https://doi.org/10.1080/0376835X.2016.1153454

Sadiq, H., Barnes, K.I., Price, M., Gumedze, F. & Morrell, R.G. 2019. Academic promotions at a South African university: Questions of bias, politics, and transformation. *Higher Education*, 78(3):423-442. https://doi.org/10.1007/s10734-018-0350-2

Sood, S. 2020. Psychological effects of the Coronavirus Disease-2019 pandemic. *Research and Humanities in Medical Education*, 7:23-26.

Statistics South Africa. 2019. *Education Series Volume V: Higher education and skills in South Africa, 2017.* Pretoria: Statistics South Africa.

Teferra, D. 2020. Imperatives and realities of doctoral education in South Africa. In: M. Yudkevich, P.G. Altbach & H. de Wit (eds.), *Trends and Issues in Doctoral Education: A Global Perspective.* Los Angeles: Sage Publications. https://doi.org/10.4135/9789353885991.n10

GENDER JUSTICE, SOCIAL COHESION, THE SOCIAL SCIENCES AND COVID-19

9

Opportunities and challenges for higher education

Cheryl Potgieter and Urmilla Bob

Introduction

Wolhuter and Chigisheva (2020) point out that the world is rapidly changing in terms of its demographics, socio-economic dynamics, and political aspects. These changes, they argue, have wide ranging consequences for scholarship, including thematic and methodological research areas for the social sciences. The Covid-19 pandemic has created unparalleled life and death challenges worldwide that was largely unanticipated. Moodley, Obasa and London (2020) assert that South Africa is currently in the midst of an unprecedented public health crisis caused by the Covid-19 virus. The response by governments the world over, including South Africa, has been to draw on the expertise of their most esteemed medical and public health experts. Dworkin (2020) comments that it is appropriate that the medical profession is "running the show" but succinctly points out that the humanities should be brought on board as they will prevent some "traps that they might do well to avoid".

In South Africa, the Academy of Science (ASSAf) recognised and congratulated the government on its response but cautioned that the challenge is not only medical, but social and thus social science and humanities academics should be members of the structures which advises government. The crucial role of the social sciences has also been pointed out by the South African National Institute for the Humanities and

Social Sciences (NIHSS, 2020). The organisation has stated that the spread of the Covid-19 virus has presented an incomparable challenge for society, academia and the social sciences. Holmes, O'Connor, Perry, Tracey, Wessely, Arseneault, Ballard, Christensen, Silver, Everall and Ford (2020) specifically state that it is evident that the direct and indirect psychological and social effects of the Covid-19 pandemic are pervasive. The NIHSS (2020) also notes, as has the ASSAF, that the medical and scientific establishment have been mobilised rapidly to respond to the outbreak, but discussions pertaining to the roles and impacts on the social sciences are subdued and ancillary to scientific concerns.

The Covid-19 pandemic has exposed an unequal world where the majority of the world's population are socio-economically and politically vulnerable. However, women, as in other pandemics, are particularly vulnerable to the health and social consequences of the virus. We write this chapter as South Africa's cases of persons diagnosed with Covid-19 are spiking and gendered data in terms of cases diagnosed and deaths are not always available. However, global data seems to indicate that more men seem to be dying from the virus, but no conclusions or generalisations can be made at this point. One cannot only look at male deaths in relation to the virus and conclude that men are more affected because of biology. Again, as in previous pandemics, women are integral as frontline workers in caring for patients as 70% of the world's health care workers are female and 80% of the world's nurses are women. In addition, women are carers not only on the frontline, but are also carers and frontline workers at home (Turquet & Koissy-Kpein, 2020).

Another consequence of the pandemic has been the rise of gender-based violence globally and in South Africa. In South Africa, the thousands of calls to help lines are indicative of the violence and we have also seen a number of murders of women. It has been argued that women are trapped in homes with their abusive partners and are thus fighting a pandemic within a pandemic. Women in higher education are part of homes and communities and they are thus affected by these gendered challenges. It is important to note in relation to the pandemic that of the 381 million care workers globally 65.3% are female and 34.7% are male. The latter figures do not include women who are responsible for care in the home as unpaid workers and in a time such as the current pandemic, their unpaid labour in the household would increase. Oosthuizen (2018) has indicated that women still do the majority of unpaid care work. One can also assume that with the lockdown and children not attending school, the need to support learning activities from home has created another job for many women and data is needed to understand how this impacts their professional position and output, as well as their physical and mental health.

Aims of the chapter

This chapter examines the role that the social sciences and humanities can play to ensure that Covid-19 impacts, which are complex and multidimensional, are sufficiently researched. The argument is made that the contributions of the humanities and social sciences should be integrated into research, policy, interventions, and curricula. The chapter thus interrogates the role which the social sciences and humanities can have in terms of various and varied responses to the pandemic. We also argue that the pandemic affects women differently and that researchers, irrespective of discipline, will not be successful in terms of interventions, both medical and social, if interventions are gender neutral. Our position is that this is a moment for the social sciences and humanities as equal partners with the medical sciences to mainstream gender justice interventions in curriculum, research, and engagement. We draw on secondary sources, as well as primary research undertaken to assess the environment for social science research in South Africa prior to the pandemic. In relation to the primary research, pertinent results are presented from a Global Development Network (GDN) funded project that the authors were involved in (Potgieter, Bob & Sooryamoorty, 2016).

State of social sciences prior to the pandemic: Key trends and issues

The progression of a critical social sciences research tradition in South Africa correlates with struggles against colonial and apartheid rule, as well as rebuilding a transformational and socially responsive post-apartheid nation. The social utility of the social sciences was also highlighted in the GDN study, particularly in relation to the social sciences driving policy critique and development in South Africa, as well as dealing with national challenges such as transformation and empowerment, vulnerabilities and social unrest.

The most recent Department of Higher Education and Training (DHET, 2020) research report indicates a diverse higher education landscape in terms of outputs with some universities that are highly research prolific (generally the historically advantaged white universities or recently merged universities). The report also reveals trends that show a growth in research output units per university and nationally.

The social sciences and humanities include the following classification of education subject matter (CESM) categories: visual and performing arts; communication, journalism, and related studies; education; family ecology and consumer sciences; languages, linguistics, and literature; law; philosophy, religion and theology; psychology; public management and services; and social sciences. The social sciences and humanities made up 29.6% of the journal research output units in 2018 (a decline from 32% in 2016), 81.2% in relation to book publications and 15% for published conference proceedings. Journal articles made up 77.2% of the total research output units followed by conference proceedings (14.7%) and book contributions (8.1%). The dominance of types of research outputs where science contributions are more discernible is evident. While the report does not disaggregate data specifically in relation to the social sciences, it is important to note that social sciences generally include education and psychology (Molotja & Ralphs, 2018).

Specifically, Molotja and Ralphs (2018) state that the social sciences include accounting; anthropology, archaeology, and history; architecture and habitat; economics; education; emerging issues; finance; geography; law; management studies; media and communication studies; political sciences and public policy; population studies; psychology; sociology; technology management; tourism and transportation studies. They further indicate that the humanities encompass arts and culture; dances; historical and civilisation studies; languages and literature; music; philosophy and religious studies. The dominance of the science, technology, engineering, and mathematics (STEM) fields in relation to research outputs in South Africa is evident in the report and correlates with global trends. The overall proportionate decline in social science and humanities research is not recent since the ASSAf (2011) found that close to a decade ago, the humanities and the social sciences constituted 38% of the annual total research output in South Africa.

The research output trends are also reflected in research funding for the social sciences. For example, the Department of Science and Technology (DST, 2012) noted that what government and higher education institutions spend on social sciences research and development at local, provincial, and national levels was 18.5% and 20%, respectively, with the rest of the investments in STEM fields. The DST (2012) indicates that when not-for-profit and business sector research and development funding is included, the picture worsens with more than 87% of expenditure allocated to natural sciences, engineering, and technology fields and only 12.5% was allocated to the social sciences. The GDN (2016) project revealed that the social sciences in South Africa (as is the case with most research), with the exception of health sciences and physical sciences which attracts substantial international funding, relies heavily on national funding. Social sciences research is also primarily concentrated in universities and research councils/centres/institutes.

As discussed earlier, these institutions have played a major role in championing the role that the social sciences can play in dealing with the pandemic, as well as initialising national research projects. The findings also reveal that the social sciences are contributing substantially to research outputs in South Africa. However, this is not matched with corresponding funding, which is disproportionately biased towards the STEM disciplines, including the natural, physical, and medical sciences (DST, 2012).

In addition to competing from a disadvantaged position for funding, within the social sciences, some disciplines have limited funding opportunities. The latter will be worsened under the current conditions where funding is shrinking and shifting to address the more direct and prioritised needs associated with dealing with the pandemic. Disciplinary differences in funding are also evident within the social sciences and humanities. For example, Molotja and Ralphs' (2018) analysis of patterns of research and development expenditure in social sciences and humanities research fields over the period 2005/2006-2014/2015 show expenditure in the 10-year reference period was targeted predominantly within just a few research fields (specifically, finance, economics, education, accounting, political science, and public policy). They found that funding in architecture and habitat, media and communication studies, psychology and transportation studies was strikingly low in the same period, and some research fields (such as dance or tourism) showed signs of being at risk of decline.

Additionally, preconceptions about the value of research and outputs which, according to Fitzpatrick and Kennison (2017), influence performance management, promotions and resource allocation persists, with lower rates of support for social scientists in terms of mentoring and networking. Similar findings to the GDN study were articulated in an earlier study by Mouton (2011) who also assessed the state of the humanities and social sciences in South Africa. Mouton (2011) found that systematic biases in the national science and higher education system tend to constrain, weaken and disadvantage the humanities and social sciences in relation to funding, publication support, expenditure on research and development and reward systems.

Li and Li (2015) examine co-authorship patterns of China's humanities and social sciences by assessing articles and reviews included in the Social Science Citation Index and the Arts and Humanities Citation Index of the Web of Science which have lessons for South Africa. Their findings were similar to trends in South Africa with most of the publications having no collaboration.

Impact of the Covid-19 pandemic on the social sciences and humanities

Funding for social science and humanities research in South Africa also reveals what we see as intra-disciplinary biases. Certain disciplines have more funding than others. Fields such as education, political science, public police and accounting receive much more funding than media studies, psychology, architecture and transportation studies (Molotja & Ralphs, 2018).

In terms of the pandemic, the disciplines which need funding to assist with non-pharmaceutical responses to the pandemic are the disciplines like psychology and transportation studies which have in the past received low research and development investments. Potgieter et al. (2016) further note that the social sciences in South Africa depend on international donors such as the Swedish International Development Cooperation Agency (SIDA), the Norwegian Agency for Development Cooperation (NORAD), governments in Europe, the International Development Research Centre (IDRC) in Canada; and various foundations in the United States of America (USA), notably Rockefeller, Mellon, Kellogg and Carnegie. All organisations are experiencing pressures to survive and prioritise funding directly to the health impacts of the pandemic. It is hoped that funding for the social sciences and humanities will not decrease because of funding for health-related disciplines, but that there will be a "balance" of funding between social sciences and humanities and health as the pandemic needs inter-disciplinary research and interventions.

An important aspect which emerged from the GDN study is that while the amount of funding available for the social sciences is lower than for STEM, the availability of funding is not the main issue, but the ability of social scientists to access funding is. Our concern is that this may again be the case for research linked to the Covid-19 pandemic, but it is too early for any assessment and it is an area which we will monitor closely. This is an important issue since, while major concerns are being raised about decreases in funding (which is likely to be of concern for most disciplines except those directly linked to the Covid-19 pandemic, especially the health sciences), there has been an increase in opportunities to respond to calls for proposals to undertake Covid-19 related research. Future research should examine the extent to which the social sciences benefitted from these funding opportunities.

As indicated earlier, the social sciences are made up of a range of different disciplines and focus areas. It is critical that these differences are understood to refrain from generalisations, which the social sciences are generally cautious of since there is recognition of context-specific dynamics. Thus, the short and long-term impacts of the pandemic on the social sciences (including research outputs and productivity) are likely to be differentiated. Specifically, those disciplines that utilise desktop study approaches, rely on secondary data sources (including large datasets such as census and geospatial data) and can shift from face-to-face to online/non-contact forms of primary data collection are likely to be minimally negatively impacted by the pandemic and may even see an increase in research. Non-contact-based approaches to data collection is also less costly and time consuming. It is important to note, however, that there are several limitations of relying almost solely on non-contact types of approaches to undertake social science research which can undermine the quality and integrity of the research endeavour.

Quality issues around research go beyond the research methodological constraints that social distancing pose for the social sciences, which are often field-based and include interactions with people. Social science research, in particular that which is generally not numeric based (although many social scientists have statistical and numerical data analytical skills), embraces engagement, debate, reflection, feedback and dissension of ideas. Online engagements as currently available are not always conducive to these types of interactions. This may further impinge on the quality of the graduates being trained under these conditions and the research outputs.

There is considerable concern that as research priorities and funding shift, disciplinary biases as noted in the previous section will be reinforced. However, this can be short-sighted and failing to address persistent societal challenges which have not subsided and, in many cases the pandemic responses have reinforced, will result in longer term health and economic impacts which could be more costly. What is required is a re-examination of how research is done to foster collaboration and partnerships to continue, and even upscale, social science research in specific areas that can have long-term positive impacts, as well as inform Covid-19 responses and measures. The benefits of a gendered social science lens to inform research in the context of the Covid-19 pandemic is therefore discussed in the next section.

Taking stock: Academic labour, gender justice and Covid-19

Van Rooyen and Zulu (2018) point out that of the 3 392 National Research Foundation (NRF) rated researchers in 2016 in the South African system, a mere 31% were women. Stated differently, 69% of NRF rated researchers in 2016 were men. In addition, 74% of rated researchers were white and the obvious conclusion is that the majority were white males. Van Rooyen and Zulu (2018) also indicate that there was an increase in women academics from 40.8% in 2009/2010 to 44% in 2013/2014. However, although the number of black women (African, coloured and Indian) are

153

increasing in academia, in 2012, African women reflected 9% of the overall number of women professors and 2% of all professors (Van Rooyen & Zulu, 2018). In the article, Van Rooyen and Zulu (2018) quote a black female academic who stated that the diversity and complexity of institutions led to feelings of disempowerment and it was compounded by balancing academic work and care-giving responsibilities.

Flaherty (2020) writes that editors of two journals reported that they had observed interesting, gendered patterns of submissions during the global lockdown and women were "losing out". A third journal editor noted that submissions by women had increased, but that single authored submissions from women had decreased. One of the editors noted that although submissions by women had increased, they did not have as much time as men to submit single authored articles. Viglione (2020), in an article published during the early months of the pandemic, reflects and supports a number of researchers' understanding that academic publication outputs among women would decline compared to men. Women take up more childcare responsibilities in the household and this holds true even when both male and female partners are university faculty.

Rethinking and re-imagining the future of higher education in the context of Covid-19

Auerbach and Hall (2020) point out that Covid-19 presents the social sciences with an opportunity to take stock of and reflect on the need for fresh approaches to rethink and re-imagine the future. They advocate for compassion and empathy being the underlying principle as social scientists re-adjust their pedagogies, as well as their teaching and research practices. This includes rethinking how students are assessed. They also suggest the need for "being inside the body and experience of Covid-19", which draws from feminist scholars who emphasise the need to focus on the personal to understand society and change. They further problematise the virtual, online world that has become the norm, arguing that online learning has the potential to reinforce inequalities and social tensions.

South Africa is one of the few African countries that has a government-funded research institute devoted to the social sciences: the Human Sciences Research Council (HSRC). The first national survey-based study on the social impacts of the Covid-19 pandemic in South Africa was undertaken by the HSRC (Reddy, Sewpaul, Mabaso, Parker, Naidoo, Jooste, Mokhele, Sifunda & Zuma, 2020). More than 19 000 respondents participated in this online perception study. The results revealed that while there was increasing understanding of the importance of the lockdown and social distancing protocols, the concerns most important to the general population was lack of money, food and health care. This research is important to develop appropriate policy and intervention strategies.

The HSRC also has a track record of undertaking research linked to health issues from a social science perspective (for example, HIV/AIDS) which reflects the expertise in the country to contribute to dealing with the pandemic. This is particularly important since increasingly, it is acknowledged that behavioural change is an important aspect of curbing the spread of the virus and co-morbidities are of major concern in countries such as South Africa with high prevalence of health ailments in the population. The effectiveness of measures to ensure these changes benefit from the insights from the social sciences is vital (NIHSS, 2020).

Social science research and data has catalysed new thinking about why we do research, what we should focus on and the methodological choices we make. The Covid-19 pandemic has exposed a range of socio-economic challenges and has brought to the fore the importance of social science research in a world where disruptions have become the norm. It is of critical importance that research is undertaken to inform policy responses which have characterised government efforts to put in place measures to deal with the pandemic. This includes the social impacts of these responses, as well as policy reviews, revisions and development as needed. The research has to be underpinned by a gendered feminist perspective that is cognisant of the intersectionality of race, sexuality, disability, and the urban/rural divide in its methodology, interpretations and interventions.

Paterson (2020) asserts that leading South African social scientists have called for increased engagement in shaping government's Covid-19 mitigation policies. There is no doubt that the pandemic has reinforced poverty and inequality in society and has resulted in new forms that require investigation and better understanding to effectively mitigate against these impacts. Schröder, Bossert, Kersting, Aeffner, Coetzee, Timme and Schlüter (2020) also indicate the need to better understand the implications of interventions on the Covid-19 outbreak dynamics in Africa, warning that socio-economic hardships, pressured national economics, and limited heath care capacities and testing capabilities will present challenges to ensure compliance to interventions to control the virus. The social sciences can add value by understanding these trends and impacts. The prominence of dire economic hardships that will trigger social strife is a key focus. Furthermore, governance and management issues are critical from policy development to ensuring and monitoring compliance. It is important to highlight that the disciplines best positioned to examine these aspects, such as economic and management studies as indicated earlier, are in the social sciences.

The role of health social scientists during this time is also important to highlight. Social scientists informing what are largely thought of as 'science' problems are not new. As the Centre for Research on Evaluation, Science and Technology's (CREST, 2014) bibliometric and survey-based analysis of social sciences in South Africa revealed, there was an increase in research outputs from 1993 to 2012, with the two areas exhibiting the highest growth being social sciences research on climate change and health-related aspects. Reid (2014) also underscored the importance of the 'medical humanities' in health sciences education in South Africa. Reid (2014:109) asserts:

> The humanities and social sciences have always been an implicit part of undergraduate and postgraduate education in the health sciences, but increasingly they are becoming an explicit and essential component of the curriculum, as the importance of graduate attributes and outcomes in the workplace is acknowledged. Traditionally, the medical humanities have included medical ethics, history, literature and anthropology. Less prominent in the literature has been the engagement with medicine of the disciplines of sociology, politics, philosophy, linguistics, education, and law, as well as the creative and expressive arts.

Furthermore, as Auerbach and Hall (2020) state, the uncertainty and disruptions associated with the pandemic reinforces the need for the social sciences whose main purpose is to grapple with the question of "how do we respond to living in a changed world?"

Paterson (2020) and Singh (2020) raise concerns about the composition of the government's Ministerial Advisory Committee (MAC) which is almost exclusively made up of 51 external medical professionals (including academics and researchers), and government ministers and officials who also mainly have medical backgrounds. They argue that the MAC had few individuals with experience and expertise in relation to broader societal impacts which is a major limitation. Singh (2020) notes that multiple revisions of South Africa's lockdown regulations show that the government is responsive to various concerns. Singh (2020), however, indicates that South Africa needs to move beyond a biomedical model in tackling Covid-19, especially in the absence of a vaccine which makes behavioural modification and compliance with rules the main measures to contain the pandemic. This requires the humanities, as well as the social and behavioural sciences to have significant representation on MAC. Similarly, Van Bavel, Baicker, Boggio, Capraro, Cichocka, Cikara, Crockett, Crum, Douglas, Druckman and Drury (2020) argue that because the Covid-19 crisis requires large-scale behavioural change and has substantial psychological burdens on people, valuable insights can be used from the social and behavioural sciences to help align human behaviour with the recommendations from public health experts and the government.

Furthermore, Yucesahin and Sirkeci (2020) caution that migratory and mobility patterns need to be monitored since this is a key mechanism that spreads the virus. The social sciences are needed to understand why people are not complying with lockdown and social distancing regulations, and what measures to use in areas (such as densely populated informal settlements) where social distancing is difficult. These issues will become more important as restrictions ease and to prepare society for future disruptions of this nature.

Messages from health officials have gone out which confuse individuals and which suggests that a mask, sanitising and social distancing can protect you, but there is the element of chance. Poor communities and vulnerable high risks individuals from all sectors of society may process the message as one that suggests that no matter what they do, they may not survive the pandemic. The latter could lead to non-compliance of non-pharmaceutical interventions. Social scientists are aware that messages need to be communicated in a way that provides hope, is realistic and is rational and can explain the "why" of interventions. There is a huge spike in positive cases and the South African Health Minister has recently suggested that a contributing factor is that people are not complying. We have anecdotal evidence that psychologists can assist in understanding the "psychology of non-compliance".

While this chapter has focused on the social sciences, the Covid-19 pandemic and its multidimensional impacts, the importance of multidisciplinary and interdisciplinary research to have a more comprehensive understanding and insights is invaluable. The social sciences are geared towards these types of orientations with many disciplines (such as education, political sciences, anthropology, sociology, psychology, human geography and gender studies) already having a strong tradition of being involved in these types of research and training in quantitative and qualitative methodological approaches. Furthermore, the NIHSS (2020) asserts that epidemiology and public health issues require and benefit from multidisciplinary fields that from the start have been influenced by several social science disciplines. Similar sentiments are expressed by Holmes et al. (2020) who argue that a key multidisciplinary priority for the Covid-19 pandemic is to mobilise expertise to deal with mental health issues. Specifically, they indicate that there is an urgent need for research to examine mental health consequences for vulnerable groups, how these can be mitigated under pandemic conditions, and on the impact of repeated media consumption and health messaging around Covid-19. Furthermore, Paterson (2020) cites Prof Crain Soudien, the Chief Executive Officer of the HSRC, who states that a major academic space has materialised around the "massive and under-theorised interface between hard science and the social sciences, and the extraordinary developments that are taking place in some knowledge fields where new questions are being asked and new frameworks are having to be developed".

Conclusion

Social science in South Africa has a rich history of exposing socio-economic inequalities and engaging in scholar-activist research. It is therefore well positioned to contribute critically to framing issues, responses and impacts during and post the Covid-19 pandemic. Thus, social science knowledge needs to be integrated into research and response efforts to ensure a better understanding of the pandemic. The knowledge is crucial to understand the impacts of both the spread and measures to stop the spread of the virus and the range of socio-economic impacts that may emerge. The lens needs to focus on the migration and mobility of populations, psychological stress and anxiety, and gender injustices. It is crucial for all within the science systems to be prepared to address other forms of conflict and violence in society (with predictions that existing forms will be reinforced, and new forms linked to the pandemic surfacing).

It is also important that in terms of integrating social sciences to deal with the pandemic (including participating in research endeavours) that the discourse should shift from funding to resourcing social sciences research and researchers. This includes developing appropriate low-cost methodologies that retain ethical and academic research integrity, pursue opportunities for skills development, and drawing on existing networks and capacity (and initiative new ones as needed). The entire global research and higher education community are re-thinking current ways of knowledge production and dissemination. Social scientists have been at the forefront of advocating for these changes, including championing transformation, decolonisation and re-curriculation efforts in South Africa. Thus, while the Covid-19 pandemic poses the worst disruptions in recent years, it also presents various opportunities for social scientists and the higher education sector generally.

In South African higher education, we have made certain limited gains in terms of gender justice and as we face and fight the pandemic, we need to ensure that these gains are not eroded by both the pandemic and Gender Based Violence (the pandemic within a pandemic). Staniscuaski, Reichert, Werneck, De Oliveira, Mello-Carpes, Soletti, Almeida, Zandona, Ricachenevsky, Neumann, Schwartz, Tamajusuku, Seixas, Kmetzsch and Parent in Science Movement (2020) argue that women being disadvantaged in science is an issue that needs urgent redress. They make a plea to ensure that women academics across all disciplines are not disadvantaged by what they label 'motherhood penalty', which essentially means all the additional responsibilities like home schooling have fallen on women to oversee during lockdown.

The current moment provides an opportunity for scholars, researchers, policy makers and implementers to work together across disciplinary boundaries to ensure a socially cohesive society. The following sentiment resonates with us:

> Lack of knowledge kills hope ... reasonable hope is sustained by peoples own confidence, as it is based on what they can accomplish if they, as individuals, so will it. Such confidence requires knowledge (Dworkin, 2020).

References

ASSAf. 2011. *Consensus study on the state of the humanities in South Africa: Status, prospects and strategies.* Pretoria: ASSAf.

Auerbach, J. & Hall, N. 2020. *A new approach to social sciences, humanities in a time of crisis.* University World News. Available at: https://bit.ly/3u2xekE [Accessed 21 June 2020].

CREST. 2014. *Mapping social sciences research in South Africa.* Stellenbosch University: CREST.

DHET. 2020. Report on the evaluation of the 2018 universities' research output. Pretoria: DHET.

DST. 2012. *Final report of the Ministerial Review Committee on the science, technology and innovation landscape in South Africa.* Pretoria: DST.

Dworkin, R.W. 2020. *To beat Covid-19, science needs the humanities.* The American Interest. Available at: https://bit.ly/31pYsFw [Accessed 23 June 2020].

Fitzpatrick, K. & Kennison, R. 2017. *Altmetrics in humanities and social sciences.* Available at: http://doi.org/10.17613/M6MW28D5J [Accessed 19 June 2020].

Flaherty, C. 2020. *No room for new ones.* Washington, DC: Inside Higher Ed. Available at: https://bit.ly/3syjVbn [Accessed 23 June 2020].

Holmes, E.A., O'Connor, R.C., Perry, V.H., Tracey, I., Wessely, S., Arseneault, L., Ballard, C., Christensen, H., Silver, R.C., Everall, I. & Ford, T. 2020. Multidisciplinary research priorities for the Covid-19 pandemic: A call for action for mental health science. *The Lancet Psychiatry*, 7:547-560. https://doi.org/10.1016/S2215-0366(20)30168-1

Li, J. & Li, Y. 2015. Patterns and evolution of co-authorship in China's humanities and social sciences. *Scientometrics*, 102(3):1997-2010. https://doi.org/10.1007/s11192-014-1471-8

Molotja, N. & Ralphs, G. 2018. A critical review of social sciences and humanities R&D expenditure in South Africa, 2005-2014. *South African Journal of Science*, 114(7/8):1-7. http://doi.org/10.17159/sajs.2018/20170407

Moodley, K., Obasa, A.E. & London, L. 2020. Isolation and quarantine in South Africa during Covid-19: Draconian measures or proportional response? *South African Medical Journal*, 110(6):1-2. https://doi.org/10.7196/SAMJ.2020v110i6.14842

Mouton, J. 2011. The humanities and social sciences in SA: Crisis or cause for concern? *South African Journal of Science*, 107(11-12):1-4. https://doi.org/10.4102/sajs.v107i11/12.961

NIHSS. 2020. *NIHSS calls for a social science response to Covid-19.* Available at: https://bit.ly/2QGyhZ7 [Accessed 21 June 2020].

Oosthuizen, M. 2018. *Counting women's work in South Africa. Incorporating unpaid work into estimates of the economic lifecycle in 2010.* Cape Town, Development Policy Research Unit: University of Cape Town.

Paterson, M. 2020. *Covid-19 response – Where are the social scientists?* University World News. Available at: https://bit.ly/2PCKWfn [Accessed 21 June 2020].

Potgieter, C., Bob, U. & Sooryamoorty, R. 2016. *Assessing the environment for social science research in developing countries: The case of South Africa.* Delhi: Global Development Network.

Pozzan, E & Cattaneo, U. 2020. *Women health workers: Working relentlessly in hospitals and at home.* Geneva: International Labour Organisation. Available at: https://bit.ly/3srPDqK [Accessed 24 June 2020].

Reddy, S.P., Sewpaul, R., Mabaso, M., Parker, S., Naidoo, I., Jooste, S., Mokhele, T., Sifunda, S. & Zuma, K. 2020. South Africans' understanding of and response to the Covid-19 Outbreak: An online survey. *South African Medical Journal*, 110(9):894-902.

Reid, S. 2014. The 'medical humanities' in health sciences education in South Africa. *South African Medical Journal*, 104(2):109-110. https://doi.org/10.7196/samj.7928

Schröder, M., Bossert, A., Kersting, M., Aeffner, S., Coetzee, J., Timme, M. & Schlüter, J. 2020. *Covid-19 in Africa: Outbreak despite interventions?* Yale: MedRxiv. https://doi.org/10.1101/2020. 04.24.20077891

Singh, J.A. 2020. How South Africa's Ministerial Advisory Committee on Covid-19 can be optimised. *South African Medical Journal*, 110(6):439-442. https://doi.org/10.7196/SAMJ.2020v110i5.14820

Staniscuaski, F., Reichert, F., Werneck, F.P., De Oliveira, L., Mello-Carpes, P.B., Soletti, R.C., Almeida, C.I., Zandona, E., Ricachenevsky, F.P., Neumann, A., Schwartz, I.V.D., Tamajusuku, A.S.K., Seixas, A., Kmetzsch, L. & Parent in Science Movement. 2020. Parent in Science Movement. Impact of Covid-19 on academic mothers. *Science*, 368(6492):724. https://doi.org/10.1126/science.abc2740

Turquet, L. & Koissy-Kpein, S. 2020. *Covid-19 and gender: What do we know; what do we not know? New York: UN Women*. Available at: https://bit.ly/39ngooO [Accessed 23 June 2020].

Van Bavel, J.J., Baicker, K., Boggio, P.S., Capraro, V., Cichocka, A., Cikara, M., Crockett, M.J., Crum, A.J., Douglas, K.M., Druckman, J.N. & Drury, J. 2020. Using social and behavioural science to support Covid-19 pandemic response. *Nature Human Behaviour*, 1-12. https://doi.org/10.31234/osf.io/y38m9

Van Rooyen, H & Zulu, N. 2018. *Navigating the academy: The perspectives of black women academics as narrated in journal articles*. Pretoria: Human Sciences Research Council. Available at: https://bit.ly/3w4pDE1 [Accessed 23 June 2020].

Viglione, G. 2020. *Are women publishing less during the pandemic? Here's what the data say. New York: Nature Research*. Available at: https://go.nature.com/2PFBbNd [Accessed 23 June 2020].

Wolhuter, C. & Chigisheva, O. 2020. New thematic and methodological research focus in the social sciences and the humanities: The BRICS countries grouping. *Space and Culture, India*, 7(5):1-2. https://doi.org/10.20896/saci.v7i5.606

World Health Organisation. 2019. *Delivered by women, led by men: A gender and equity analysis of global health and social workforce*. Geneva: Human Resources for Health Observer Series no. 24. Available at: https://bit.ly/3sxb2Ps [Accessed 24 June 2020].

Yucesahin, M.M. & Sirkeci, I. 2020. Coronavirus and migration: Analysis of human mobility and the spread of Covid-19. *Migration Letters*, 17(2):379-398. https://doi.org/10.33182/ml.v17i2.935

10

THE ROLE OF AFRICAN HIGHER EDUCATION INSTITUTIONS IN DRIVING A COVID-19 RESPONSE THROUGH INNOVATION TECHNOLOGIES

Linda Linganiso and Nobathembu Faleni

Introduction

The epidemic of the coronavirus disease 2019 (Covid-19), originating in Wuhan, China, has become a major public health challenge for not only China, but also countries around the world. While the early transmission appeared to affect China, South Korea, much of western Europe, and the United States, the virus is now spreading rapidly across the African continent, presenting a major threat to already-stressed health systems. When the World Health Organisation (WHO) declared the Covid-19 pandemic to be a Public Health Emergency of International Concern on 30 January 2020, countries around the globe were prompted to make means to prepare. Preparation for Covid-19 was difficult, more especially in developing countries such as the African countries. Not all African countries were well equipped with appropriate diagnostic kits and Personal Protective Equipment (PPE) to handle the pandemic so WHO became concerned. WHO, realising the challenge, identified 13 top-priority countries; Algeria, Angola, Cote d'Ivoire, the Democratic Republic of the Congo, Ethiopia, Ghana, Kenya, Mauritius, Nigeria, South Africa, Tanzania, Uganda, as well as Zambia which have direct connections to China.

Over the last decade, 87% of the continent has had at least one epidemic (Kapata, Ihekweazu, Ntoumi, Raji, Chanda-Kapata & Mwaba, 2020). West Africa experienced an Ebola epidemic outbreak between 2014 and 2016 (Out, Ameh, Osifo-Dawodu, Alade,

Ekuri & Idris, 2017). Due to previous experience with an Ebola epidemic outbreak, significant improvements in digital technology, as well as clinical and laboratory capacity across the African continent were observed. The challenges included the lack of diagnostic equipment, as well as strategies to flatten the curve.[1] We hope that the 2020 pandemic will give rise to improved technologies, increasing digital technology innovations, as well as entrepreneurship in higher education institutions. And the students will learn to create and tackle every challenge which perplexes the world today. Our focus in this chapter will be ground-breaking innovations from the African countries from Higher Education Institutions (HEIs).

Through a desk study via Google Scholar, using keywords such as Covid-19, Africa, higher education, innovation, and technology, this chapter discusses how innovation technologies can drive Africa's response to Covid-19 by mirroring the role of higher education. By reviewing relevant literature sources, documents and news items, the chapter examines the readiness of the higher education sector in South Africa by focusing on the status quo and how the sector has been handling Covid-19 related issues. The chapter also addresses the response of academics to the shift and the preparedness of South African institutions in order to capacitate academic staff members. The challenges and response strategies of the HEIs in the current spectrum are also discussed and recommendations are provided.

HEIs in South Africa: Status quo and sector readiness

HEIs are expected to change due to external factors such as:
1. socio-economic issues,
2. political & economic issues and (Fraser 1997), and
3. globalisation (Fraser 1997, 2000 and 2003).

Internal factors driving the change include:
1. policy makers and
2. standardised curriculum.

These changes encouraged the academics to embrace a learning society in all aspects. It was also crucial to implement both formal and informal ways of teaching and establish collaborative projects in order to create a platform for students to exchange practical and theoretical knowledge abroad and encourage the learners to be innovative. Due to the aforementioned factors, the world is transitioning towards a knowledge economy.[2] The HEIs in response to both internal and external

---

1   A public health strategy to slow down the spread of Covid-19.
2   An economy where growth is determined by the quantity, quality and accessibility of available information instead of the means of production.

factors have now focused on development of technology innovations. In the past, the HEIs used to only focus on traditional learning approaches and basic research at technology readiness level one (Figure 10.1). Socio-economic, political, and economic issues have redirected the focus of the academics towards generating new commercial products (Fraser 1997, 2000, 2003 & Mowery 2005). Research and development conducted in academic institutions must be redesigned in such a way that the research begins from basic level, Technology Readiness Level 1 (TRL1), and escalates through other levels to TRL9. And the resulting innovative products must be sold in local and international markets. Technology readiness levels (TRLs) are a method for estimating the maturity of technologies during the acquisition phase of a program, developed by National Aeronautics and Space Administration (NASA) in the 1970s. The use of TRLs enables consistent, uniform discussions of technical maturity across different types of technology. A technology's TRL is determined during a Technology Readiness Assessment (TRA) that examines programme concepts, technology requirements, and demonstrated technology capabilities. TRLs are based on a scale from 1 to 9 with 9 being the most mature technology.

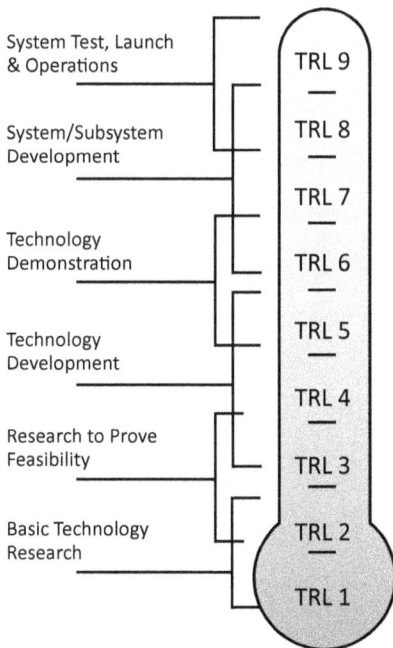

Figure 10.1   Heder (2017) Technology readiness level (TRL)

This approach to research encourages generation and commercialisation of patents which is essential for the economic growth of the country (Hawkins, Langford & Sidhu 2007). Tech transfer officers assist in technology transfer operations. Academic institutions have a tech transfer officer to channels these transactions. The institutions are also encouraged to establish spin-off companies to generate the third stream of income in line with the National Development Plan. Currently, the University of Cape Town (UCT) and Stellenbosch University (SU) have established several spin-off companies in response to this change and we expect other universities to also transition towards knowledge economy as it is essential for economic growth in South Africa.

Public academic institutions are funded by big corporations such as the World Bank. External drivers to the change include initiatives set up by United Nations Environmental Program (UNEP), Millennium Development Goals, Africa Agenda 2063, as well as the 17 Global Sustainable Developmental Goals, to name but a few. The national priorities are shaping the research focus areas in the academic space. The academic staff members are required to identify the "niche areas" which are priority sectors in South African government, write proposals and secure funding for creative projects (McMeekin, Green, Tomlinson & Walsh 2002). Areas of focus include Fourth Industrial Revolution (4IR) topics, data modelling projects, bioeconomy initiatives, renewable energy, climate change, waste beneficiation, water scarcity, HIV-AIDS, big data management and other health related projects.

In addition, the South African government has also established agencies to encourage the academics including the researchers to focus on specific areas of research. The agencies do this in the form of competition for funding, which only funds directed and relevant research to drive the outcomes towards the targeted areas of research. To secure funds, academics are required to pitch ideas in writing and verbally in line with South African government priorities. Several funding agencies and incubation programmes to assist academics and students are, but not limited to the following:
1. Technology Innovation Agency (TIA) for SMMEs
2. Department of Science and Innovation (DSI)
3. Global CleanTech Innovation Program (GCIP)
4. Leaders in Innovation Fellowship (LIF)
5. Transnet Enterprise Development Hub
6. Red Bull Amaphiko Academy
7. Aurik Business Accelerator
8. The Techstars Foundation
9. Anglo's Zimele
10. Shanduka Black Umbrellas
11. SEDA Ekurhuleni Base Metals Incubation Programme, etc.

Exhibition programmes such as Innovation Bridge and trade conferences are hosted in South Africa to help academics showcase their products for marketing and to attract investors. These platforms are made available to both scholars and the private sector with the mission to drive the country towards income generation. The approach is mandated to train the younger generation to create sustainable income/jobs, as well as establish a profitable Small, Medium and Micro Enterprise (SMME). To be quite honest, academics are under increasing pressure to respond to the rapidly changing market environment. The unique growth, complicacy, and competitiveness of the global economy along with its consequential socio-political changes have been placing pressure on HEIs to adopt market-oriented initiatives. As the anointing flows from the head to the tail, academic staff must be well trained and prepared for the workforce.

The response of academics to the shift and the preparedness of South African institutions to capacitate the academic staff

Target skills and competency are now required in order to build and develop highly skilled human capital. As much as this will bring the academics under pressure, they must adjust to accommodate the change. Bilateral collaborative projects with developed countries, such as the United States and the European Union, as well as developing countries, such as China and India, are some of the approaches academics must embrace to build and develop highly skilled human capital. Such collaborations will allow exchange programmes where the learners are sent abroad to broaden their perspectives and exchange knowledge.

Global economy, the new managerialism[3] and corporatism[4] on institutional structures put the academics under pressure and the academics were obliged to comply. For example, the impact of globalisation has stimulated the academic institutions to transition towards entrepreneurial economy for the purpose of generating profit. The HEIs have adopted the strategy in order to help the university to generate the third stream of income. The higher education system adopts the principles emanating from the corporate world in response to the external factors such as changes in economic spheres. HEIs are aggressively engaged in the knowledge-based economy and the academics continue to analyse the efforts of the institutions to develop, market, and sell research products, educational services, and consumer goods in the private marketplace.

Managerialism allows the staff members in the academic space to shift towards an entrepreneurial culture. Government entities, such as the Technology Innovation Agency, have been indirectly used to encourage the academics to innovate in a competitive manner in order to drive this theory. Innovative projects whose TRL is

---

3   The reliance on the use of professional managers in administering or planning an activity.
4   The control of an institution by large interest groups.

closer to technology demonstration or prototypes development are often funded. There is an organised consortium in place to drive and implement South African government concern from the funding entities to the academic management. Managerialism is a great initiative as it also teaches the students to learn to translate research and development findings into new products for commercialisation. However, the value of academics is affected by the institutional changes taking place. As this seems like a beautiful initiative, providing the academics with better opportunities, they are also facing increasing student enrolment due to increasing demands for higher education and expansion of the sector.

Academic institutions are taking the entrepreneurial side of things in a post-industrial economy; they focus on knowledge less as a public good than as a commodity to be capitalised on in profit-oriented activities. This theory also allows changes in policy and practice, revealing new social networks and circuits of knowledge creation and dissemination, as well as new organisational structures and expanded managerial capacity to link HEIs and markets.

Changes in the academic space due to academic capitalism, managerialism, as well as corporatism are as follows:

1. There was a significant increase in the national student enrolment which resulted in increased workloads.
2. The workload of the academic staff teaching undergraduate studies was significantly increased as opposed to those supervising master's and PhD students.
3. There were observed changes in the academic profession as the academic staff were forced to take duties related to administration and management.
4. The academic institutions rely heavily on hiring staff on a part-time basis. The idea behind hiring academic staff on a part-time basis is the need to save costs. In addition, the students, master's and PhD, are given departmental duties, to serve respective departments eight hours every week to balance the rising workload due to political and economic factors. Key Performance Indicators (KPI) have changed drastically in response to these external factors. Conformity seems like the best approach. We will then learn to deal with uncertainties, overcome and prevail.
5. The workload also affects the research outputs and therefore the academic profile. It was however reported that the young academic staff feel the effect more as they are tasked to teach the undergraduate students. The effect is less significant with regards to senior lecturers and professors as they are mainly tasked to supervise master's and PhD students. One's career development takes time as a result. So, most academic staff prefer the supervision of post-graduate students as opposed to teaching undergraduates as the demand and pressure in terms of planning and administration continues to increase.
6. The standards and the quality in terms of supervision and teaching are therefore compromised as the number of students increases and therefore there is a need for manpower. The line managers also put pressure on the academic staff members to improve the pass rates.

HEIs challenges and responses

The HEI with the aid of local universities has reflected on the impact of the Covid-19 pandemic and has devised tools which activate magnificent digital transformation in education. The study pursues the 4IR tools that were implemented by various institutions. The concept of 4IR tools introduced in this study are technological innovations that are meant to serve specific purposes by reducing incidents of human error and operational disruptions, especially within the context of Covid-19. The admission of students to higher education has been a challenge in South Africa, due to limited number of spaces and funding provided. This pandemic has intensified human suffering in the world. This has offered an opportunity in increasing and presenting successful practice of technologies, outlays, and improvement of these technologies (World Economic Forum, 2016).

These technologies (4IR) represent the latest ways of learning which involves being introduced to our society and our human nature. Teaching and learning is expected to be a face-to-face interaction with students and teachers. In the unforeseen circumstances, such as this Covid-19 pandemic, teaching and learning activities were disrupted and turned to digital learning. The students in higher institutions were required to incorporate distance education which does not require teachers and learners to be in the same classroom. The learners were expected to do self-learning. The teaching and learning materials are offered online using platforms such as Microsoft Teams, Zoom, Skype and WhatsApp. Data has been a challenge in African HEIs, and research facilities are scarce. Zero-rated data was provided for students through different network coverages, but this was also a challenge. The national financial aid assistance provided student with laptops to facilitate teaching and learning.

The above-mentioned learning platforms have increased access to digital content and continuous assessment activities are conducted in supporting curriculum delivery with Information and Communications Technology (ICT) facilities. This pandemic has transformed teaching modes in the education sector. The pandemic has influenced all education sectors in South Africa to use various 4IR tools. The delays in learning were experienced in rural areas in which data and computers must be provided to students. The Walter Sisulu University (WSU) in the Eastern Cape, South Africa is a historically black disadvantaged institution that experienced challenges with online learning as no systems were active. The laptops for students and lecturers must be arranged for learning to continue. The distribution of laptops for students was funded by the National Student Financial Aid Scheme (NSFAS). Collection of the laptops was a challenge as many of the students are from deep rural areas.

The university was working with local police stations and the nearest schools for collection of the laptops and students were notified. The data is sent through their cell phones for learning and teaching to occur. A technical task team was formed which is pioneering the project. The experienced lectures in online teaching are working together with ICT. The staff members were trained in online teaching and learning, including how to upload study materials for students. A research and innovation team could not be formed at this institution as there is a lack of resources and structure. The lack of funding has limited researchers creating and implementing new ideas/technologies that would benefit society. These technologies will bridge the lines between InfoTech and biotechnology. The novel coronavirus has swept around the continent affecting millions of citizens. The authorities in health, scientists and innovators have rushed into discovering ways to minimise the spread of the virus. The universities contribute a part in preventing and regulating this virus by being part of innovation teams which could devise tools for assisting our society and creating long-lasting healthcare systems.

The African universities in higher education also took part in online learning. The colleges in Ghana were operative in making sure e-learning programmes continue smoothly. However, some students in the Gambaga College of Education would walk two kilometres to attend classes due to lack of accommodation on campus. They have experienced challenges with online learning such as poor internet connectivity, irregular power outages which disrupt synchronous lessons and damaged electronic gadgets when power is active again. The Makerere University in Uganda faced similar challenges as other education institutions in Africa. The different online programmes are continuing, though not yet successful. The research and innovation unit are focused on immunity responses and their implications in the prevention of Covid-19 infections. The social and economic structure of the world has suffered, and the United Nations Secretary General has highlighted that Covid-19 is the worst global crisis since World War II. The Covid-19 pandemic not only affects health issues, it is also a contributing factor in disrupting learning, cultural and economic accomplishments.

In response to the lockdowns and the challenges of responding to the pandemic, the innovative use of technology and new ways of working in health and other non-health sectors are being piloted. For instance, drones are being used to transport test kits and samples from hard-to-reach areas, thus reducing the sample transport time from many hours to minutes; there is a boom in locally manufactured face masks; an explosion of locally produced soap and hand sanitisers; and training, meetings, and workshops have moved online. Many governments have realised the need to improve hazard payments and provide insurance for staff on the frontline of the infection. African businesses have teamed up to donate in cash and kind to support country efforts, such as the $70 million donated by a coalition in Nigeria.

Technology has shown the potential to drive the response to the pandemic in different ways from the rise of e-Health, Telehealth, Telemedicine, mHealth, e-learning, robotics, drones, etc. This subsection focuses on technologies deployed to ease the response against Covid-19 in different sectors across the African continent, in higher education and the private sector. Besides innovations, Africa has seen the paced adoption of some technologies, which were not mostly used before Covid-19. Through a desk study which involves the collation of information already available mainly on the internet, an overview of how different universities developed technology innovations to combat Covid-19 is outlined below:

e-learning

South African universities have implemented multi-faceted solutions including the adoption of e-learning as an appropriate alternative since the banning of contact learning, boosting the pace of future classrooms, which are virtual but more efficient. The most-reported challenge with e-learning across South African universities has been technological readiness, especially those in rural areas, which includes connectivity issues and lack of electronic devices for students. Various measures, including the distribution of electronic devices and internet service provision to students were taken to accommodate students with various backgrounds through this technological transformation in the higher education sector.

Artificial intelligence and big data

Big data, one of the major 4IR technologies, has gained more applications during the pandemic to collect, process, analyse and interpret Covid-19 related data, and to help generate heatmaps, trace contacts and make useful projections for experts to advise relevant authorities and communities. Certain universities, like Nelson Mandela University (NMU) have implemented projects specifically focusing on this (NMU, 2020). The modelling of viral activity studies and guiding of policymakers are highly assisted by big data-analytics. Deep learning and Artificial Intelligence enhance the diagnosis and detection of Covid-19. This is important as some African countries do not have tests and resources to accurately distinguish between common flu and Covid-19 (Ting, Carin, Dzau & Wong, 2020).

3D printing

Some companies, universities and government institutes use 3D printing to print medical equipment, face masks and PPE. The Durban University of Technology (DUT), Central University of Technology (CUT), NMU, UCT and North-West University (NWU) are among the South African universities who either already have prototypes and are undertaking research projects on its potential use to curb the Covid-19 pandemic or are currently producing medical equipment using 3D printing. The materials printed include face masks, face shields, PPE, autoclavable swabs, and oxygen connectors to aid large scale manufacturing processes, oxygen splitters, valves for Continuous Positive Airway Pressure (CPAP) and Bilevel Positive Airway Pressure (BiPAP) functionality, etc. (Universities South Africa, 2020). Durban University of Technology (DUT) already has raw materials for 3D printing of their respective medical equipment. Two hospitals have reviewed over 20 face shield prototypes produced by the University of Djibouti using 3D printing and laser cutters, with their government already benefiting from their supplies, respectively (Africa Renewal, 2020).

Self-sanitising mask (South Africa, Uganda)

The masks that are widely used physically minimise the number of exhaled droplets reaching surrounding individuals, objects or surfaces. Researchers at North West University (NWU) are designing masks that can deactivate viruses on contact using anti-viral chemicals built into the masks that sanitise passing respiratory droplets, minimising the number of viruses in the droplets exhaled by an infected wearer, and consequently protecting anyone around. Students at Makerere University, Uganda have also developed a self-sanitising face mask.

In addition, experts at Central University of Technology (CUT) in the Free State contributed their innovation in fighting the Covid-19 pandemic. The university contributed towards protective equipment demand and designed a non-invasive ventilation helmet/mask. The ventilation masks were produced and certified through the Centre for Rapid Prototyping and Manufacturing (CRPM), the Product Development Technology Stations (PDTS), and the Centre on Quality of Health and Living (CQHL) and CUT Innovation Services (CUTIS).

Ventilator unit (Ghana, Kenya, Somali, South Africa, Zimbabwe)

Uganda are modelling the Covid-19 pandemic to organise and intervene with environmental studies and sampling for public health at risk. They have discovered a low-cost ventilator using an open-source design collaborating with the University of Florida. The Kenyatta University in Kenya with vibrant researchers responded to

Covid-19 innovation by building a mechanical ventilator that assists patients that have difficulty breathing. It operates in two modes, Intermittent Positive Pressure Ventilation (IPPV) mode for patients who cannot breathe on their own and Synchronised Intermittent Mandatory Ventilation (SIMV) mode to assist patients who can breathe on their own but cannot acquire sufficient volumes of oxygen. The machine comprises pressure sensors, flow sensors and oxygen sensors to monitor and regulate the respective parameters based on the settings. The Harare Institute of Technology in Zimbabwe also manufactured a prototype of an oxygen ventilator unit which is currently undertaking clinical tests, to serve as a first response unit for less critical cases to address the shortage of Intensive Care Units ventilators.

The Jomo Kenyatta University of Agriculture in Kenya added another contribution by inventing two portable solar powered ventilators, which uses 12 voltage batteries with contact tracing applications. A team from the Academic City University College in Ghana has developed a mechanical ventilator prototype, while a Somalian engineer developed a home-made respirator with autonomous ventilators (PLOS, 2020). The students of NMU and the Engineering Design Group also invented the intubation units. The ventilators were delivered to the Anaesthesiology staff at Livingstone Hospital, a local hospital in Port Elizabeth. This assisted in minimising the tension experienced by the local hospital because of shortages of ventilation systems. It could be argued that Covid-19 revealed hidden potential going by the many technology innovations devised by African researchers to respond to the pandemic.

Mobile payments (Ghana, Kenya, Nigeria)

As banknotes may be spreading the virus, technologies that minimise the physical exchange of money have received recommendation and adoption in some African countries as part of the measures to curb the spread of Covid-19 (Shahbaz, Bilal, Moiz, Zubair & Iqbal, 2020). Kenya and Ghana are two of the first African countries to turn to mobile money. The Bank of Ghana, mobile money operators, and other banks agreed to promote digital payment platforms for more efficient payments (Bank of Ghana, 2020). Safaricom, the largest Kenyan telecommunications provider, implemented a fee-waiver on M-Pesa, the leading mobile-money product in East Africa, for person-to-person transactions under 1 000 Kenyan Schillings (TechCrunch, 2020). The President of Kenya, Uhuru Kenyatta, pleaded with banks "to explore ways of deepening mobile-money usage to reduce the risk of spreading the virus through physical handling of cash" (TechCrunch, 2020). Paga, a mobile money company based in Nigeria with over 15 million users, lowered fees in response to a call to minimise cash exchange (Thomson Reuters Foundation, 2020).

Telehealth, e-Health, mHealth, telemedicine (Ghana, Nigeria, South Africa, Uganda)

Widespread national lockdowns have impacted the accessibility of health services, leading to the high adoption of digital health technologies to deliver health information to patients. Telehealth modalities such as teleconsultation, telepsychiatry, call centres and smartphone health information sharing have increased across the continent since the Covid-19 pandemic (Kamulegeya, Bwanika, Musinguzi & Bakibinga, 2020). E-Health, telehealth, m-Health and telemedicine minimise doctor/physician-patient visits and utilise efficient means to share Covid-19 related information, such as Short Messaging Services (SMSes), smartphones, apps and the internet. South Africa and Uganda are some of the many countries that have adopted this transformation. Redbird, a Ghanaian e-health startup, provides epidemiologists with data for Covid-19 contact tracing in real-time. The platform collects user data when users report their symptoms and it instantly tags the user location and contact number. Identified potential cases are mapped and sent to hospitals for records and triage (PLOS, 2020). Two UCT alumni developed an app, Coronapp, to provide users with reliable information about Covid-19 in South Africa to help prevent unnecessary panic (Thomson Reuters Foundation, 2020).

The development and adoption of smart digital solutions plays a crucial role in efficiently responding to the pandemic in different ways, including mobile apps, AI-powered e-health assistants and chatbots. The mobile apps deployed allow health professionals to communicate with patients through Video Observational Therapy (VOT) which plays an important role in enhancing social distancing and pace the adoption of e-health, and mHealth, across the continent (University of Zululand, 2020).

Monitoring, surveillance, and detection (Nigeria, South Africa)

A free online Covid-19 Triage Tool, developed by a Nigerian company, Wellvis, uses users' disclosed symptoms and their exposure history to assess their coronavirus risk. The user then receives remote medical advice or is directed to a nearby healthcare facility. The platform has helped to drop the number of curious callers. South Africa uses a WhatsApp service, which runs an interactive chatbot that provides answers to common Covid-19 related myths, symptoms, treatment, and stats (World Economic Forum, 2020). These tools form part of e-health and m-health, which also plays a crucial role in responses to the Covid-19 pandemic across the continent. Internet of Things (IoT) platforms, such as Worldometer, have been used to allow public health authorities to access data to monitor the Covid-19 pandemic more efficiently.

Worldometer gives access to real-time updates on Covid-19 related statistics worldwide, such as daily new cases and distribution by countries (United Cities and Local Governments, 2020).

Testing (Ghana, Nigeria, Senegal, South Africa)

Countries have scaled up molecular testing progressively across the continent for Covid-19 testing, with the likes of South Africa and Nigeria leveraging and scaling up the diagnostic capacities currently used for certain diseases such as HIV, Lassa fever and drug-resistant Tuberculosis. Ghana addresses the shortage of diagnostic reagents by pioneering pooled testing, which is faster and increases population coverage (Ihekweazu & Agogo, 2020). Researchers at the Pasteur Institute in Dakar, Senegal are developing a 10-minute testing kit for potential use across the continent. They collaborated with a British company, Mologic, to develop a saliva swab test and a finger prick test for identifying previous exposure to non-infected people (The World, 2020).

Sanitisers

Hand sanitisers have the highest demand in the continent with many private and government institutions producing their sanitisers. South African universities currently producing or undertaking projects on the production of sanitisers involve NMU, CUT, Rhodes University, Tshwane University of Technology (TUT), University of Johannesburg (UJ) and University of Cape Town.

In addition, Kenya has developed a digital system which predicts Covid-19 infections and an automatic solar-powered hand washing machine. The materials to manufacture these innovations were brought from local equipment suppliers. The material is reliable and can operate for two weeks without maintenance. Another group of students devised a Contact Tracing and Case Management app that identifies where and when a person gets into contact with a Covid-19 positive person. Also, another student developed Rona, an AI solution that responds to Covid-19 pandemic inquiries (IEEE Entrepreneurship, 2020).

CUT responded and accepted the call from WHO to increase their manufacturing of protective wear (masks) by 40% in order to assist the government with protecting human lives against the spread of Covid-19 globally. Currently, patients, healthcare workers, doctors and frontline workers depend on PPE against infection of the life-threatening disease (IEEE Entrepreneurship, 2020).

The hand sanitisers in KwaZulu Natal, approximately about 1 000 litres, have been supplied and produced by DUT. The pioneer of the project emphasised that FastSan uses 80% ethanol as opposed to other sanitisers that contain 70% ethanols. A humectant moisturiser is added to prevent drying of hands. Hydrogen peroxide is added to sterilise the bottles and sanitiser.

Face shield and oxygen machine

Additional PPE is needed and should be increased in production. Face shields are manufactured at TUT to assist medical staff in the Tshwane district. The different staff members have formed a team to produce these protective wears and donated them to local hospitals in the region, such as Kalafong Hospital. A CUT team manufactured an additional oxygen connector, referred to as a "Christmas tree connector". It has a two-way splitter with an added safety feature that ensures the pipe does not dislodge from an oxygen machine. The oxygen machine is needed for admitted patients in need of an additional oxygen supply due to Covid-19 related complications.

The research unit producing Covid-19 testing materials and prototypes positions South African scientists in global biotech innovation. The reliable reagents material must be accessed locally to produce research material, which are safe, reliable and strengthen product market and cooperation globally in fighting pandemics and saving lives. The expansion of locally researched projects will be effective in applications far beyond this current virus. The students' exposure and experience in partnering with local and global market environments develop critical understanding of what is needed in society (real life) and encourages the application of theoretical knowledge. The National Ventilator Project led by the government to produce medical goods assist students in entailing these skills. The ventilator prototype is a required health item and as the number of positive cases increase, so do the number of patients who need ventilators.

The interactive app which provides real time data on Covid-19 infections, including number of people infected, recovered or those that have passed away, was invented. This was done in affiliation with WHO and the Centres for Disease Control and Prevention in the United States of America, via GitHub, which uses an online repository tracker. The Centre for Epidemiological Modelling and Analysis from SU, in collaboration with researchers at the London School for Hygiene and Tropical Medicine, developed models to evaluate the spread of Covid-19 in African countries. The model predicts which countries will encounter cases between 1 000 and 10 000 when not adhering to the measures taken for minimising the spread of Covid-19.

The University of Witwatersrand (Wits) has performed tests in tracking, modelling, and testing for the virus. The National Institute for Communicable Diseases and WHO collaborated with the university to develop an intuitive and interactive dashboard to track and model the spread of the virus based on information provided, such as demographic information and cases of the various transmission routes. The dashboard shows a day-by-day account of the tests and recorded infections and variations in the data by province.

Concluding remarks

In response to the challenges posed by the Covid-19 pandemic, innovative use of technology and new ways of working in HEIs and in the Department of Health are being piloted. Drones are being used to transport test kits and samples from rural areas, thus reducing the sample transportation time. University students on the African continent have been driving the development of technology. Innovation from mechanical ventilators to medical equipment, PPEs, face masks, sanitisers, as well as smart digital solutions to boost online trading and facilitate online learning for higher education students. It is the argument of this chapter that innovative technologies could help control the spread of Covid-19 as we have seen in the efforts of HEIs in combatting the virus. In countries such as South Africa, Nigeria, Uganda and Ghana, certain innovative measures have been established and it is the recommendation of this chapter that HEIs in South Africa should invest heavily in technological innovations that will gradually lead to the end of the Covid-19 insurgence. Importantly, future research could dwell on aspects of innovation not mentioned in the chapter and how such innovative ideas contribute to the fight against Covid-19.

Health authorities, policymakers, scientists, and innovators in Africa are racing to invent ways to contain the further spread of the virus. Innovative technologies and connectivity are critical keys to fight the novel coronavirus disease on the African continent. Advanced machine learning models present solutions for data management from areas where data has been historically difficult or impossible to access in Africa. Digital technology has been used to help businesses boost online trade, build intelligent networks to support agriculture and food chain delivery, practice online medical consultancy, carry out online job searches and provide contactless loans to SMMEs. With ground-breaking university innovations, including autonomous robots to help deliver care and services, a steriliser that removes up to 99.99% of different infectious viruses, creative solutions to screen pupils for Covid-19 using cell phones and more, the ideal technological response to tackle the insurgence of the coronavirus is just on its way.

References

Africa Renewal. 2020. *Digital space for migrants supplies 3D-printed face shields to hospitals treating Covid-19 cases in Djibouti*. Available at: https://bit.ly/31qUuMX (Accessed 11 June 2020).

Bank of Ghana. 2020. *Monetary policy committee press release*. Available at: https://bit.ly/2QMaEyx (Accessed 21 July 2020).

Ebenso, B. & Out, A. 2020. Can Nigeria contain the Covid-19 outbreak using lessons from recent epidemics? *Correspondence*, 8(6):E770. https://doi.org/10.1016/S2214-109X(20)30101-7

Fraser, N. 1997. *Justice interruptus: Critical reflections on the 'postsocialist' condition*. London: Routledge.

Fraser, N. 2000. Rethinking recognition. *New Left Review*, 3:107-20.

Fraser, N. 2003. Social justice in the age of identity politics: Redistribution, recognition and participation. In: N. Fraser & A. Honneth (eds.), *Redistribution or recognition? A Political-Philosophical Exchange*. London: Verso, 7-109.

Gray, L. 2018. Exploring how and why young people use social networking sites. *Educational Psychology in Practice*, 34(2):175-194. https://doi.org/10.1080/02667363.2018.1425829

Hawkins, R.W., Langford, C.H. & Sidhu, K.S. 2007. *Science, technology, and innovation indicators in a changing world: Responding to policy needs*. Ottawa: OECD Publishing.

Heder, M. 2017. From NASA to EU: The evolution of the TRL scale in public sector innovation. *The Innovation Journal*, 22:1-23.

IEEE Entrepreneurship. 2020. *Kenyatta university students innovate ventilator in response to Covid-19*. Available at: https://bit.ly/3fnKHiP (Accessed 3 June 2020).

Ihekweazu, C. & Agogo, E. 2020. Africa's response to Covid-19. *BMC Medicine*, 18(151):1-3. https://doi.org/10.1186/s12916-020-01622

Kamulegeya, L.H., Bwanika, J.M., Musinguzi, D. & Bakibinga, P. 2020. Continuity of health service delivery during the Covid-19 pandemic: The role of digital health technologies in Uganda. *The Pan African Medical Journal*, 35(2):43-46. https://doi.org/10.11604/pamj.supp.2020.35.2.23115

Kapata, N., Ihekweazu, C., Ntoumi, F., Raji, T., Chanda-Kapata, P. & Mwaba, P. 2020. Is Africa prepared for tackling the Covid-19 (SARS-CoV-2) epidemic. Lessons from past outbreaks, ongoing pan-African public health efforts, and implications for the future. *International Journal of Infectious Diseases*, 93:233-236. https://doi.org/10.1016/j.ijid.2020.02.049

McMeekin, A., Green, K., Tomlinson, M. & Walsh, V. 2002. *Innovation by demand: An interdisciplinary approach to the study of demand and its role in innovation*. Cheltenham: Edward Elgar. https://doi.org/10.7228/manchester/9780719062674.001.0001

Mowery, D.C. 2005. The Bayh-Dole act and high-technology entrepreneurship in U.S. universities: Chicken, egg, or something else? In: G.D. Libecap (ed.), *University Entrepreneurship and Technology Transfer (Advances in the Study of Entrepreneurship, Innovation and Economic Growth)*. Bingley: Emerald Group Publishing Limited, 39-68. https://doi.org/10.1016/S1048-4736(05)16002-0

Nelson Mandela University. 2020. *Data analytics and research information*. Available at: https://bit.ly/2PGvjne (Accessed 10 June 2020).

Out, A., Ameh, S., Osifo-Dawodu, E., Alade, E., Ekuri, S. & Idris, J. 2017. An account of the Ebola virus disease outbreak in Nigeria: Implications and lessons learnt. *BMC Public Health*, 18:3-11. https://doi.org/10.1186/s12889-017-4535-x

PLOS. 2020. *African countries set the tone in technological innovation to fight Covid-19.* Available at: https://bit.ly/3u5c4lQ (Accessed 18 July 2020).

Shahbaz, M., Bilal, M., Moiz, A., Zubair, S. & Iqbal, H.M. 2020. Food safety and Covid-19: Precautionary measures to limit the spread of coronavirus at food service and retail sector. Journal of Pure and Applied. *Microbiology*, 14(6203):749-756. https://doi.org/10.22207/JPAM.14.SPL1.12

Shilo, S., Rossman, H. & Segal, E. 2020. Axes of a revolution: Challenges and promises of big data in healthcare. *Nature Medicine*, 26:29-38. https://doi.org/10.1038/s41591-019-0727-5

TechCrunch. 2020. *Kenya Turns to Safaricom's M-Pesa Mobile-Money to Stem the Spread of Covid-19.* Available at: https://bit.ly/31rCLVM (Accessed 21 July 2020).

The World. 2020. *Researchers in Senegal are developing a coronavirus test kit to be used across Africa.* Available at: https://bit.ly/3u2SYwY (Accessed 5 June 2020).

Thomson Reuters Foundation. 2020. *Coronavirus seen as trigger for mobile money growth in West Africa.* Available at: https://tmsnrt.rs/3dgoqRs (Accessed 15 June 2020).

Ting, D.S.W., Carin, L., Dzau, V. & Wong, T.Y. 2020. Digital technology and Covid-19. *Nature Medicine*, 26(4):459-461. https://doi.org/10.1038/s41591-020-0824-5

United Cities and Local Governments. 2020. *Digital technologies and the Covid-19 pandemic.* Available at: https://bit.ly/3m3LN4H (Accessed 15 April 2020).

University of South Africa. 2020. *Research projects in support of the struggle against Covid-19.* Available at: https://bit.ly/39niaGv (Accessed 30 May 2020).

Wilmott, C., Fraser, E. & Lammes, S. 2018. I am he. I am he. Siri rules: Work and play with the Apple Watch. *European Journal of Cultural Studies*, 21(1):78-95. https://doi.org/10.1177/1367549417705605

World Economic Forum. 2016. *What is the fourth industrial revolution?* Available at: https://bit.ly/3rtnyhC (Accessed 25 May 2020).

World Economic Forum. 2020. *Here's how Africans are using tech to combat the coronavirus pandemic.* Available at: https://bit.ly/3cuVG8D (Accessed 25 May 2020).

www.ingramcontent.com/pod-product-compliance
Lightning Source LLC
Chambersburg PA
CBHW080542090426
42734CB00016B/3182